SCRIPTURE READINGS IN ORTHODOX WORSHIP

Scripture Readings In Orthodox Worship

GEORGES BARROIS

ST VLADIMIR'S SEMINARY PRESS

CRESTWOOD, NEW YORK

LIBRARY OF CONGRESS CATALOGING-IN-PUBLICATION DATA

Barrois, Georges Augustin, 1998-
    Scripture readings in Orthodox worship.
    Includes bibliographical references.
    1. Liturgics—Orthodox Eastern Church. 2. Bible—Liturgical use.
    I. Title.

BX350.B37   264'.01'901   77-24018
ISBN 0-913836-41-9

copyright © 1977 by
ST VLADIMIR'S SEMINARY PRESS
575 Scarsdale Road, Crestwood, New York 10707
1-800-204-2665
www.svspress.com

ISBN 0-913836-41-9
ISBN 978-0-913836-41-5

PRINTED IN THE UNITED STATES OF AMERICA

Table of Contents

Foreword

The object of this book is the use which the Orthodox liturgy makes of the Holy Scriptures. Is our worship scriptural and, if so, how and to what extent? In order to answer this question, a thorough study of ancient Christian liturgies would go a long way. We need only quote such important works as A. Baumstark, *Comparative Liturgy* (Westminster, Md., 1958); Gregory Dix, *The Shape of the Liturgy* (London, 1964, reprint of the 1945 edition); Dom O. Casel, *The Mystery of Christian Worship* (Westminster, Md., 1962). Fr. A. Schmemann, in his *Introduction to Liturgical Theology* (London, 1966), discusses the theories of these scholars and analyzes in depth the spirit and order of the Byzantine liturgy, an outstanding member in the family of Christian liturgies, though not the oldest. Fr. A. Kniazeff is the author of a substantial essay on "La lecture de l'Ancien et du Nouveau Testament dans le rite byzantin" in *La Prière des Heures,* edited by Msgr. Cassien (Bezobrazof) and Dom Botte O.S.B. (Paris, 1963).

Our purpose is different. We do not intend to investigate the remote sources of our liturgy, the influences which may have conditioned its development, nor do we presume to foretell whether or not it will remain unchanged in the future. We start from the liturgical usage as we know and practice it today; we shall examine our Scripture lessons for content and in relation to the liturgical seasons and feasts through the year. The usage to which we refer is that of the Orthodox

7

Church in America, a daughter of the Orthodox Church of Russia. Divergences from the Greek usage are minimal, at least from our own point of view, and we shall mention them whenever necessary or useful.

We aim at placing into the hands of our readers a study of the scriptural fragments which are used in our services, as an introduction into the mind of the Church, inasmuch as our liturgists, most of the time anonymous, chose psalms, prophecies, parables, lessons from the apostles or from the Gospel and fitted them into the framework of public prayer and the celebration of the Christian mysteries. In order to fulfill our program, we must remain true to God's word and to the voice of the praying Church in our interpretation; we have need of an hermeneutics based on Tradition, and we cannot but deplore that such a one may elicit little response in those academic circles still committed to an obsolete ideology of positivism.

Liturgical piety admits of a high degree of flexibility. "It can accept the cult in a key other than that in which it was conceived and expressed as text, ceremony or rite," writes Fr. Schmemann (*op. cit.*, p. 77). The same can be said of the Scriptures, as they are interpreted and incorporated into the liturgy; a considerable adaptation of the general rules of hermeneutics takes place here. Tradition has recognized the validity of types from the Old Testament finding their fulfilment in the person and the work of Christ: the sacrifice of Isaac, the burning bush, the water from the Rock "which was Christ," as St. Paul writes. We have to go one step further. The authors and compilers of our liturgies, following the example of the majority of the Fathers, cared little to distinguish sharply between typical exegesis, which yields an indirect but authentic sense of Scripture, and allegory, which is the product of human ingenuity, limited only by the instinct of faith, common sense and good taste, the latter two being variables. Allegory, of itself, does not make authority in theology; yet it offers some historical interest, and it occupies too important a place in the liturgical complex to be overlooked by us.

The plasticity of the liturgical tradition to which Fr.

Schmemann refers is manifested here to the extreme. The authors of our canons have drawn their inspiration from the Old Testament odes and Gospel canticles. The very same motifs which captured their attention, for instance the vision of Habakkuk, the sign of Jonas, the dew sprinkled on the fiery furnace in Babylon, have yielded an incredible diversity of hymns or stanzas according to what the feast, the Sunday or the season demanded; according also to the genius of the hymnographers whose canons are used in the liturgy. There enters in these matters a measure of arbitrariness which is bound to affect our presentation. Here is not the place for being dogmatic, and all we may do is to keep the conjectural within acceptable limits.

I have always kept in mind, while writing this little book, the needs of our seminarians, our educators and parish readers. Are we not all exhorted to "sing with understanding," ψάλατε συνετῶς, and to apply ourselves "to the study and the reading of the divine words in wisdom and with discernment, through him who shall keep us in blamelessness of life"? I was greatly encouraged by my colleagues who suggested the topic, and my gratitude goes to those who took care of the editorial work and of the proofreading.

Biblical references, including references to the Psalms, are indicated according to the King James version. Whenever necessary, we shall add the references according to the Septuagint. As for quoting, we shall use—eclectically—the text of the King James (KJ) or of the Revised Standard Version (RSV), or eventually other translations from the original texts. In quoting from the Old Testament, we have often used "Yahweh" as the personal name of God—the likely reading of the sacred letters Y-H-W-H—or its rendering in the versions: "The Lord," Κύριος, Dominus. Quotations from the liturgical books reproduce the translations approved or authorized by the hierarchy. We stand greatly indebted to Mother Mary, of the Monastery of the Veil, and Archimandrite Kallistos Ware, for their Festal Menaion (Faber and Faber: London, 1969). I have not neglected such stand-bys as Isabel Hapgood's Service Book or the voluminous Divine Prayers and Services translated by Rev. Seraphim Nassar and published by the Antiochian archdiocese. These translations have been severely criticized and some of the criticisms were justified; but the truth of the matter is that they have not been replaced thus far, and they have proved most serviceable, even to their critics.

Calendar dates, that is the ordinal numbering of a given day within the month, are indicated according to the so-called Gregorian calendar (new style) which since 1900 is thirteen days in advance of the Julian calendar (old style). This has no bearing on the determination of the date of Easter and the paschal cycle. But the discrepancy between the old and the new calendar affects the observance of fixed feasts and fasts. Thus, for instance, the churches, parishes and monasteries which have adopted the new calendar celebrate the Exaltation of the Holy Cross on September 14, the Nativity of Our Lord on December 25, St. George on April 23, etc., whereas those which have kept the old calendar observe these feasts respectively on what we would call September 27, January 7, and May 6.

Occasional allusions to the liturgical usage of the western church reflect generally the Roman or monastic practice before the reform of the liturgy initiated in the Second Vatican Council. This reformation was not consistently implemented everywhere and the situation at this time remains fluid.

CHAPTER ONE ⚒ **The Liturgical Year**

Cycles and Seasons. Two factors determine the course of the liturgical year: the revolution of the earth around the sun, and the centrality of Pascha. The succession of days, years, and seasons is of itself indifferent and derives its meaning from its relation to human happenings. Our "fix" in the amorphous flow of days is Pascha, foreshadowed by the biblical Passover. The yearly course of liturgical celebrations owes its ultimate significance to the unique event of the Resurrection of Our Lord as its center.

The revelation of God's design through providentially controlled occurrences and the "Christ event" justify the dual structure of our liturgical ordo: on the one hand, the commemoration of the temporal birth of God's eternally begotten Son and the travail of the saints; on the other hand, the Passion, the Tomb and the Resurrection, in anticipation of the triumph on the Last Day. In other terms, there are two series of celebrations: the annual cycle of feasts, dated more or less conventionally; and the dominical cycle, centered on the date of Easter, namely the Lenten Triodion, Great and Holy Week, Pascha, the seven weeks to the Sunday of Pentecost, and the Sundays from Pentecost to the Sunday of Zacchaeus. This second cycle urges us forward beyond the limits of history, "till He come" (1 Cor. 11:26).

In ancient Palestine, the calendar year began in autumn with the moon of *Tishri* (September-October). It marked the start of a new agricultural cycle: the harvest had been long

11

threshed and stored, the fruits gathered, and the new wine pressed. In spring, the moon of *Nisân* (March-April) would give the signal for the observance of Passover, originally a rural celebration of peasants and shepherds, which had received its definitive consecration as the memorial of the liberation of Israel from Egypt.

Our liturgical year follows a similar rhythm. The church year, with its fixed feasts and fasts, begins on the first of September. The festal cycle does not run separately from the paschal or dominical cycle, but concurrently. The sanctification of the historical time of the Menaion must not be opposed to the eschatological time of the Triodion and the Pentecostarion. They combine with each other, and we are not permitted to drift aimlessly from day to day, from saint to saint, from feast to feast, and forget the goal that is set before us, the kingdom which Christ ushered in and which He will consummate on the last day. It is important to note that the long series of the Sundays after Pentecost, which bridges one calendar year over to the next, from All Saints to Zacchaeus Sunday, does not indicate a break away from the paschal cycle, which somehow is extended indefinitely through the weekly recurrence of the "Day of the Lord," its vigil with the Resurrection Gospel, and the weekly hymns of the eight tones, the Oktoechos. The fact that certain feasts, in a given year, may fall on a Sunday, poses a number of practical problems such as, for instance, whether the festal Scripture readings will supplant the Sunday lessons altogether or be read together with them. These problems are not of our competence; we leave it to the liturgists in charge of preparing the annual ordo to decide, according to the rules of the Typicon.

How were the Scriptures selected and distributed through our services? Fr. Kniazeff, prior to entering into the discussion of the problem, notes that by reason of the hymnographic development proper to the Byzantine liturgy, "the office in its actual form consists almost entirely of diverse troparia and stichera, thus reducing the proportion of the other elements constitutive of the office, and especially the passages of Holy Scripture read or chanted in the course of

the various services."[1] Only a few verses of the Psalms of
Vespers are used at "Lord, I have called upon thee"; the biblical odes which form the theme of our canons are generally
omitted, except the *Magnificat*, "My soul magnifies the
Lord," and the *Nunc dimittis*, "Lord, now lettest thou thy
servant depart in peace," which are sung or read respectively
at Matins and at Vespers. The integral celebration of the divine office is left to the monks in large monasteries or in
quasimonastic centers, such as our seminaries, with some
abridgments or adaptations at the discretion of the celebrant.
While taking these modifications into account in the following chapters, we shall deliberately avoid considering the arbitrary simplifications—at times deformations—of the divine
liturgical services.

The Psalms in the Byzantine Liturgy. The Book of Psalms
was the Temple prayer book and was bequeathed as such to
both the Synagogue and the Christian Church. It is a collection of inspired religious poems to which the name of David
became attached. The historical books of the Bible did in fact
attribute to the prophet-king a charism of poetic inspiration
and credit him with the organization of the cult in the national sanctuary and of the musical program entrusted to the
Levites. In addition to the psalms of David or traditionally
ascribed to him, the Psalter contains a number of psalms
which, according to their titles, were composed by prominent
choir-leaders whose names appear in the genealogies of the
Levites. The entire collection, far from representing an organic unity, appears to have been put together without a
systematic design.

If we survey the Psalter as a whole, we recognize easily
the following themes: psalms of praise and acclamations,
namely the "Alleluia Psalms" (*hallelû Yab*, "Praise ye Yahweh!"); didactic poems extolling the glory of God in the
creation and his providence toward Israel his people; prayers
for the king and the nation; collective or individual laments
over human miseries, persecutions, sickness, death, apparent
failures of justice, and an ardent appeal for deliverance and
redress; confession of sins, national or personal, and an appeal for mercy. According to their titles, the authenticity of

which is often problematic, numerous psalms in the latter two
categories would relate to circumstances of David's life as an
outlaw in the Judaean wilderness, or to tragic episodes of his
reign. A number of psalms had been especially composed in
view of the ceremonies at the Temple, or assigned to daily or
weekly services and to the annual festivals.

In the canonical book, the psalms are not consistently
grouped according to topic or presumed origin. The division
of the Psalter in several books is late and arbitrary. The entire collection seems to have grown through successive addi-
tions or insertions. It happens rarely that a few psalms following each other in the Psalter deal with the same, or a
similar, topic. The homogeneous group of the "Psalms of
the Degrees" (Ps. 120-134) constitutes a notable exception.[2]

The Church uses the Book of Psalms in two ways. The
first way consists in reading or chanting the psalms according
to their numerical succession regardless of content; the second
way, in selecting certain psalms in relation to the particular
mood of a given liturgical service or the theme of a feast.
The periodic reading of the entire Psalter in continuous order,
a primitive feature of monastic life, early became widespread
in the Church at large, inasmuch as its canonical worship
aimed at the sanctification of time, as distinct from the eucharistic celebration. In the Byzantine rite, the Psalter is divided
into twenty *kathismata*, meaning etymologically "sessions,"
for distributing the one hundred and fifty psalms among the
daily services of Vespers and Matins.[3] The recitation of the
integral Psalter continues in the traditional reading of the
psalms at a funeral wake, as practiced in Orthodoxy and in
some western religious orders. However, the necessity of ab-
breviating the services in our parish churches and in small
monasteries has generally resulted in the omission of the
psalmody except during the pre-Nativity season and the Lenten Triodion, or in the reduction of the kathismata to a few
verses, as for instance at the Vespers of the Sunday vigil:
"Blessed is the man that walketh not in the counsel of the
ungodly, for the Lord knoweth the way of the righteous.
Serve the Lord and rejoice unto him. Blessed are all that put

their trust in him. Arise, O Lord, and save me!" (Ps. 1 and 2), representing the first kathisma.

Most of the western churches follow the principle of continuous reading, the *lectio continua*, of the Psalter, in order that it may be read or chanted virtually in its entirety during a specific period of time. Successive revisions of the monastic, or of the Roman and diocesan breviaries have introduced many variations in the application of the principle, especially with regard to the distribution of the psalms among the daily services. A Jewish origin for the practice of the *lectio continua* seems probable. It has been suggested that the Psalter had been divided into a number of liturgical sections analogous to the sections of the Pentateuch and of the prophets, aiming at a three-year course of reading. However the midrashic texts on which this hypothesis rests are not decisive. The massoretic notes of the Hebrew Bible make no mention of such an arrangement for the Psalter, nor do the modern prayer books of the Synagogue.[4]

We need not seek an internal harmony between the psalms of the kathismata and the proper significance of the days unto the sanctification of which they were assigned. At any rate, the lack of systematic order of the Book of Psalms would preclude any attempt at attaching a specific meaning to each kathisma, as if the psalms it contains were organically related. The homogeneousness of the Psalms of the Degrees (120-134), forming the eighteenth kathisma, assigned to the Friday Vespers through the year and weekday Vespers during Great Lent and the pre-Christmas season, is a-symptomatic. These psalms show no particular relation to the days on which they are read. They may indeed be regarded as suggesting the approach of the Christian Church to the mysteries of the Incarnation, Passion and Resurrection, but it is by no means certain that this symbolism was actually intended by the compilers of our liturgies.

The other mode of utilization of the psalms for the liturgical worship of the Church is topical. A limited number of psalms was chosen on account of their content, in relation to the rationale of a given service or according to the mood of the day, the feast or the season. Some psalms are seldom used and some others frequently, but this is totally immaterial. The essential point is their relevance in view of the liturgical context.

However, the poetic versatility of the psalms, the multiplicity of themes and the sudden changes of mood not only from one psalm to another, but often in the same piece, the cries of passion breaking out in the midst of a lyric, make it difficult to justify objectively the choice of a given psalm for inclusion in a particular service. Only in rare instances is this possible, and we are most of the time reduced to guesswork and subjective hypotheses. Exceptionally the psalms or fragments of psalms which belong to the structure of Vespers (outside of the kathismata) demonstrate a definite relation to the symbolical character of the service, at least in a general way. Psalm 104, "Bless the Lord, O my soul; O Lord my God, thou art very great," being a description of the marvels of creation from the first day onward,[5] is particularly appropriate as an introductory psalm, as the Church blesses a new liturgical day, since days are counted from sunset to sunset, following the ancient Jewish custom.

The psalms and verses (Ps. 130, 141, 142) which we read at "Lord, I have called upon Thee," are cries of fervent supplication from human beings in a state of despondency, physical and moral, conscious of their sinfulness: "If Thou, O Lord, shouldst mark iniquities, O Lord, who shall stand?" May our prayer "ascend as incense, and the lifting up of our hands be as the evening sacrifice!" This verse refers obviously to the holocaust offered every evening on the altar of Solomon's Temple. Psalm 51, the *Miserere*, "Have mercy on me, O God, according to thy lovingkindness," which is used in diverse liturgical contexts, belongs in the same family of psalms. Psalm 34 concludes Great Vespers as a fervent prayer of thanksgiving.

Psalms 20 and 21, "The Lord hear thee in the day of trouble," and "The king shall rejoice in thy strength," which are read when Matins is not served following Great Vespers at the all-night vigil, are relics of a historical past and of archeological interest. Originally prayers offered in the Temple of Jerusalem for the Davidic kings, they became prayers for

the Byzantine emperor in the liturgical order of certain monasteries of imperial foundation. Their strong messianic accent retains its full value.

The "six psalms" at Matins (3, 38, 63, 88, 103, 143) are
the desperate prayer of men aware of their wretched condition when the grace of God does not uphold them, and the
six psalms at Great Compline (4, 6, 13, 25, 31, 91) are an
ardent appeal to God for protection, and end on a note of
filial trust, as the night closes upon us. The verses of praise
from Psalms 135-136 and from Psalms 148-150 are particularly fitting at the Polyeleos and in conclusion of Matins, before
the Great Doxology.

The difficulty of accounting for the choice of psalms to
be read in the church services is due in part to the fact that
the hermeneutics of the liturgists is noticeably different from
modern biblical scholarship. Erudition and biblical criticism,
higher or lower, no matter how necessary, still are not the
proper keys to the hidden values of the liturgy. We need a
special optics, akin to that of the Fathers. We have to re-
acquaint ourselves with the typological method, which the
exegesis of the sixteenth-century Reformers, the rationalism
of the Enlightenment and the historicism of the nineteenth
and twentieth century have recklessly discarded, but which
makes us able to penetrate the continuous reality of the living
mystery, beneath the phenomenal level of history or the neat
theologoumena which may satisfy our curiosity but which
leave us spiritually starved.

Typology as a means to understanding the selection of
psalms or verses of psalms in relation to the liturgy may be
illustrated by a few examples: the verses of Psalm 114 on the
crossing of the sea and of the Jordan by the Israelites liberated
from the bondage of Egypt, which are read at the Theophany
as the first antiphon of the Divine Liturgy; or from Psalm 22,
a "Passion psalm," at the Exaltation of the Precious Cross.
Similar verses of psalms form the substance of most of the
prokeimena and Alleluia verses at the Divine Liturgy. Whereas some of the verses thus borrowed are of a very general
nature, a number of them are immediately applicable to the
theme of the feast or of the day: "Be thou exalted, O Lord,

above the heavens, and thy glory over all the earth" (Ps. 57:11) on the feast of the Ascension; "The rulers of the peoples have assembled against the Lord and his anointed" (Ps. 2:2) on Great and Holy Thursday.

Another aspect of what may be termed "liturgical exegesis" of the psalms is the emphasis laid on the letter, as they are read for inspirational value rather than for contextual relation. Some striking verse, deemed vital for Christians, was so valued that our liturgical books would prescribe that it should be repeated,[6] for instance the verse, "I laid me down and slept and rose up again, for the Lord sustained me" (Ps. 3:5)[7] or, "In all places of his dominion, praise the Lord, O my soul!" (Ps. 103:22).

Readings from the Old Testament. Byzantine liturgy limits the reading of the Old Testament to certain seasons and to a restricted number of feasts throughout the year. The Scriptures to be read are appointed in two ways. First, according to a course of lessons in more or less continuous sequence, following the order of chapters in the books of the Bible, with the exception of necessary cuts, since time obviously precludes the reading of the entire text, and with less rigor than the continuous reading of the Psalms in the kathismata; second, according to the particular theme of a given Old Testament passage set in relation, historical, typological or prophetical, with the character of the day or the feast.

The regular course of continuous Old Testament readings begins in the week following the Sunday of the Last Judgment. In Holy Week proper Old Testament lessons are added to the running lectionary of Lent. These lessons are prophecies and chapters of the Old Testament foreshadowing the events of the Passion and the Crucifixion, for the edification of the faithful and the preparation of the catechumens for baptism, according to the usage of the early churches. The vigils of the Entrance of Our Lord into Jerusalem (Palm Sunday), of the Ascension, and of the Sunday of Pentecost, have also their own Old Testament lessons.

The detailed contents and significance of the above mentioned Old Testament readings for the Triodion and the Pentecostarion will be examined in the following chapters.

The Old Testament lessons for the fixed feasts of the Menaion, especially the feasts of Our Lord and of the Theotokos, of the Holy Cross, and major feasts of the saints, will be presented and analyzed in chapter VII.

Surveying the lectionary as a whole, we may notice that nothing is read of the following: Ruth, Samuel, Chronicles, Ezra and Nehemiah, Tobith and the Maccabees among the historical books; Ecclesiastes, the Song of Songs and Ecclesiasticus among the wisdom and poetic books; Lamentations, Hosea, Amos, Obadiah, Nahum and Haggai among the prophets. The development of Byzantine hymnology may partly explain the limitation of our liturgical Bible to a restricted number of Old Testament books.[8] Our apparent neglect of the "historical" books from Joshua onward, except for Kings, which is read sparingly, contrasts with the relatively abundant use which the Latin liturgy makes of them, as if it invited the faithful to thumb through the pages of an illustrated Bible. The latter approach is definitely retrospective. The Byzantine lectionary, on the contrary, tends forward. The perspective of the Scriptures, by assigning a divine *telos* to an indifferent succession of days, alone makes sense of history. We move toward an eschatological future, the new aeon ushered in by Christ and awaiting consummation. Is it even a "future" in the common sense of this word? Is it not rather a shift to another level of reality which transcends the present order? Recently Professor John D. Zizioulas compared this sublimation of historical, "linear" time with the "epicletical" change of the bread and wine in the eucharistic liturgy.[9]

Readings from the New Testament. Lessons from the New Testament, *viz.* the Gospels and the apostolic writings, St. John's Apocalypse excepted, are read at the celebration of the Divine Liturgy throughout the year and on the feasts of the saints or other commemorations. The New Testament readings for the feasts and for services other than the Divine Liturgy are generally chosen for content, in harmony with the proper character of the feast or the occasion. The running course of Scriptures selected for the period extending from the Sunday of All Saints, *i.e.* from the second Sunday after

Pentecost,[10] to the beginning of the Triodion in the following
calendar year, is organized on the general principle of continuous reading. The order of chapters is generally respected
save a few exceptions and eventually with intervals of vari-
able length between the pericopes, especially on Sundays.

The New Testament lectionary for the time extending
from the beginning of the Lenten Triodion to Pentecost dem-
onstrates the special concern of the Church with the preparation of the faithful for the celebration of the paschal mystery.
The instruction of catechumens preparing for baptism and of
the newly baptized had been the common practice of all the
ancient churches, Rome, Jerusalem, Antioch, Constantinople,
the Orientals and the Africans. The Byzantine Church reads
the Gospel of Mark during the liturgical season of Lent.
Likewise, the Acts of the Apostles and the Fourth Gospel
provide the New Testament lessons for the fifty days following Easter, in a quasi-continuous sequence.

The principle of the *lectio continua*, however, is applied
most freely or even set aside altogether on major days of the
pre- and post-paschal season, as well as on the great feasts
listed in the calendar of months. We could hardly read anything else but John 12:1-18 on Palm Sunday, the Passion
Gospels on the three major days of Holy Week, John 20:19-
31 on Thomas Sunday, or Matthew 2:1-12 on the Nativity
of Our Lord.

The purpose of this preliminary chapter was merely to
outline the mechanics of our system of Scripture reading and
the general principles which seem to have guided the compilers of our liturgical books. The detailed examination of
the Byzantine lectionary in relation to the structure of the
liturgical year itself according to days, seasons and festal
occasions on fixed calendar dates will be the object of the
following chapters.

CHAPTER TWO

The Triodion

THE FIRST THREE WEEKS

The Triodion, *Postnaya Triod*, is the liturgical book which contains the services from the Sunday of the Publican and the Pharisee, tenth before Easter, to Great and Holy Saturday. The seven weeks of Great Lent are preceded in the present practice of the Byzantine Church by four Sundays named for the salient features of the Gospel read at the Divine Liturgy, *viz.* the Sunday of the Publican and the Pharisee, the Sunday of the Prodigal Son, the Sunday of the Last Judgment, and the Sunday of Forgiveness. But it was not always so. The three weeks thus delimited were added successively, in reverse order, to the forty-eight days of the Great Fast.[1] The week after the Sunday of the Last Judgment was the first to be added in preparation for the Lenten fast in Constantinople; the week after the Sunday of the Prodigal Son, in the ninth or tenth century; and last of all, the week after the Sunday of the Publican and the Pharisee, in the twelfth century.[2]

Dietary prescriptions prepare us gradually for the fast of Great Lent, marking the rhythm of these weeks, in conformity with the hymnology and the scriptural readings. The week following the Sunday of the Publican and the Pharisee is fast-free.[3] The week following the Sunday of the Prodigal Son is a normal week, with no other abstinence than that of the Wednesdays and Fridays observed throughout the year. The Sunday of the Last Judgment, "Meat-Fare Sunday," is followed by the week of the tyrophagy, "Cheese-Fare Week," when meat is forbidden, but milk products may be used, up to the Sunday of Forgiveness inclusively, after which the Lenten fast proper begins.

The significance of the weeks preparatory to Great Lent is concentrated in the Gospel readings of the four Sundays, which spell out the essence and objectives of true fasting overagainst its perversions. The lessons have been selected in order to express the views of the Church regarding the chosen means by which we may participate in the mystery of our salvation, as we draw nearer to the Cross and the Resurrection. Their object is our preparation for Great Lent and the paschal season rather than the general course of instruction which runs throughout the Sundays and weeks of the year. The fact that the services of the preparatory Sundays were added successively to the Byzantine ordo, of which they were not original components, may explain why the corresponding New Testament lessons, instead of being parts of the series organized on the principle of the *lectio continua*, are "proper" lessons. As for the Epistles and Gospels of the intervening weekdays and Saturdays, they follow their own continuous order.

We ought to be reminded here that Scripture readings are only one element of the total liturgical complex, the hymns and prayers of the Church being the others. Obviously none of these elements should be given precedence over the others. Our concentrating on the biblical element does not mean at all that we regard the hymnody and the liturgical prayers as secondary or negligible.[4]

Sunday lessons from the New Testament. The liturgical themes of the first four Sundays of the Triodion arise unambiguously from the lessons of the Gospel and the Apostle. The selection from the Epistles either reinforce the basic teachings of the Evangelists or complement it, or spell out its implications for Christians. No historical sequence is to be sought here: the parables of Jesus present us with a truth which is of and above all times. The intention of the liturgist is to prepare us spiritually for the Lenten fast, not as a ceremonial observance, but in relation to our religious and moral living as a whole, in conformity with the requirements of the Sermon on the Mount, beyond which we are urged to raise our sights toward the cosmic perspective which the Resurrection of Christ will open to us.

The theme of the first Sunday is centered on the parable of the Publican and the Pharisee (Lk. 18:10-14). On the eve of the Great Fast, it comes as a warning: by all means fast, but let your fast be a true fast, and not a show! The story told by Jesus is not to be construed as an indictment of the Pharisees as a class, nor as a plea for the Publicans. Jesus had no prejudice toward either, nor did he object to the teaching of the Pharisees and the Rabbis: "Whatever they tell you, do and observe, but do not do as they do, for they preach, but do not practice" (Mt. 23:3). His resentment was against their involving the people in a futile casuistry, and against the relentless hostility of those who spied on him at each step he took with his disciples. He vented his anger once and for all in the "Woes" recorded by the Evangelists (Mt. 23:13-33; cf. Lk. 11:46). The detractors of Jesus, when they reproached him for consorting with Publicans and sinners (Mt. 9:11; Mk. 2:16; Lk. 5:30), evidently tried to make capital of the instinctive hatred of the crowd for corrupt tax collectors and petty government officials always ready to extort bribes. The fact that St. Matthew belonged to that body or St. Luke's picturesque sketch of the conversion of Zacchaeus (Lk. 19:1-9) would certainly not justify us to absolve the Publicans as a body, nor to indict all the Pharisees. But the point of the parable is clear, and it certainly hit the target: fasting is in itself a salutary discipline and should not be turned into exhibitionism, all the more if scorn for others is added to it. This was precisely the sin of our Pharisee, when he boasted of being "different." He did fast twice a week (Lk. 18:12). Very well! The Law of Moses had never ordered this. The Jews fasted in times of public danger or in commemoration of disasters which had befallen their nation, but fasting was by no means a common practice. The ascetic display of the man was totally uncalled for. The Talmud reports as an unusual fact the case of one who had taken to fasting regularly in the course of an entire year, and expresses no judgment of value.[5]

The Epistle for this first Sunday (2 Tim. 3:10-15) does not seem, at first sight, to be closely related to the Gospel reading. St. Paul, writing from Rome in lonely detention to his beloved disciple Timothy, reminisces on his past ordeals, the common lot of the apostles: how, as he and Barnabas preached in the synagogues at Antioch of Pisidia, Iconium and Lystra, they met with the opposition of a party of Jews who aroused the pagans against them. Mobbed by the crowd, Paul and Barnabas had barely escaped with their lives (Acts, chapters 13 and 14). Similar persecutions await Timothy, who is urged to beware of those men "swollen with conceit . . . who hold the form of religion but deny the power of it . . . evil men and seducers . . . deceiving and deceived." The situation will grow worse as the present age is running out.[6] The message is for us as well, and its eschatological connotation should not escape us as we enter the time of the Triodion. In a few weeks, the Resurrection of Christ will have changed invisibly the very nature of time, and the new aeon will dawn over his glorious sepulcher.

The Gospel of the second Sunday is the parable of the Prodigal Son (Lk. 15:11-32). A young man, the cadet of two brothers, having obtained from their father the share of the family good that should come to him by inheritance, journeys to a foreign country where he squanders his possession in loose living. Reduced to abject poverty, he resolves to go back home and beg his father for pardon. Touched with compassion, the father, overjoyed by the return of his lost child, orders a big feast to be prepared, much to the displeasure of the older son who gripes at what he considers a shocking extravagance: "These many years I served you . . . and you never gave me a kid, that I might make merry with my friends!" The many faceted parable has been diversely commented by Christian exegetes according to whether they focused their attention on the father, on the prodigal son, or on his older brother.[7] The condition of the prodigal before and after his conversion, rather than the psychology of the father and the sour reactions of the other son, is obviously what interested most the compiler of the lectionary, seeing that the Lenten season calls for change of heart and return.

The far-off country where the prodigal wandered is the figure of a world in which the activities of men, even their duties, are disconnected or antagonistic to each other and not ordered to an end, a τέλος; a world of incoherent pursuits, of illusory strivings, of craving for foods that satisfy not and drinks which quench not our thirst, a world where nothing ultimately makes sense, engulfed as it is in untruth, deceit and sin; the exact opposite of the world as created by God and potentially re-created by his Son and Spirit. There is no cure for the evils of our age unless we return to God, since the world in which we live is not the normal world, but a waste land. This is why the Church prescribes that we should add to the psalms of the polyeleos at Matins, on this and the following two Sundays, the nostalgic lament of the exiles: "By the streams of Babylon we sat and wept as we remembered Zion. On the willows we hung our harps, for how could we sing the Lord's song in a strange land?" (Ps. 137). St. Ambrose of Milan comments on our parable with these words: "It is possible indeed that one would remove himself further away from his own people through his way of life, than by mere distance . . . For he who separates himself from Christ is in exile from the fatherland and becomes a subject of the world. But we are not aliens and foreigners; we are fellow citizens with the saints and of the household of God; we were some time afar off, but we were made nigh by the blood of Christ."[8]

The Epistle (1 Cor. 6:12-20) goes very far in spelling out the bearing of the parable on the mores of the Apostle's contemporaries, and it might as well have been written for us. The prodigal son had sought an escape from the unexciting routine of the family life. He had not found it, and was lucky enough to be welcome again in the father's home. St. Paul's Corinthians had shared the first part of the prodigal's experience, but they loathed drawing the proper conclusion and refused to heed the call of the Church for a change of heart unto the fulness of Christian life. St. Paul begins on a

note of irony: "To me, everything is permitted."[9] But some
things are unhealthy, and I, Paul, have no intention of becoming slave to anything, nor should we. Food and drink are
needed as long as we are in our mortal body; but we are called
to rise up with Christ to life eternal, and our bodies are definitely not for gluttony, drunkenness, or wenching. And "do
we not know that our body is a temple of the Holy Spirit . . .
and that we are not our own?" St. Paul's question aims
straight at those among us who let themselves be obsessed
with morbid sexuality under a false pretense of liberation.

If we were still tempted, after the first two Sundays of
the Triodion, to consider the Lenten fast as a cheap legal
observance, the liturgy of the last two Sundays before Great
Lent would open our eyes and dispel any illusion we might
entertain. We are in the midst of a fallen mankind, unaware
of our predicament; at best seeking palliatives to the evils
that beset us, but minimizing or refusing to admit any feel-
ings of guilt, rejecting the idea of a cosmic judgment which
would restore the order whose existence our sins denied, and
not being ready to accept God's offer of forgiveness, through
unbelief, pride, or stubborn despair.

The Gospel reading on the Sunday of the Last Judgment
(Mt. 25:31-46) is a prophetic discourse of Christ, which
preceded the events of Great and Holy Week. It stages the
solemn spectacle envisioned by the apocalypses of the Old
and New Testaments. On the last day of the world, the "Son
of Man" appearing in glory shall sit on his throne and judge
all nations, πάντα τὰ ἔθνη, gathered before him from all
lands and all ages, for the dead also shall rise to stand judgment (as may be deduced from Matthew 10:15, 11:22-24,
12:41-42). The "Son of Man," like a shepherd who divides
his sheep from the goats, shall place the blessed ones of his
father on his right, and the evil ones on his left, so that they
might hear the sentence: an irrevocable sentence of life or
death, unto eternal blessedness or eternal perdition. On the
sharp line of demarcation stands the Cross, toward which our
eyes are turned during this season. "In the midst between
two thieves was thy cross found to be the balance-beam of

righteousness, for while the one was led down to hell by the burden of his blaspheming, the other was lightened of his sins unto the knowledge of things divine."[10] We are reminded of three words in a hymn of Venantius Fortunatus (sixth century) which the Latin Church sings at Vespers during Passiontide: the beam of the cross from which the Savior hangs, is the balance of our redemption in his flesh, *statera facta corporis*. We wonder whether it is not possible to find here an answer, among others, to the question frequently asked, "Why is the lower bar of the traditional Russian cross not at a straight angle with the vertical beam?" We may observe that it rises at one end toward the right hand of the Crucified, the side of the repentant thief, and sinks at the other end, the side of the reprobate.[11] It is somehow significant that the judicial function of Christ was recognized even in Islam, and is abundantly illustrated in the folklore of the Dome of the Rock in Jerusalem, the so-called Mosque of Omar.

Love to others is the ground on which the sentence of the Judge is to be pronounced; not a mere benevolent disposition, but out-going love, love-service. It had never been totally absent from mankind in spite of the ravages of selfishness and enmity. Through God's grace, heroes of charity have been known in all times. Moses' command was: "Love thy neighbor as thyself" (Lev. 19:18), and our Lord quoted it on par with the first commandment (Deut. 6:5; Mt. 22:37-40). The Gospel opens a new vista: love for our fellow men is, on account of the Incarnation, love for the whole Christ, head and members. What we do to the least of us, the poor and the underprivileged, is done for him who will be our judge, and what we fail to do will be counted against us: sins of omission may be worse than sins of commission, and would cause us to be rejected with the crowds of the left hand. It may be appropriate to quote here a picturesque anecdote of St. Gregory the Great, the sixth-century Bishop of Rome. A certain monk Martyrius, on his way to visit the abbot of a nearby monastery, came upon a traveller lying exhausted by the roadside. Martyrius, moved of compassion, wrapped the man in his own cloak, loaded him on his back, and took him to the monastery. The abbot, who watched them as they drew near, called on his monks with a loud voice: "Make haste, open the gate, for our brother Martyrius is coming; 'tis the Lord he is bearing."[12] The primacy of love, ἀγάπη, is constantly re-affirmed in the Sermon on the Mount, and what we hear on this Sunday echoes the fierce preaching of Amos, the rude eighth-century prophet of Judah, and the voice of the great inspired ones in Israel. But it has become so familiar to us that we have to be shaken out of our heedlessness. Life events may do it, unless they merely confirm us in our callousness.

St. Paul had to spell out some immediate applications of the general principle for the benefit of the Corinthians, and the Church has us read at the Divine Liturgy a passage from 1 Corinthians 8:8 to 9:2. Some discussions had arisen regarding Christian freedom and the reluctance of some brethren to eat the meat of victims which their neighbors had offered to the idols; this had been regarded in Israel as a major sin of *communicatio in sacris*. The Christians who chose to abstain are called by Paul the "weak brethren," weak in their faith which should have made them understand that they were no longer subject to the "ceremonial" precepts of the Law. Objectively speaking, the "strong brethren," who had no qualm about partaking of those meats—this was almost unavoidable in a pagan country—were right. After all, idols are nothing, and nothingness cannot be a basis for prohibitions from which the Gospel has liberated us. But the superior precept of love should have impressed upon them the duty of respecting the scruples of the weak, until they would know better. Did not the Apostle circumcise Timothy lest he be found objectionable to the Jews they were evangelizing? (Acts 16:3). And when he ascended to Jerusalem after his farewell to the elders of the Church at Ephesus, hearing of four men who had taken the Nazarite vow, did he not pay their expenses, lest he be charged with disrespect toward bona fide observant Jews? (Acts 21:23-26). And are we not brought back on this Sunday to the theme of the parable of the Publican and the Pharisee? But it is no longer an exhortation to humility that

we hear. It is, in the form of a dilemma, the unqualified proclamation of the law of charity.

The last Sunday before Great Lent is commonly known
as Cheese-Fare Sunday, after which dairy products, which
were still permitted following the Sunday of the Last Judgment, will disappear from our tables until Easter. The Church
wishes us to be gradually weaned from our habitual fare in
preparation for the oncoming fast. The Synaxarion notes that
"this Sunday, we remember the expulsion of Adam from the
Paradise of bliss," and this remembrance is the theme of the
hymns of the vigil. Our thoughts are directed beyond the
material observances of Lent toward the final goal, when
time as we know it will be absorbed in the splendor of the
Eternal Day. The same Sunday is also called Sunday of Forgiveness: forgiveness, so difficult to achieve in our fallen
state, yet the indispensable key to the kingdom!

The Gospel at the Divine Liturgy is a part of the Sermon on the Mount, recorded by St. Matthew (Mt. 6:14-21).
Three points are made. First, the Lord says: "If you forgive
men their trespasses, your Father in heaven will also forgive
you. But if you forgive not their trespasses, neither will your
Father forgive yours." Any commentary would only weaken
the impact of that "if" and "if not." Secondly, and this is
appropriate in this season, "when you fast, be not of a sad
countenance, like the hypocrites, who disfigure their faces,
that they may appear unto men to fast," in colloquial English,
"Don't make a show!" Fasting is a means, not an end in itself; it should merely express our readiness to liberate ourselves from needs, often imaginary, which hold us captives.
Thirdly, "Lay not up for yourselves treasures upon earth . . .
but lay up for yourselves treasures in heaven . . . for where
your treasure is, there will your heart be also." The applications and implications of this third point are many in our personal and social life and need not be enumerated here. We are
simply not allowed to let our heart be choked "in its own
fat," like those "who have their portion in this life and whose
belly Thou fillest with their hid treasures," of whom we hear
in the psalm at the Third Hour (Ps. 17-14).[13] I suddenly think

of a picturesque Old Testament character, Nabal, a rich cattle owner, glutton, foul-mouthed, stupid, bullying his wives and anybody else. In the course of a drunken bout with his cronies, "his heart died in him, he became as a stone, and he died about ten days later" (1 Sam. 25:36-38).

The lesson from the Apostle (Rom. 13:11 to 14:4) stresses the eschatological perspective: the time of our salvation draws every day nearer. "The night is far spent, the day is at hand." St. Paul, like all the early Christians, had been in the dark regarding the day and the hour—unknown to Christ himself according to his human knowledge—of his return in glory.[14] At any rate, time seemed to be running out. As Christians we cannot afford a way of life implying that our existence on earth, no matter how long its duration, is "terminal," if I am permitted to use a gruesome medical jargon, no matter how we live, whether on pleasure-seeking or on altruistic principles. St. Paul spells this out in no ambiguous terms, and the Church insists on a measure of austerity, seeing that we "have put on the Lord Jesus Christ." At the same time, the last verses of the Epistle should be a forewarning against pharisaism and ostentation, and this appears equally important, if our fasting is to be the true fast unto Pascha.

New Testament readings on weekdays and Saturdays. On weekdays during these first three weeks of the Triodion, the Church completes the course of regular lessons from the New Testament which had begun after Pentecost of the preceding calendar year (see below, chapter VI), whereas two "a-liturgical days," the Wednesday and the Friday of cheese-fare week, have no New Testament lessons. The Apostle is read in continuous order, except for some cuts and appropriate spacing, from the second Epistle of Peter and from the Epistles of John and Jude. These lessons as a whole are not specifically related to the theme of the pre-Lenten season. The reading of the Gospel according to St. Mark during the first two weeks of the Triodion (Mk. 13:9 through 15:41) terminates the yearly course of Gospel lessons and makes us hear the so-called eschatological discourse in which the

themes of the destruction of the Temple and the end of the
present aeon are intertwined, various episodes of the last week
of Jesus in Jerusalem, the Passion and the Crucifixion. Lessons from Luke, excerpted from chapters 19-23, which record
the final days of Jesus, from his triumphal entry into Jerusalem to his burial, are provided for the liturgical days of the
last week before the fast. The fact that the Evangelists recorded whatever came to pass during the days preceding the
Resurrection in an approximate chronological order causes
the choice of weekday Gospel lessons for the first three weeks
of the Lenten Triodion to harmonize with the method of the
lectio continua. In a sense, this choice was imposed upon the
liturgists by the events themselves.

The series of Saturday readings at the Divine Liturgy is
independent of the weekday course of Scriptures, the sections
being determined either according to the order of chapters or
according to theme, so as to express the spirit of the season
or somehow to harmonize with the reading of the corresponding Sunday. Thus the New Testament lessons for the Saturday Liturgy of the weeks preceding Lent can be defined, in a
sense, as proper lessons. The pericopes from the Gospel express the doctrine of the Church on the prescriptions of Lent,
and the spirit in which they must be observed: do fast, but
beware of formalism, ostentation, and covering under a veil
of austerity a brazen disregard of moral living; in other
words, heed the teaching of Christ in the Sermon on the
Mount and the inspired voice of the prophets. The parable
of the judge who feared neither God nor man (Lk. 18:2-6),
no doubt one of those power-seeking Sadducees who used the
Law for gaining personal influence and promoting their social and political objectives, is read on the Saturday before
the Publican and the Pharisee. That lawyer finally agreed
to take the case of a wearysome widow, not out of a sense of
duty, justice or compassion, but simply to get rid of her. On
the next Saturday, we hear of the scribes parading in their
judicial robes, who loved to be greeted in the market-place
and claimed reserved seats in the assemblies, yet had no
scruple at "devouring widows' houses." The caricature
sketched by St. Luke contrasts with the parable of the poor

widow casting her two pence into the treasure box of the
Temple (Lk. 20:45 to 21:4). On the Saturday preceding the
Sunday of the Last Judgment, the Gospel lesson is a cento
of verses from Luke relative to the signs portending the destruction of Jerusalem, the general conflagration, and the
second advent of Christ (Lk. 21:8-9, 25-27, 33-36). This
lesson resumes the theme of Mark ch. 13, which was the object of the Gospel readings during the week of the Publican.
We return to Matthew (6:1-13) for the Saturday in cheese-
fare week: do not blow the trumpet when you give alms or
when you pray, "that you be seen of men."

The Epistles for these Saturdays are similarly oriented.
On the Saturday before the Publican, we are urged to consort
with Christ in his Passion, and forewarned against impostors
and charlatans, who will proliferate in the latter days (2 Tim.
2:11-19).[15] A similar note is sounded on the Saturday of the
Prodigal: Flee licentiousness, unruliness, and beware of ex-
travagant theories and uncontrolled mysticism or supersti-
tions (2 Tim. 3:1-9). The principle of Christian liberty in
matter of legal observances is re-affirmed on the Saturday
before the Sunday of the Last Judgment (1 Cor. 10:23-28):
nothing created is impure, for "the earth is the Lord's and the
fulness thereof" (Ps. 24:1), but Christian liberty remains
subject to the superior duty of charity. Then we turn back to
Romans (14:19-26),[16] where the Apostle draws the practical
conclusion: "Let us follow after the things that make for
peace and mutual edification." Legal observances are useful
as means; food and drink, of themselves, are indifferent. So,
eat or abstain in good faith, above all avoiding scandal.

Memorial Saturdays. Saturday is traditionally the day for
commemorating the dead at the altar. The liturgical observance of the Saturdays during the time of the Triodion is
marked by a series of commemorations, and a special set of
New Testament readings is added to the Saturday Liturgy,
for the Church is acutely conscious of the mystery of death
during the pre-Paschal season. Is not the resurrection of
Lazarus a prophecy of the Resurrection of our Lord? This
sets the tune for our remembrance of the dead. Death, which

Christ has trampled under foot, has lost its power, and we remember the departed in hope and with thanksgiving as we would wish ourselves to be remembered, rather than in mourning and wailing.

On the Saturday preceding the Sunday of the Judgment, we commemorate "our fathers and brethren who have fallen asleep in the Lord," and this will be repeated on the second,[17] third, and fourth Saturday of Lent. The Gospel is from John 5:24-30, "The hour is coming and now is, when the dead shall hear the voice of the Son of God, and they that hear shall live." The Epistle is from 1 Thessalonians 4:13-17, in which St. Paul reassures those who fear for the destiny of the brethren who would fall asleep before the return of the Lord, or from 1 Corinthians 15:47-57, a paean, not a lamentation: "Death is swallowed in victory. O Death, where is thy sting? O Grave, where is thy victory?" On cheese-fare Saturday, we remember especially all those who have been illumined by fasting: we read St. Paul's enumeration of the fruits of the Spirit and the Gospel according to St. Matthew 11:27-30: "My yoke is easy, and my burden is light."

The prophecies in the third week. The Divine Liturgy is not served on the Wednesday and Friday in cheese-fare week, in anticipation of the Fast, which begins on the following Monday. Instead of Scripture readings from the New Testament, Old Testament prophecies are prescribed at the Sixth Hour and Vespers of the two "a-liturgical days," lessons from Joel being read on Wednesday, and from Zechariah on Friday.

We know little about Joel, one of the so-called "Lesser Prophets." The book which bears his name gives no date, nor any indication of his personal identity. It was probably composed in post-exilic Judah, when the exiles returning from Babylon had resettled the country, and when the service in the Temple restored by Zorobabel had been resumed.[18] The book professes the moral-social Yahwism of the earlier prophets like Amos and Isaiah, and expects a future vindication of justice which is to happen beyond history, on the "Day of Yahweh," described in apocalyptic terms. There is no cogent reason for regarding it as resulting from the fusion of two original pieces of writing. The common theme of the "Day of Yahweh" unites both parts of the book, as does also the recurrent reference to the occasion which prompted the prophet to raise his voice. A cloud of locusts had befallen the entire countryside, a not uncommon happening in Palestine and Transjordan, but reaching catastrophic proportions in that particular instance. The prophet describes how those animals had gnawed at every growing thing, "laying waste the vineyards, attacking the fig trees, stripping them of their bark and making their branches like dead wood" (Joel 1:7).[19] There is not much one can do about such things. The Jewish peasants regarded them as a punishment sent by God for their sins, and the prophet called them to a public fast in order to placate God's anger against his people. But it had to be a true fast, and not some kind of magic ritual which would leave the people unconverted and soon reverting to their sinful ways.

We read at the Sixth Hour Joel 1:12-16. The gloom spread over the land by the "cloud" of locusts—by no means a hyperbola—turns the imagination of the prophet toward the ominous darkening of the sky which shall herald the Day of the Lord. The ravage wrought by the invasion of locusts causes the prophet to reminisce over past invasions of the country by their enemies, and similar disasters would be the prelude to the day of vengeance. "Yet even now, says the Lord, return to me with all your heart, in fasting, and weeping, and mourning . . . Rend your hearts, not your garments, and turn unto the Lord your God, for He is gracious and merciful, slow to anger, and abundant in mercy . . . Between the porch and the altar the priests shall weep saying: Spare thy people, O Lord!"[20] The response of God to a sincere prayer will be favorable; the lesson ends on the picture of an idyllic restoration of the land: no more swarms of locusts. Yahweh will send rain in due season: "the early rain, the later rain"—the so-called rain of St. George at Lydda—which makes possible the autumn ploughing. The threshing floors will be loaded with a rich harvest, the vats filled with wine and oil, "and you shall know that I am the Lord."

The lesson at Vespers (Joel 3:12-21), develops the eschatological perspective. We are transported into the Valley of
Jehoshaphat,[21] theater of the Last Judgment, and the vision
of the heavenly Jerusalem rises over the horizon. We have
passed beyond history. We know in our Christian faith that
we have entered the new aeon since the night of the Resurrection, but the final realization is still ahead of us as it was for
the contemporaries of Joel. Zion, the holy mountain, is the
symbol, and the prophet sees a spring of water gushing forth
from the "House" unto a regenerated people. Ezekiel had
seen the same vision (Ezek. 47:1), and the Latin liturgy ap-
propriates his words at the sprinkling of holy water before
the Sunday Mass, from Easter to Pentecost: "I saw water
flowing from under the Temple on the eastern side, and all
whom that water reached have been made whole. Alleluia,
Alleluia, Alleluia!"—an allusion to the baptism of the catechumens who in Rome laid aside the white robes of their
baptism on the second Sunday of Pascha, *Dominica in Albis.*

On Friday of cheese-fare week, we read from the Book of
Zechariah, the first part of which, chapters 1-8, is explicitly
dated to the autumn of 520 B.C., "in the second year of
Darius, in the eighth month" (October-November).[22] It records carefully dated visions of the prophet relative to the
post-exilic reconstruction, for us a flash-back on Israel's past:
it opens messianic perspectives of which the people of Jerusalem and the House of Judah would be the beneficiaries,
and it answers discussions on the practice of fasting. The
second part, chapters 9-10, is a collection of undated, anonymous, heterogeneous fragments, reflecting late messianic speculations among whose features is the prophetic announcement of the advent of a son of David, humble and peaceful
(9:9-10), and a lamentation on "him whom they have
stabbed" (12:10). These two fragments drew the attention
of the Evangelists, who quoted them in relation to the entry of
Jesus into Jerusalem (Palm Sunday), and of the transfixion
of the Crucified by the spear of the centurion.

In this third week of the Lenten Triodion, the Church
wishes to impress upon us how our fast will enable us to
reach our goal. At the Sixth Hour, we read of an era of pros-

perity and universal peace under God, "in truth and righteousness" (Zech. 8:7-17). For the prophet, the restoration of the
Temple of Jerusalem would be the portent of the establishment of the messianic kingdom in an indefinite future.[23] And
Zechariah states, in the spirit of the ancient prophets, the indispensable condition to be fulfilled, that God might realize
his promise of salvation: "Speak the truth to one another,
render in your gates judgments that are true and make for
peace; do not devise evil in your hearts against one another,
and love no false oath, for these things I hate, says Yahweh."

The lesson at Vespers is 8:19-23. Zechariah had previously been directed to consult with the priests on fasting in remembrance of the calamities which had befallen the nation
seventy years before. There was a fast in the fourth month in
memory of the fall of Jerusalem (cf. Jer. 39:2 ff.); in the
fifth month, destruction of Jerusalem and the Temple (cf.
2 Ki. 25:8 ff.); in the seventh month, the murder of Gedaliah
(cf. 2 Ki. 25:25 ff.); in the tenth month, beginning of the
siege by the Chaldaeans (cf. Jer. 39:11). Zechariah made no
comment on the decisions of the priests, but stated instead
how the Jews could make fasting profitable and turn days of
penitence and mourning into days of joy and good cheer:
"Love truth and peace; then your fast will be genuine."

CHAPTER THREE

The Triodion

GREAT LENT, TO THE SIXTH FRIDAY

An outline of the liturgical structure of the Lenten period from the first Monday of the Great Fast to the end of the sixth week will provide the setting for our study of Scripture readings during that season.[1] It may not be superfluous at the beginning of this chapter to remember that the weeks of Lent *precede*, rather than *follow*, the corresponding Sundays. Thus the first Sunday after the first week of Lent is followed by the second week, the second Sunday by the third week, and so on. The Church has always understood Great Lent as a time for repentance and for spiritual awakening. We test our faith looking toward the Cross of Christ, that by following him in his Passion we may have part in his Resurrection.

The eucharistic service is suspended during the weekdays of Lent; it is limited to the Saturdays, when the Liturgy of St. John Chrysostom is served, and to the Sundays, when the Liturgy is that of St. Basil. Twice a week, on Wednesday and Friday, the Liturgy of the Presanctified Gifts, Λειτουργία τῶν προηγιασμένων, is served; additional altar breads have been consecrated on the preceding Sunday and kept in the ἀρτοφόριον. The Christians are invited to partake of the sacred body of Christ, "lest they faint in the way" (Mt. 15: 32).[2] We should keep in mind that the Liturgy of the Presanctified is in reality a Vespers service, though frequently it is served in the morning so that the eucharistic fast—total

37

abstinence from food and drink—would not aggravate those
who wish to partake of the holy gifts. There is a strong movement for restoring the service to its normal time and for
giving to the faithful an opportunity to attend the service and
receive communion at the close of the working day.

The forty days of Lent[3] are an image of our journey toward our eternal destiny and the last link in a chain of typical
events: the forty years of the Israelites in the desert, the
forty-day march of Elijah to Mount Horeb, and the forty-day
fast of our Lord. The particular structure of Byzantine worship during Lent explains the distribution of Scripture readings. The weekdays lessons of the Office are taken exclusively from the Old Testament and read in the general order of
the text with due spacing. The Book of Isaiah is read at the
Sixth Hour, Genesis and Proverbs at Vespers, including
Wednesdays and Fridays, when Vespers is combined with the
Liturgy of the Presanctified. The purpose is obviously a didactic one. In the early Christian centuries, catechumens received instruction preparatory to their baptism at Easter, and
the reading of these books was part of the Church's pedagogy,
still fit to counteract our twentieth-century ignorance or neglect. At any rate, the choice is appropriate. The oracles of
the Book of Isaiah converge toward the person and saving
work of Christ the Messiah. Genesis describes the Creation
and the early phase of God's plan for the ultimate association
of man with himself, in spite of sin and its sequels. The
Proverbs are a collection of maxims for realizing a modicum
of human wisdom and make our basic cooperation with God
possible. These three Books belong to the traditional divisions
of the Hebrew Bible: the Law, *Tôrah*; the Prophets, *nebî'im*;
and the (sacred) Writings, *ketûbim*. A table of the lessons
from Isaiah, Genesis and Proverbs will be found at the end of
this chapter, for the sake of easy reference.

On the "liturgical days," namely on Saturdays and Sundays, nothing is read of the Old Testament.[4] At the Divine
Liturgy, the Epistles are from the Epistle to the Hebrews, a
systematic demonstration to Christians of Jewish background
of the superiority of the new dispensation of grace over the
old one. The Gospels are from Mark, a straight record of

what Jesus did and said, in which the author shows himself particularly aware of Jesus' apparent defeat by the forces of evil, which must be regarded as an integral part of his way on earth, freely accepted and ultimately vindicated by the triumph of the Resurrection.

The Isaiah prophecies. Old Testament scholars are generally agreed in regarding the Book of Isaiah as a collection of oracles pronounced at diverse times and in diverse circumstances, either by Isaiah himself, who prophesied during the second part of the eighth century B.C., or by anonymous prophets who ministered to the Jews exiled in Babylon after the fall of Jerusalem to the Chaldaeans (586 B.C.),[5] and to those who were repatriated following Cyrus' "Edict of Return" (538 B.C.). The canonical book shows forth an undeniable unity of inspiration. On the one hand, the presumed continuators of Isaiah were moved by the same Spirit which had made him speak. On the other, the doctrine of moral Yahwism preached by the eighth-century prophets, and the essentially Jewish phenomenon of messianism under its successive reinterpretations, run from one end of the book to the other.

A short description of its contents may be useful at this point. The major divisions of the book correspond to three periods in the history of the people. The first division, chapters 1-39, contains oracles pronounced by Isaiah himself, denouncing the moral and social evils of his time. In the chapters immediately following the prophet's fiery invectives, appears a messianic figure, the Immanuel, whose birth, childhood and coming of age are given as signs of divine protection at a time when the nation was threatened by the kings of Samaria and Damascus and when, a few years later, Jerusalem was besieged by the Assyrians and miraculously delivered of her enemies as foretold by the prophet.

The second part of the Book, chapters 40-55, a collection of oracles commonly called by modern exegetes the "Book of the Consolation of Israel,"[6] is related to historical events of the sixth century B.C., long after Isaiah's death. The kingdom of Judah had definitely lost its independence, Jerusalem had been destroyed, and the elites of the nation had been deported to Babylon. An anonymous prophet arose to foretell a mass return to the homeland in a near future. Cyrus, the Persian ruler who had supplanted the Neo-Babylonian dynasty, would be the providential agent of the liberation. There appears in this general context a mysterious "Servant of the Lord," the 'Ebéd Yahweh, in four poems which may be integral parts of the "Book of the Consolation," or later insertions.[7]

The third part of the Book, chapters 56-66, is a gathering of post-exilic fragments reflecting the situation of the re-patriates in the homeland. Not all the exiles had availed themselves of the liberal provisions of the Edict of Cyrus. Many, through industry and the resilience characteristic of their people, had created for themselves, in Babylon and in the diaspora, a more than tolerable situation. The homecoming of those who chose to return was far from what they had hoped for. The low-class Jews, whom the Babylonians had not deported, and throngs of foreigners had occupied their homesteads. Reviving the courage of the "Holy Gôlah" was the burden of a third generation of prophets who raised their sights to a future transcending the vicissitudes of history.

The literary analysis of the Book of Isaiah which we have tried to outline is complicated by the fact that some early fragments do open, beyond the historical conditioning, long-range prospects such as are normally found in the later chapters, and by the interpolation of some odd pieces out of context by the compiler, often on account of purely verbal clues or accidental similarities. It would be pointless, therefore, to seek a strict logical order in the medley of oracles of the book or in our liturgical sections, which were determined according to the principle of continuous reading.

Isaiah's early oracles, chapters 1-4, provide the material for the liturgical readings from the first Monday of Lent to the second Wednesday. The corruption and sinful stupidity of the people had prompted the prophet to raise his voice to call them unto repentance. "The ox and the ass recognize their master, but Israel does not ... From the sole of the foot up to the head there is no health in him, but bruises, sores,

and open wounds" (1:3-6).[8] The worst is that they esteemed
themselves to be sheltered from God's vengeance by the practice of a ritualism totally divorced from moral concern:
"What is to me the multitude of your sacrifices, says the
Lord . . . Your new moons and your convocations, my soul
hates. I am weary of them" (1:14).

The oracles of the first four chapters present the message
of Isaiah by way of antithesis, a favorite pattern of Hebrew
poetry. Each of our lessons confronts us with the choice: the
way of obedience, leading to deliverance from sin, to peace
and blessedness, or the way of rebellion and obstinacy, calling
for temporal and eternal malediction. The visions of gloom
begin with a lamentation over Jerusalem. The rhythm of this
piece is that of a *Qînah*, dirge, threnody, a poetic form of
which numerous examples are found in the prophetic literature. "How did the faithful city turn into a harlot, she that
was full of justice . . . her silver has become dross" (Is. 1:21-
22). Everywhere corruption and bribes; the judges have no
regard for the fatherless; "the widow's case does not even
reach them" (Is. 1:23); everywhere idolatry, superstition, ar-
rogance, jingoism, presumptuous reliance of the nation upon
arms and military might,[9] injurious to Yahweh who mean-
while is forgotten. The retribution will be terrible. "Enter
into the rock, hide in the dust . . . in the caves of the rocks
and the clefts of the cliffs . . . from before the terror of the
Lord" (Is. 2:10, 19). Do we not hear, by anticipation, the
very words of Christ? "Days are coming . . . when they shall
say to the mountains: Fall on us, and to the hills: Cover us!"
(Lk. 23:29-30; cf. Apoc. 6:15-16).

Alternating with each dark frame of that film-strip, come
the bright pictures: "Though your sins are like scarlet, repentance shall make you white as snow" (Is. 1:18). Jerusalem will be tested by fire: "I shall smelt away thy dross . . .
restore thy judges and counsellors as in the beginning" (Is.
1:25-26). The divine blessings shall be extended to all nations, for "out of Zion shall go forth the Law, and the Word
of the Lord from Jerusalem" (Is. 2:3); here the prophet refers to him, still unknown, who is to come and proclaim
God's truth, Christ the Teacher. The divine protection shall

be over the city, "a cloud by day and a flaming fire by night; the glory of God, a canopy and a pavilion," as in the days of Moses (Is. 4:5; cf. Ex. 13:21-22).

The human response had too often been sheer ingratitude. In the lesson of the second Monday of the fast, we are given to hear a tale of woe: "Let me sing," intones the prophet in the person of Yahweh, "the song of the vineyard.[10] My beloved had a vineyard on a fertile hillside. He had fenced it, cleared it of rocks, and planted it with choice plant... He had built a watchtower and made a wine-press in the midst of it. He expected it would bring forth muscat; what it yielded was sour grapes" (Is. 5:1-2). "Now judge, I pray you, between me and my vineyard. What more could I do for it that I have not done?... I tell you what I will do... I will let it go to waste... briers and thorns shall grow in it, and the clouds will I order that they rain no rain over it" (Is. 5:4-6).

The song of the vineyard is the prelude to a chain of imprecations in the following verses, resumed from time to time in the course of the book: Woe unto those who usurp the land, "joining house to house, field to field, till there is no space left." Woe to them who live in continuous revelry. Woe to those who defiantly challenge God, saying: "Let him speed his work... that we may know what he can do." Woe unto those who reverse the moral order, "calling evil good and good evil... Woe unto those that are wise in their own eyes and shrewd in their own sight... Woe unto the heroic wine-bibbers and the valiant mixers of strong drinks... Woe unto those who sell justice for a fee" (Is. 5:8-23). The Evangelists have recorded similar "Woes" pronounced by Christ himself (Mt. 23:13-29; Lk. 11:42, 47, 52).

From the second Thursday of Lent to the Thursday of the third week, we read from the chapters containing the Immanuel oracles, which moderns incline to regard as an originally independent unit of authentic Isaian origin, chapters 6-11. The compilers of the lectionary did not clearly single out the immediately messianic Immanuel fragments, either for lack of a sufficient attention to Hebrew prosody, or because they professed to consider the whole span of God's economy rather than to focus on single oracles, no matter how important for the "pre-history" of our salvation. They proceed in much the same way when dealing with the poems of the Servant in the second part of Isaiah.

At any rate, the Immanuel section is prefaced in the actual text of the book by Isaiah's description of his own call to the prophetic ministry, which we read on the second Thursday of the fast. "In the year that King Uzziah died,[11] I saw the Lord (*Adônai*) sitting upon a throne, high and lifted up, and his train filled the Temple. Above him stood the Seraphim . . . and one called to the other and said: Holy, holy, holy is the Lord of Hosts, the whole earth is full of his glory. And I said: Woe is me, for I am lost, for I am a man of unclean lips, and my eyes have seen the King, the Lord of Hosts! Then flew one of the Seraphim to me, having in his hand a burning coal from the altar, and he touched my mouth and said: Lo this has touched thy lips, thy guilt is taken away and thy sin is forgiven.[12] And I heard the voice of the Lord saying: Whom shall I send, and who shall go for us? Then I said: Here I am, send me! And He said: Go!" (Is. 6:1-12). The significance of the vision, reminiscent of the theophanies on Mount Sinai, when Yahweh spoke to Moses and Elijah, prototypes of the prophetic order, will escape no one. It is a solemn proclamation of God's transcendence and universal sovereignty.

A first Immanuel prophecy is read on the second Friday of the fast (Is. 7:1-14). The historical context is the critical situation of Jerusalem and Judah attacked by their northern neighbors, the kings of Samaria and Damascus. Isaiah, sent by God to re-assure King Ahaz of Judah, offers him, in the name of Yahweh, a sign at first declined by the king: "The *'almah*—ἡ παρθένος, the virgin—is with child and shall give birth to a son whom she will call (or, in Greek, whom thou wilt call, καλέσεις) Immanuel, 'God with us'." The lesson stops here, unaccountedly. The biblical text gives the meaning of the sign in the following verses, which are part of the oracle: the child will not yet be able to tell bad from good, "and already the land of the two kings who threaten thee shall have been laid waste." Since the birth of Immanuel is meant to be a sign of such a nature as to strike the imagination of the people, it must have been easily recognized by Ahaz, his courtiers, and the burghers of Jerusalem, no matter which interpretation is given to the Hebrew *bâ-'almah*, the virgin.[13] But we just do not know what the contemporaries of Isaiah did understand. The attempts at identifying the *'almah* and the Immanuel with known figures of the eighth century B.C. have proved abortive. We would rather think that, beyond the immediate context of the Immanuel oracle, the prophet himself foresaw dimly, and was ordered to announce, the birth of a messiah in an undetermined future. This is how it was interpreted by the Evangelists and received by the Church, not arbitrarily, but because here was the real event to be expected, of which the enigmatic birth of the child witnessed by the king and the people was the type. "All this took place," writes St. Matthew, "that it be fulfilled that which the Lord had spoken by the prophet" (Mt. 1:12). What had been for Isaiah prayerful hope is for us the full truth of the Incarnation of Christ, the Messiah.

On the third Monday of Lent, the lesson at the Sixth Hour is also from Isaiah's Immanuel prophecies (8:13 to 9:7). Like the preceding one, we shall hear it again on the eve of the Nativity (see chapter VII). The emphasis in this Lenten season is less on the miraculous birth of the Christ-child than on his future messianic labours. Immanuel would be unto his people a leader, whose light would shine upon those "who walk in darkness," even "in the shadow of death"; the invaders would be destroyed, "as in the day of Madian."[14] It becomes clear that the personality of the young ruler, son of David, whose royal protocol is recited by the prophet, "Wonderful Counsellor, Mighty God, Prince of Peace," transcends his immediate mission in history. We are invited to look higher and further ahead, no matter who the still unidentified type of our Messiah may have been. This was certainly the feeling of the Greek translators—Alexandrian Jews—when they interpreted "Wonderful Counsellor" as "the Angel of the Great Counsel." As for the categorical affirmation of the Hebrew text, that "his reign shall have no end," we may and we must understand it literally.

The Lenten lectionary bypasses unaccountably a third Immanuel prophecy, "There shall come forth a rod out of the root of Jesse" (Is. 11:1-9). This is all the more surprising because the lesson for the third Thursday is Isaiah 11:10 to 12:2, a post-exilic fragment misplaced among the Immanuel oracles and inserted by the compiler of the book on account of its mention of the root of Jesse in verse 10; the fragment is a long-range prophecy announcing that under a messianic leader, the people will find a permanent "resting place" (Hebr. *menûhah*, Gr. ἀνάπαυσις). The hieronymian Vulgate, *et erit sepulchrum eius gloriosum*, "and his tomb will be glorious," namely the tomb of Christ, is a forced translation which neither the biblical text nor the context authorize.

The prophecies which follow, up to chapter 39, and from which we read widely spaced excerpts from the Tuesday of the third week of Lent to the fifth Monday, continue on the themes common to the first part of the book: moral Yahwism, with its blessings and sanctions, the universal sovereignty of God over the nations, and dynastic messianism within the boundaries of the history of Israel, though with an extended vision to a distant future. Some oracles, verging on the eschatological, are most likely late insertions by the final redactor or compiler of the book.

A step by step commentary would be unduly repetitious, and the outline which we have just drawn should suffice for a correct understanding of our lessons. We may note the growing emphasis on Zion,[15] originally a topographic designation, becoming the capital of the Davidic monarchy and ultimately a religious symbol to the nation. "What will one answer to the messengers? The Lord has founded Zion" (Is. 14:32); "I lay in Zion for a foundation a stone, a tested stone, a precious cornerstone" (Is. 28:16; cf. Mt. 21:42; Eph. 2:20; 1 Peter 2:6). We hear, from time to time, a veiled yet unmistakable prophecy of the Messiah's triumph over death: "On this mountain . . . he will swallow up death forever" (Is. 25:8).

We read from the so-called Book of the Consolation of Israel (Is. 40-55) from Tuesday of the fifth week to the following Tuesday, the liturgical sections being separated from

each other by considerable intervals. A series of oracles announces the return of the exiles as if it were a new Exodus.
The events thus foretold, however, are conceived not as mere
historical material, but as heavy with religious implications.
The return is not merely a march along high roads providentially opened in the wilderness (Is. 40:3); it implies a conversion. The restoration is not a mere resuscitation of the
Davidic monarchy; it is meant to be a revival of the theocracy
instituted by Moses. This transformation is demanded by
God, whose counsel is unsearchable. "Have you not known?
Have you not heard? . . . It is He who sits above the circle of
the earth . . . the Eternal God . . . the Holy One" (40:21-28).
In this context, "Holy" is not a mere qualifier, but the very
essence of the Thrice-Holy acclaimed by the seraphim in
Isaiah's vision (6:3). Nothing that exists or that is conceiv-
able can possibly be compared with him. In him is the truly
unshakable foundation of our hope, for "they that wait for
him shall renew their strength and grow wings like the
eagles" (Is. 40:31).[16] The theme continues in the lesson of
the fifth Wednesday (Is. 41:4-14). "Who has called the
generations from the beginning? I, Yahweh, I am He; I, before the first, and after the last of them."[17] We may feel that
the imprecations against the manufacturers of idols in verses
6 and 7 are only a commonplace topic little in tune with the
rest of the oracle. But in reality, they express in terms which
Jewish masses could readily understand the ineffable Transcendence which no likeness can possibly represent. One day
St. Paul would teach that only Christ is the perfect image
of the Invisible God (Col. 1:15), the icon not made by hands,
equal to the Father.

The policies initiated by Cyrus had made the return possible. They had been more than an act of political wisdom
of the Persian overlord. Cyrus was a providential agent,
Yahweh's anointed (Is. 45:1).[18] The theme "service" is now
in the forefront: Cyrus is a servant, Jacob-Israel is a servant
(Is. 41:8 and 42:19), in the latter instance, however, a me-
diocre servant, blind and deaf. But here arises the figure of
the Servant par excellence.[19] The Church reads of him beginning on Thursday of the fifth week. His identity is as myste-

rious as the identity of the Immanuel, unless we agree to step out of the Old Testament boundaries. The authors of the New Testament had no hesitation in identifying him with our Lord Jesus Christ. The poems of the Servant provided the Evangelists with a powerful argument to convince the Jews in their audience, and this is how they were understood by the Church Fathers. St. Jerome even called Isaiah "an evangelist rather than a prophet."

The messiahship of the Servant is all spiritual. He comes not as a conqueror by force of arms, but in the strength of his own righteousness, kindness and meekness, his only weapons. He is sent "to open the blind eyes, bring out the prisoners from the prison and them that sit in darkness out of their dungeon" (Is. 42:6-7). These verses from the first poem are echoed in the oracle of chapter 61:1-2, which Jesus read in the synagogue of Nazareth on the first day of his Galilaean ministry (Lk. 4:16-22): "The Spirit of the Lord is upon me . . . ," the Spirit who inspired the prophets and descended upon Jesus when he was baptized in the Jordan.

The second poem (Is. 49:1-6) is included in the lessons of Monday and Tuesday of the sixth week. The text of 49:3 presents a problem thus far not solved. It reads: "Thou art my servant, Israel, in whom I will be glorified," a reading not easily compatible with verse 5, in which the Servant is clearly a physical person, whose task is "to bring back Jacob." Now Jacob is the beneficiary, not the agent, of messianic redemption.[20] At any rate, the messianic ideal of God's salvation reaching unto the end of the earth—"Hearken, O isles of the sea!"—is envisioned for a distant future, as the realization of the type, namely the return of the exiles from Babylon. To this purpose, Yahweh has called his Servant from the womb: "From the bowels of my mother he has named my name" (Is. 49:1); prophets and heroes had often been the objects of such providential calls. The reading of the two major Servant poems (Is. 50:4-9 and 52:13 to 53:12), in which the Church recognizes types of the Passion of the Savior, is postponed until Great and Holy Week (see chapter VI).

We wind up our reading from the Book of Isaiah during the last three days of the sixth week with post-exilic prophe-

cies in the latter part of the book. The pattern is similar to
that used by Isaiah in his early oracles: a series of diptychs
in which the retributions for the crimes of men alternate with
the blessings on those who listened and obeyed. But the stage
has changed. Isaiah had announced foreseeable punishments
and rewards within a few generations. Now the disillusion-
ment of the repatriates, the drab realities of the resettlement
and of the reconstruction, caused the continuator of Isaiah to
look ahead beyond historical contingencies. The hoped-for
reign of peace would not be realized until the latter days, and
the prophecy gives way to apocalyptic visions: either the final
cataclysm of which the destructions wrought in the past by
the enemies of Israel were but pale figures, or a glorious renewal of all things (Is. 65:8-16; 66:10-24).

The evolution of messianism, from dynastic, to futuristic,
to eschatological and apocalyptic, would have remained open-
ended, and our faith would have been in danger of "passing
out" in a rarefied atmosphere, had it not been for the Incarnation, which is the hard fact on which we can securely lean.
This is why the reading of Isaiah, the prophet of the Incarnation, is particularly appropriate in this season of Great Lent,
when our sight is arrested by the rock of Calvary and the
tomb from which Christ will arise, having conquered death
by death. We are back on the earth of men and, lest we
would be tempted to forget it, the Church has us read on the
Wednesday of the sixth week of Lent an authorized description of what is the true fasting, and a biting caricature of the
ludicrous comedy which we sometimes dare to call a fast
(Is. 58:1-11).

The reading of Genesis. The Book of Genesis is read at
Vespers. The lessons follow the order of chapters and are
irregularly spaced. The liturgical sections were apparently
determined by the positive role which the biblical narratives
played in the history of salvation and their appropriateness
to Lenten objectives. Whereas our survey of the Isaiah fragments demanded that they be replaced in their literary and
historical context, we have from the start, with Genesis, the
benefit of a unified composition in a systematic framework,

genealogical and, to a measure, chronological. The final redactor of the book has made every effort to weld together the traditions he found in his various sources.[21]

The main divisions of the book are as follows: (1) The creation of the world in six "days"—the so-called *Hexaemeron*. (2) The first human couple, the garden in Eden, and the Fall. (3) Early mankind, the Flood, the dispersion of peoples. (4) The deeds of the Hebrew patriarchs, from Abraham to Joseph.

We shall not read Genesis as an illustrated story-book, but as the revelation of man's unique destiny in the eyes of God. The book is neither a collection of legends nor a scientific discourse on origins, but rather a theology and an anthropology in terms intelligible to the ancient Hebrews. The narrative of Creation is related to the cosmogonies of the Near and Middle East, but these have been expurgated and transposed in order to express the faith of monotheism in its uncompromising purity and to define our relationship to God. The complex of modern sciences dealing with the origin of the cosmos, the appearance of life on earth and the early stages of mankind, would fall short of the objective of the Church, which lies beyond both the scientific interest or retrospective erudition. What we are aiming at is existential knowledge, unto the fulfilment of God's dream for his chosen creature.

The Genesis account of the work of Creation, namely the *Hexaemeron* and God's rest on the seventh day,[22] is the object of our readings on the first three days of Lent. We are taught that God created the world from nothing. We are not to imagine that there was, prior to Creation, a pseudo-being which we would call "nothingness," out of which God would have drawn all things into existence; in other words, the Creator is not to be thought of as organizing a pre-existing, shapeless material to which he would give form and order, and communicate a measure of power. Prior to Creation, there was God Eternal, and there is no such thing as an emptiness into which God would cause things successively to appear. God made light and divided light from darkness, "and the evening and the morning[23] were the first day . . . the second day . . . the third day," and so on. God's will is the only

cause of Creation. The Bible knows of no instrumentality
which could possibly concur in the production of the creature.
"God said . . . and it was so." A solemn announcement precedes the creation of man: "Let us make man in our image,
after our likeness!" (Gen. 1:26). Patristic tradition has interpreted this plural in express reference to the societal nature
of God, the Triune.[24]

We end the first week by reading Genesis 2:4-19 and 2:20
to 3:20: the story of Adam in the garden of Eden, literally
"the garden in the steppe"; the creation of the woman; the
temptation, fall, and expulsion from Paradise. A verse in
the first chapter of Genesis occurs over and over again like
a refrain: "And God saw that it was good." At the end of
the sixth day, the formula changes into: "Behold it was very
good." That excellence shows up after the creation of man,
whom Yahweh placed in the garden "to tend it and keep it"
(Gen. 2:15), and to whom he gave, in the person of the
woman, "a help meet for him" (2:18). Now Adam was en-
dowed with all he needed to do whatever God required of
him. He shared in the divine privilege of freedom, rather
than being driven by a blind law of nature and the compul-
sion of animal instinct. But he failed precisely here. His
failure is nigh unto incomprehensible; it is not imputable to
the Creator, into whose likeness he was to have grown, even
unto a participation of divine life—the "deification" or
θέωσις of our patristic tradition. Enticed by a mysterious
tempter and deceived by the illusion of a short-cut to reach
that goal, Adam and Eve claimed a false autonomy and,
through the misuse of their freedom, broke the pact of obedience which bound them to God. The biblical text spells out
the consequences of their rebellion: general disorder and un-
balance; hard toil and "the sweat of your brow"; loss of con-
trol over the sexual instinct; for the woman, the pangs of
childbirth; hostility and feuds breaking the unity of the human race; and death, instead of the unlimited life which could
have been their own. Yet evil will not prevail. A ray of hope
shines in this chaos. A descendent of Eve shall crush the
head of the deceiver (Gen. 3:15).[25] This, however, does not
mark the end of the struggle. Men will continue to face,

sooner or later, the ruin which threatens them inexorably. But God's grand design cannot possibly be thwarted; sin will be overcome, and death will lose its sting. Our own future is at stake, for we are all Adam and Eve. We do not read these chapters of Genesis as a picturesque tale from the past, but as our own destiny in Christ and through Christ.

Our reading continues during the second week with the vicissitudes of the first generations of men as the Hebrews imagined them, from Cain to Noah (Gen. 3:21 to 6:8). The redactors of the book have loaded what seems at first sight folkloric material with religious, nay theological values, under the inspiration of the Holy Spirit. They describe the fight between good and evil in diptych fashion, by way of simple allusions or extended dramas: on one side the rebels; on the other those men who, through obedience, have found grace in God's eyes. It is the latter whom the author of the Epistle to the Hebrews will eulogize (Hebr. 11:4-7). We are confronted with the mystery of election and rejection which has not ceased to baffle men, whose only recourse is in the justice and mercy of God. A succession of pre-Mosaic figures files off under our eyes: Abel, the first martyr; Cain, his brother's murderer, in defiance of God's answer to his complaint: "If thou doest well, shalt thou not be accepted? And if thou doest not well, sin crouches at thy door!" (Gen. 4:7); Seth, of whom it is said that "in his time, men began to call upon the name of Yahweh" (Gen. 4:26); Enoch, "who walked with God, and (then) he was not, for God took him" (Gen. 5:24).

From Monday of the third week to the fourth Thursday, our Vespers lessons are excerpts from Genesis 6:9 to 11:9. The composite story of Noah saving himself, his family, his three sons and the wives of his sons, eight persons in all out of the mass of sinners destined to perish in the waters of the Flood, has singularly impressed the New Testament writers (1 Peter 3:20; 2 Peter 2:5). Patristic tradition saw in the ark of Noah a type of the Church, in which all who are to be saved would find a safe refuge. We survey the various episodes of the story of Noah from the construction of the ark to the receeding of the Flood waters, the rainbow and the sacrifice of thanksgiving. We finish reading from early mankind with the Hebrew version of the scattering of people throughout the earth and the confusion of tongues, which evoke by contrast the effusion of the Holy Spirit on the day of Pentecost and the gathering of the Church.

On the fourth Friday of Lent, we pass to the history of the Hebrew patriarchs, an epic extending over several generations, from the day when Abraham departed from Ur of the Chaldees in Mesopotamia, nomadized through the pasture grounds of Canaan, to the sojourn of Jacob and his sons in Egypt. One day Moses would bring Israel into what had been thus far the Land of the Promise. In the perspective of our liturgy, we are given to understand that their journey is our journey; for we are called to enter, after the struggle of an existence which we insist on regarding as normal, into a radically new way of life in which the temptations and uncertainties of a fallen world will be overcome as we pass-over into the kingdom and are united to the risen Lord. Our readings converge toward that ultimate goal, set before us by the Evangelists and Apostles and the entire patristic tradition.

We hear successively the call to Abraham: "Go from thy country and thy kindred and thy father's house to a land I will show thee" (Gen. 12:1-7); God's promise to Abraham at the Oaks of Mamrê (Gen. 13:12-18); the solemn pact by which Abraham and Yahweh, the latter hidden under symbolic appearances, bind themselves by oath as they pass between the rows of sacrificial victims neatly quartered by Abraham (Gen. 15:1-15).[26] The promise thus sealed is solemnly reaffirmed in chapter 17:1-9: the true posterity of Abraham is to be blessed forever. The bargaining of Abraham pleading before God for the people of Sodom—"And if only ten just men should be found there?"—brings back with special insistence a basic feature of moral Yahwism: the rigor of God is in reality forced upon him by the sinners themselves, unto whom he is ready to extend his mercy, if only they are willing to accept it (Gen. 18:20-33). The series of episodes of which Abraham is the hero ends with the story of the sacrifice of Isaac, read on the fifth Friday. The typological transfer to the sacrifice of Jesus Christ on the Cross is transparent. The innocent victim rescued at the last minute by the hand of an angel is the figure of him who came to bear the sins of the world (Gen. 22:1-18). The basic relevance of the Old Testament is compelling, even if we question some of the allegorizing details relished by the Fathers and the hymnographers.[27] This lesson is repeated on Great and Holy Saturday—"repeated", unless, as Fr. Kniazeff suggests, the liturgical structure of the office during Great Lent, especially the lessons at the Sixth Hour and at Vespers, represent an extension of the readings selected for Holy Week.[28]

The sacrifice on Mount Moriah (Gen. 22:1-18) is the only episode which the Lenten lectionary has retained of the stories in which Isaac appears as one of the principal personages. Otherwise, his role is rather that of a mere link in the chain of succession from Abraham. The Byzantine lectionary passes immediately from the deeds of Abraham to the widely spaced episodes of which Jacob and Joseph are the heroes. Thus, on the sixth Monday, we read of Jacob being blessed by his dying father unto the line of election, preferentially to his brother Esau who had forfeited his birthright (Gen. 27:1-41). St. Paul argues from the competition between the two brothers in support of his doctrine of gratuitous election of the saints: "Jacob I have loved, but Esau I have hated" (Rom. 9:13), which is an explicit quotation from Malachi 1:2.[29] The Fathers have recognized in the substitution of Jacob for Esau his elder brother a figure of the accession of the Church to the privilege of the Jewish nation under the Covenant. Jacob's stratagems to secure his father's blessing to the detriment of Esau seem to have caused some embarrassment to the Church Fathers, for instance to St. Augustine, who concluded an unconvincing argument by saying that there was here no crookery, but rather mysteries, *non mendacium, sed mysterium.*

The lesson for the sixth Tuesday stages the return of Jacob from Transjordan and the definitive separation of the Hebrew clans from the Aramaeans (Gen. 31:3-16).[30] Verse 13 recalls the vision which Jacob saw in a dream when, journeying away from his father's home, he heard the voice of God saying: "I am the God of Bethel, where thou didst anoint the pillar and vowed a vow unto me." The allusion is to Genesis 28:10-22, Jacob's ladder and the stone pillar of Bethel, which the Byzantine liturgy reads for the Nativity of the Theotokos (see chapter VII).

Selections from the life of Joseph form the Vespers lessons on the last three days of Great Lent, prior to Lazarus Saturday (Gen. 43:26 to 50:26). We hear of Joseph the Provider, welcoming his brothers—a mixed lot—down in Egypt, the land of refuge, but also of exile, where many an Asian tribe had emigrated, by the mercy or at the mercy of the Pharaonic rulers.

Jacob himself, now known under the God-given name Israel, would join his sons in Egypt, after God had spoken to him "in the visions of the night," saying: "I am God, the God of thy fathers; fear not to go down into Egypt. There I will make thee a great nation . . . and Joseph's hand will close thine eyes" (Gen. 46:1-7). As we are preparing to witness the resurrection of Lazarus before entering Great and Holy Week, we hear of the death and solemn funerals of Jacob-Israel and of Joseph, whose remains would be laid to rest in the soil of Canaan: Jacob in the cave of the Machpelah, the burial grounds which Abraham had purchased from Ephron the Hittite (Gen. ch. 23).[31] As for Joseph, according to a tradition still alive in the Nablus district, he was buried under the walls of Shechem, in the shadow of the Oak of Moreh, where Abraham had first pitched his tent.

We may have noticed the irregular spacing of the fragments selected for reading in the Church. The "continuous reading" is far from continuous. A considerable part of the patriarchal history was omitted. Some reasons for this are fairly obvious: some lengthy stories are definitely marginal to the theme of the covenant of grace, such as the idyl of Isaac's betrothal to Rebekah, or the description of the somewhat too ingenious methods used by Jacob to increase his flocks. Other episodes come up in the book in duplicate or triplicate, for instance Genesis 12:10-20; 20:1-18; 26:7-11. The lengthy novel of Joseph and his brethren abounds in repetitions, due to the inability of the final redactor of Genesis to fuse his various sources into a satisfactory unit. The compilers of our lectionary skipped much of such material, irrelevant from their own viewpoint.

They had however deeper reasons for by-passing sections which may appear at first significant material. The theme of divine election unto salvation has certainly guided their choice; the counterpart of election is reprobation, and the Book of Genesis involves an essential process of elimination at every step of the history of the Hebrew patriarchs. It is precisely the episodes relative to the foreigners who have no valid claim, and to the "drop-outs," which have been systematically omitted from our lectionary: Lot and his descendants Moab and Ammon; the clans issued from Abraham's concubines relegated "in the East"; Ishmael and the Arabs; the in-laws of Isaac and Jacob; Esau and the Edomites, Judah's turbulent neighbors. This may explain, at least in part, the otherwise unaccountable intervals that exist between the liturgical sections from the Book of Genesis.

Lessons from Proverbs.[32] The Book of Proverbs, Παροι-μίαι, is composed of several collections of maxims, and was circulated under the name of Solomon, of whom it was said that "he surpassed all the wise men of the East and the sages of Egypt... He spoke three thousand proverbs, and his songs were a thousand and five" (1 Ki. 4:30, 32).

The first collection, chapters 1 through 9, is entitled "Proverbs of Solomon, son of David, king of Israel." It contains admonitions of a father to his son, or his sons. The title "Proverbs of Solomon," is repeated in 11:1 to introduce a series of impersonal maxims, up to 22:16. The following section, 22:17 to 24:34, is attributed to anonymous sages: "Hear the words of the sages" (22:17), and "These also are from the sages" (24:23). Chapters 25-29 are a collection of proverbs ascribed to Solomon, "which the men of Hezekiah, king of Judah, copied out." They are followed by the "Words of Agur" (30:1-33) and of "King Lemuel" (chapter 31), unidentified representatives of the legendary wisdom of the East. This type of literature had been cultivated in Mesopotamia and in Egypt by the Assyro-Babylonian scribes and the Pharaonic government officials. Solomon, inasmuch as he

had organized the administration of the Hebrew kingdom on
the model of the Egyptian chancery, may rightly be called the
father of gnomic poetry in Israel.[33]

The liturgical sections of our lectionary are divided most
arbitrarily. It is almost impossible to determine why some
fragments of the mosaic were used and the others left out.
The ascription of the principal parts of the Book of Proverbs
to Solomon as their author may have been the criterion of the
compiler of the lectionary. As a matter of fact they did not
draw on the material collected by the scribes of Hezekiah nor
on the Words of the Sages and the Words of Agur and
Lemuel. The table at the end of this chapter will help surveying the lectionary as a whole. We shall content ourselves
here with a few introductory remarks and a summary of the
didactic values of the book. The general object of the liturgists was to present the Book of Proverbs as a primer of practical wisdom for daily life and the moral instruction of believers.

In the Vespers lessons of the first Monday and the first
Wednesday of Lent (Prov. 1:1-19 and 2:1-22), the origin
and working of human wisdom are epitomized in the following correlation: on the one hand, the fear of the Lord is the
principle of wisdom; on the other, the quest for wisdom leads
to fearing God. Such a fear is not the fear of slaves under a
ruthless master, but respect for a God whom we hate to
offend.

The canonical book, and the lectionary as well, aim at
demonstrating the precepts of ethics by means of familiar
maxims, no matter how humble our activities are. They always presuppose a free choice on our part, and this free
choice is expressed in striking antitheses. Two ways are open
before us, the way of life and the way of perdition. "Hear,
my son, and heed my words . . . I have taught thee the way
of wisdom and led thee in the right path" (4:10-11); but "a
man who strays from the way of understanding will rest in
the assembly of the dead" (21:16). The horizon being that
of the Old Testament, the retributions and sanctions are normally conceived as temporal (cf. 3:9-10; 4:10).[34]

The moral precepts are scattered through the various collections, whose ordering defies every logic. A large number of fragments are relative to the caution which men should observe in their dealing with women. "Foreign" women are to be shunned. They had led Solomon astray (1 Ki. 11:1); Nehemiah, in the days of the post-exilic restoration, saw in them a danger to ethnic purity and the faith of the nation (Neh. 13:26-27). But the Proverbs state the problem in more familiar terms, denouncing the luring ways of loose women, especially dangerous for young men (Prov. 2:16-19; 5:3-8). The vivid picture of a prostitute enticing a young son ends with the warning: "Her house is the way to the She'ol, down to the chambers of death" (Prov. 7:6-27).[35] Beware of becoming involved in adultery and promiscuity; the ideal is a monogamous union: "Drink water from your own cistern, live water from your well... Let your fountain be blessed, and rejoice in the wife of your youth" (Prov. 5:15-16, 18).

We shall hear miscellaneous principles of moral action and advices of down-to-earth wisdom as they occur in the lectionary: on sobriety (Prov. 20:1; 23:20-21; 23:30-35), with a masterful description of the physiology of drunkenness; on laboriousness vs. idleness (Prov. 6:6-11; 19:15); on the right use of riches, which are not the supreme good (Prov. 11:28; 27:24); on prudence in business: be slow in becoming surety for your neighbor (Prov. 6:1-5, 17-18);[36] on honesty and justice (Prov. 11:1, 3, 6; 20:10, 17; 23:10-11); on generosity, charity, compassion (Prov. 11:25; 22:22; 24:11-12; 31:9).

There is no denying that the moralistic wisdom of the Hebrew bureaucrats, in spite of its picturesque, occasionally humorous insights into human behavior, is often short-winded, and their moral precepts less than sublime, which we need not deplore; they speak, after all, to our common lot. It would be unjust, however, to see in the Book of Proverbs nothing more than a treasury of Polonius' truisms.

The passages which depict Wisdom attain to a rare elevation. Christian tradition has been prompt to identify divine Wisdom with the Logos.[37] It was actively present in the act of creation: "The Lord possessed me in the beginning of his way... I was set up from everlasting, from the beginning ere the earth was ... When there were no depths, I was brought forth, when there were no fountains gushing forth with water, before the mountains were firmly rooted, earlier than the hills was I begotten ... I was at his side as master builder, making his delight day by day, playing before him always, playing on the surface of the earth, and my delights are with the sons of men" (Prov. 8:22-25, 30-31). Wisdom calls on men at the crossroads (Prov. 1:20-33), inspires kings, rulers and law-givers. "I love them that love me, and those who seek me early find me ... for who finds me finds life and obtains favor from the Lord" (8:17, 35). "Wisdom has built her house, set up her seven pillars, slaughtered her beasts, mixed her wine, set her table ... sent her maidens to call on the high places of the city ... Come, eat of my bread and drink of the wine I have mixed" (Prov. 9:1-5). Do we not hear in this call of Wisdom the very voice of our Lord in the parable of the wedding feast? (Mt. 22:1-10). The latter passage from Proverbs, which is part of the lesson for the third Tuesday, is also read at Great Vespers on the feasts of the Theotokos (see chapter VII). The angle from which it is approached, however, is quite different. In the Lenten perspective, we think of divine Wisdom as the transcendent source and model of human wisdom. In the perspective of the Marian feasts, divine Wisdom is considered in function of the total economy of salvation, leading directly to the Incarnation, as the Word became flesh, "finding his abode in the Virgin."[38]

The series of our Lenten lessons ends with the praise of the "virtuous woman" (King James), "good wife" (Revised Standard Version), "a valiant woman," *'esbeth hail* (Hebrew) (Prov. 31:10-31). According to form, it is an acrostich poem; this literary device, the first letter of each stich following the traditional order of the Hebrew alphabet, *aleph, beth, ghimel, daleth,* etc., was used in some poetic compositions, as for instance Psalm 119 and the Lamentations. The matron of Proverbs epitomizes in her person and activity the qualities and virtues described in the previous chapters. A "Martha" type, certainly not a "Mary"; she is not, however, to be regarded as a busy-body, for her excellence proceeds from a deeper source: "Grace is deceitful and beauty is vain, but a woman that fears the Lord, she is to be praised" (Prov. 31:30).

There should be no question regarding the relevancy of Proverbs as a practical course of morals for neo-Christians. Of course, catechumens do not exist any more as a distinct body of persons to be instructed in view of a mass baptism on Great and Holy Saturday. Yet the advice and precepts of the Book of Proverbs have lost nothing of their propriety. They are neither more nor less significant than the precepts and advice of St. Paul to the Corinthians, who thought themselves above the level of elementary morals, and they should also correct the vagaries of the so-called "new morality" of our time.

New Testament readings. The series of New Testament readings, Epistles and Gospels, on liturgical days shows a number of modifications of the regular course of the liturgy, without immediate relation to the original rhythm and the spiritual dialectics of the Lenten season. The commemoration of the victory of the Church over iconoclasm and the restoration of the cult of images in A.D. 843 has been substituted for the liturgical service of the first Sunday in Lent. St. Gregory Palamas, who had been instrumental in the victory of Orthodoxy in a fourteenth-century crisis, is commemorated on the second Sunday. The third Sunday is entirely devoted to the veneration of the Holy Cross, and the memory of St. John of the Ladder and of St. Mary of Egypt is associated with the fourth and fifth Sunday, respectively.

The introduction of such motifs to the Sunday liturgy in Lent has its origin in the usage of Constantinople. Fr. Kniazeff, who refers to a study of Karabinov on the Triodion,[39] states that the character of the Byzantine *ordo* may be explained, at least partly, by the common belief in the supernatural origin and nature of the imperial power, following which a correspondance was sought between the Old and New Testament economy of Revelation, and the history of Byzantium and the Church, which was regarded as the incipient phase of the Kingdom of God. The system of readings in the Church of Jerusalem as we know it from a Sinaitic Gospel book of the ninth-tenth century shows in fact a much lesser concern with historical parallels than the Byzantine lectionary now in use and a more exclusive interest in the penitential character of Great Lent as a preparation for Easter.

The complexity of design resulting from the introduction of votive elements into the liturgical worship is particularly noticeable in the distribution of scriptural readings. The regular course of common lessons from the Epistle to the Hebrews and from the Gospel according to St. Mark is interrupted by the proper lessons of Orthodoxy Sunday and the Sunday of the Cross. The best approach for us will probably be to follow, week by week, the order of the liturgical calendar, even if it breaks up, unavoidably, the continuity of our exposition.

First Saturday of Lent. The regular course of readings from the Epistle to the Hebrews begins on the Saturday before Orthodoxy Sunday with the first twelve verses of the Epistle, where the entire economy of divine Revelation is spelled out: God had spoken to the "Fathers" through the prophets, from Moses to John the Baptist. He now speaks to us through his Son, the eternally begotten, "expressed image of his substance" χαρακτὴρ τῆς ὑποστάσεως αὐτοῦ, who together with the Father created and upholds the universe, who became man to purge away our sins and, having accomplished his task, is forever glorified "on the right hand of the Majesty on high."

The Gospel of the first Saturday of Lent (Mk. 2:23 to 3:5) displays the enmity which Jesus met on the part of the Jewish intelligentsia, and which would finally lead him to the Cross. On a certain sabbath, in a synagogue, Jesus healed a man who had a "withered hand." This was enough to provoke the anger of the Pharisees who, on another sabbath day, had sourly commented on the disciples passing through a field and plucking a few ears of grain to nibble: a sacrilegious violation of the Law! Jesus retorted that the sabbath is made for man, not man for the sabbath. "Therefore, the Son of Man is Lord also of the sabbath." St. Mark notes that from that time onward, the Pharisees and the Herodians, Jewish supporters of Herod Antipas, Tetrach of Galilee, "took counsel against Jesus, how they might destroy him." A strange caucus of ritualists hypnotized by the letter of the Law, and of politicoes who could not care less about religious matters, but became panicky at the plausibility of a messianic upheaval! Yet Jesus was not a contempter of tradition nor a revolutionary firebrand.

Orthodoxy Sunday. The Epistle (Hebr. 11:24-26, 32; 12:1-2) is the encomium of the heroes who, through their life and their faith in the Promise, testified to the virtue of the divine Revelation: a "cloud of witnesses" who surround us and leave us without an excuse for shying away from "the race that is set before us." Let us rather look toward Jesus Christ, "the author and finisher of our faith, who for the joy that was set before him endured the Cross, despising the shame, and is set down at the right hand of the throne of God." The same Epistle, cut differently, is also read on the first Sunday after Pentecost (All Saints), and on the Sunday before the Nativity (the Holy Fathers).

Exceptionally, the Gospel lesson is not from Mark, but from John (1:43-51). Fr. Kniazeff, *op. cit.* pp. 230 ff., explains this exception by the following hypothesis. On the one hand, the Gospel of Mark is by-passed when the calendar shifts from the "Sundays of Matthew" to the "Sundays of Luke"; on the other hand, there is a strong evidence for a primitive Palestinian course of readings from John, which is continued in the weeks of the Pentecostarion; the Byzantine Church may have wished to make a place for Mark in the dominical Lenten readings by substituting his Gospel for an older course of lessons from John. The actual reading of John 1:43-51 on the first Sunday of Lent would then be a vestige of the presumed older system of Gospel lessons. The substitution would have taken place before the proclamation of Orthodoxy (843), with which the pericope of John has no specific relation.

The Evangelist describes the calling of the Apostles, those of Bethsaida, lake fishermen, and of Nathanael, the guileless

Israelite who could not figure out how a Messiah could possibly come out of Nazareth. This balances and completes the mustering of the Old Testament saints in the Epistle to the Hebrews. In a sense, the call is addressed to all of us, and the lesson ends on the Savior's promise that "we shall see the heaven split open and the angels of God ascending and descending upon the Son of Man" (John 1:51). This last verse is heavy with associations with the Old and the New Testament: Jacob's ladder (Gen. 28:12), the heavens split open when Jesus was baptized in the Jordan (Mt. 3:16; Mk. 1:10; Lk. 3:21), and when St. Stephen was stoned by the Jews (Acts 7:55).

The second Saturday. The Epistle of the second Saturday (Hebr. 3:12-16) is an appeal to conversion, mutual edificattion, and perseverance to the end. The author quotes from Psalm 95:7-9: "Today, if you hear his voice, harden not your hearts as in (the day of) exasperation," ἐν τῷ παραπικρασμῷ, an allusion to the seditious murmurs of the Israelites against Moses.[40] None of them would enter the Promised Land. Could we dare, then, decline the invitation or, having heard and accepted it, fall away from the Living God through unbelief?

The Gospel of the second Saturday (Mk. 1:35-45) relates how Jesus went preaching in the synagogues and "casting out devils." In that particular instance, he "cleansed" a leper, made ritually impure by the disease, and to be shunned by all. Jesus charged the man "not to publish it much and blaze abroad the matter," lest it be misinterpreted, and to present himself to the priest, according to the prescription of the Law (Lev. 14:1-32). Once Jesus was gone, the ex-leper started to broadcast the news, little concerned with the policy of so-called Messianic secret.[41]

The second Sunday. The Epistle of the second Sunday (Hebr. 1:10 to 2:3) points to the constancy of God as the guaranty of our faith. Heaven and earth may pass; God's Word abides forever. His purpose cannot possibly be defeated. The Son, who was sent to all that are called and is enthroned on the right hand of the Father, holds "the scepter of righteousness, the scepter of royalty" (Hebr. 1:8, quoting Ps. 45:7). We are saved by an act of his sovereignty, which is above the ministry of the angels, mere instruments in God's hand. The author of Hebrews argues from the belief that the Law, a temporary organ in the economy of salvation, was brought to men by angels (Hebr. 2:2, cf. Gal. 3:19). As a matter of fact, the "angel" who conversed with Moses on Mount Sinai (Acts 7:38) is properly the "Angel of Yahweh," that is to say Yahweh manifesting himself to his creatures (cf. Gen. 16:7; Ex. 3:2; Judges 2:1). The argument in Hebrews reflects a later tradition of Jewish origin which aimed at safeguarding God's transcendence by a distinction between Yahweh and his Angel.

In the Gospel (Mk. 2:1-12), we hear of another of the healings which so infuriated Jesus' adversaries. This one did not happen on the sabbath, nor could it be suspected of being an incitement to revolt against the Romans, but hostile by-standers were not slow in finding a motive for grievance. The people of Capernaum had brought to Jesus a paralytic lying on his couch, whom he absolved from the sins which, according to popular belief, were the cause of the disease. A few scribes[42] who had witnessed the miracle objected loudly: everybody knows that only God can forgive sins; did that fellow make himself God? The time and place were inopportune for doing anything more than murmuring, but it was obvious that this blasphemer and rabble rouser ought to be silenced, the sooner the better.

The third Saturday. The pre-paschal instruction continues on the third Saturday with an exhortation of the author of Hebrews to neo-Christians (Hebr. 10:32-38), that they persevere in the fervor of their "illumination," a term frequently used in the New Testament and in Patristics to designate baptism. It enabled Christians to endure suffering and withstand persecution; it should make them overcome every temptation of discouragement in the days ahead. Faith strives toward the future: "A little while yet, and He that is to come will come and not tarry," for "the just shall live by faith" (Hebr. 10:37-38, quoting Habbakuk 2:3-4; cf. Rom. 1:17).[43]

The scribes of whom we heard in the Gospel of the second Sunday of Lent were probably Pharisees and not little proud of their theology. Continuing the reading of Mark (2:14-17), we find them again charging Jesus for having attended a banquet which St. Matthew, the ex-tax collector now called to be an apostle, was offering to his fellow publicans (cf. Mt. 9:9-13; Lk. 5:27-32). Such people are notoriously bad company, and our self-appointed guardians of morals felt it their duty to warn the disciples. Jesus' retort (he had overheard them): "They that are whole have no need of the physician, but they that are sick. I came not to call the righteous, but sinners to repentance."

The third Sunday. The dual character of the third Sunday, which doubles as a commemorative Sunday devoted to the "Veneration of the Cross," Σταυροπροσκύνησις, sets it apart from the rest of the series of Saturdays and Sundays in Lent. We shall therefore proceed in the same manner as we did for Orthodoxy Sunday. The case, however, is different. Orthodoxy Sunday, first in Lent, recalled the triumph over iconoclasm, celebrated in Constantinople in the ninth century, but the Veneration of the Cross on the third Sunday does not relate to any definite event in the life of the Church, in contrast with the feast of the Universal Exaltation of the Holy Cross, the Ὕψωσις, on September 14, anniversary date of historical events in Constantinople and Jerusalem (see chapter VII). The Latin Church also celebrates two feasts of the Cross: the *Exaltatio Sanctae Crucis* on September 14, and the *Inventio Sanctae Crucis*, that is, the discovery of the Cross by St. Helen. The latter was originally part of the September celebration, but was transferred to May 31 in the course of the eighth century. The feast of the Σταυροπροσκύνησις in the East marks the middle point of the Great Fast and is announced in the Synaxarion as follows: "Today in the midst of fasting and of our perilous and strenuous journey, the Life-giving Cross was erected by the Holy Fathers to give us rest

and refreshment, to lighten our burden and give us courage
for the remaining task."

The proper Epistle for the Sunday of Holy Cross is also
taken from Hebrews (4:14 to 5:6), like the Epistles of the
other Saturdays and Sundays in Lent. It directs our thoughts
toward the sacrifice of Christ whose High Priesthood will be
the subject-matter of the Epistles selected for the latter part
of Lent, prior to Palm Sunday. For we have in him a High
Priest who, unlike the Aaronic priests of the Old Testament,
can be touched with feeling for our infirmities, "being in all
points tempted as we are, yet without sin." The author of
Hebrews never tires of this theme, comparing the priesthood
of Aaron with the priesthood of Christ. The call to the priesthood is not of human institution. Aaron was called of God.
Christ was ordained on the eternal day when the Father said
to him: "Thou art my Son, today have I begotten thee" (Ps.
2:7, cf. Hebr. 5:5); for God had foreseen the Incarnation
from all eternity. The priesthood of Christ is not by delega-
tion, but in his own name. It would be incorrect to conceive
the priesthood of Christ as derived from the priesthood of
Aaron. On the contrary, the archetype is the eternal priesthood of Christ, of which the priesthood of Aaron is a passing
shadow, and this is expressed in a sentence which comes up
again and again in our Epistle readings: "Christ is priest forever after the order of Melchisedech" (cf. Ps. 110:4), the
mysterious king-priest of the Most High, of whom it is said
that he was "without father, without mother, without genealogy, having neither beginning of days nor end of life, but
made like unto the Son of God" (Hebr. 7:3).

The Gospel (Mk. 8:34 to 9:1) falls in place in the current series of the Sundays of Mark, and also orients us toward
the Cross, as the time draws near to the sacrificial death of
Christ, to whom we are urged freewillingly to associate ourselves, having been incorporated in him through baptism.
The Crucifixion is not merely one moving spectacle which we
contemplate with a shudder, but a personal drama in which
we are existentially involved. "Whoever will come after me,
let him deny himself and take his cross, and follow me!"

The fourth Sunday. We resume our survey of the New Testament readings for Great Lent in their serial order. The steady progression of the Epistles until Lazarus Saturday is, to a large extent, explained by the systematic composition of the Epistle to the Hebrews, which is perhaps the most homogeneous piece of writing of the entire apostolic corpus. The lesson for the fourth Saturday (Hebr. 6:9-12) repeats with renewed emphasis the theme of faith, inspirer of every good work.

This Gospel, like the preceding one, takes us along the shores of the Lake of Gennesareth, as Jesus returned from a journey in the districts of Tyre and Sidon, perhaps in order to escape the crowds for a while (Mk. 7:31-37). They brought to him a man who was deaf and whose speech was impaired —evidently the work of some devil! The Evangelist describes in detail the healing of the patient. Once more, the formal recommendation not to noise the thing abroad was unheeded. "The more Jesus charged them, the more loudly they spread the news."

The fourth Sunday. The Epistle immediately follows what was read yesterday (Hebr. 6:13-20). The Apostle stresses the infallibility of a promise sealed by oath, as the foundation of our faith, "for when God made promise to Abraham, since he could swear by no greater, he swore by himself." The prospect open to us is that of a new life, a life of consecration: the Christian lives in this world, but he is not of this world; leaving behind the obsession with things profane, he is already anchored in a firmer ground; in his true self he lives already "within the veil," the veil of the Holy of Holies (Ex. 26:31-34; Lev. 16:2; Mt. 27:51)," where Christ, our High-Priest, entered once and for all in his own blood, shed for us. The same symbolism is further developed in the Epistles of the fifth Saturday and Sunday, respectively Hebrews 9:1-7 and 9:11-14. The portable sanctuary built by Moses in the desert after the model which Yahweh himself had shown to him "on the mountain" is the figure of the eternal sanctuary, not made by hands, and from which it derived its mystical significance. The sacrifice of Christ on the

Cross and our eucharistic sacrifice on the Christian altar, behind the veil of the iconostasis, is now consummated in heaven. We would like to recall here the prayer *Supplices te rogamus* in the Roman anaphora—perhaps a former epiclesis: "We beseech thee, God Almighty, command that these things be borne by the hand of thy Holy Angel to thine altar on high, that as many of us as shall partake of thy body and of thy precious blood may be filled with every blessing and grace."

The healing of a boy possessed of a demon, whom the disciples of Jesus had vainly tried to exorcize (Mk. 9:17-31), is the theme of the Gospel on the fourth Sunday. It all happened immediately after the Transfiguration of Our Lord on Mount Tabor (see chapter VII). The description of the miracle by the Synoptics is unusually detailed (cf. Mt. 17:14-21; Lk. 9:37-42); this has induced modern translators and exegetes to diagnose the condition of the boy as epilepsy. Whatever it may have been, the Evangelists took care to register accurately the attitude of the bystanders, including that of the father and of the Apostles, in fact an attitude of total incomprehension of the role of Jesus. The crowds were disposed to believe in him, tentatively, as some of our contemporaries believe in charlatans and quacks. Just think of the marvelous cures advertized in the newspapers and of the bizarre theology underlying some speculations on faith-healing! What interests most people is "whether it works"; but they do not care much to know the real source of the healing power. This may explain the reaction of our Lord when he was first approached by the father. "O, faithless generation, how long shall I suffer you?" (Mk. 9:19).[45] The request was granted, but not before the father declared his faith: "Lord, I believe; help thou my unbelief!" What about the disciples? Faith they had, but also they thought of themselves as apprentice exorcists, since they were of the retinue of the Master, and they felt dismayed at their failure: "Why could we not cast that devil out? And Jesus said unto them: This kind cannot be driven out by anything but prayer" (Mk. 9:29). A marginal note in some manuscripts adds: "and fasting," καί νηστεία, cf. Vulgate, *nisi in oratione et ieiunio.* The lesson ends with Jesus' prediction of his forthcoming Passion, Death, and Resurrection. This was the second announcement he made of these. The first time, according to Mark 8:31-32, had been after the profession of faith of St. Peter at Caesarea Philippi.

The fifth Saturday. Following the allusion to the veil of the Temple in the Epistle of the fourth Sunday, we read today the description of the Mosaic sanctuary, the Temple of Solomon and its reconstructions. It was a permanent replica of the tent—the "Tabernacle"—which sheltered the Ark of the Covenant (Hebr. 9:1-7). What prompted the Apostle was not archaeological interest, but the value of the earthly Tabernacle as a figure of the heavenly sanctuary into which Christ entered for our salvation.

Whereas the lectionary abides consistently by the reading of Hebrews until Lazarus Saturday inclusively, it interrupts the reading of Mark, as if the Church were drawn irresistibly by an accelerating current into the tragical events of Great and Holy Week. Thus the Gospel of the fifth Saturday (Luke 10:38-42 and 11:27-28) introduces Martha and Mary, Jesus' hostesses, who will play a major role in the final drama. We shall comment briefly on that pericope at the beginning of chapter IV. Fr. Kniazeff thinks that the sudden turn taken by the Gospel lectionary on this Saturday, the Saturday of the Acathist, is the hypothetical trace of an ancient feast of the Annunciation, shifted later to its present date on March 25.[46]

The fifth Sunday. The Epistle (Hebr. 9:11-13), continues the theme of the passage read yesterday. The High Priest entered once a year into the sanctuary with the blood of victims, to make expiation for his sins and the sins of the people. Now Christ "the High Priest of the good things to come . . . entered once and for all into the holy place, having secured by his own blood an eternal redemption."

This is the mystery which we will celebrate after two weeks hence, and today's Gospel (Mk. 10:32-45) begins with Jesus' third announcement of the forthcoming Passion: "Behold, the Son of Man is delivered unto the chief priests, and

they shall condemn him to death and deliver him to the
Gentiles. And they shall mock him, and scourge him, and
spit on him; they shall kill him, and the third day he shall
rise again." It does not seem that the Apostles understood
fully what this implied, judging from the incongruous request
of James and John: "Might we sit one on thy right hand, and
the other on thy left hand, in thy glory?"

TABLE OF OLD TESTAMENT READINGS
FOR WEEKDAYS IN LENT

	Isaiah (Sixth Hour)	Genesis (Vespers)	Proverbs (Vespers)
First week			
Monday	1:1-20	1:1-13	1:1-20
Tuesday	1:19 to 2:3	1:14-23	1:20-33
Wednesday	2:3-11	1:24 to 2:3	2:1-22
Thursday	2:11-21	2:4-19	3:1-18
Friday	3:1-14	2:20 to 3:20	3:19-34
Second week			
Monday	4:2 to 5:7	3:21 to 4:7	3:34 to 4:22
Tuesday	5:7-16	4:8-15	5:1-15
Wednesday	5:16-25	4:16-26	5:15 to 6:3
Thursday	6:1-12	5:1-24	6:3-20
Friday	7:1-14	5:32 to 6:8	6:20 to 7:1
Third week			
Monday	8:13 to 9:7	6:9-22	8:1-21
Tuesday	9:9 to 10:4	7:1-5	8:32 to 9:11
Wednesday	10:12-20	7:6-9	9:12-18
Thursday	11:10 to 12:2	7:11 to 8:3	10:1-22
Friday	13:2-13	8:4-21	10:31 to 11:12
Fourth week			
Monday	14:24-32	8:21 to 9:7	11:19 to 12:6
Tuesday	25:1-9	9:8-17	12:8-22
Wednesday	26:21 to 27:9	9:18 to 10:1	12:23 to 13:9
Thursday	28:14-22	10:32 to 11:9	13:20 to 14:6
Friday	29:13-23	12:1-7	14:15-26
Fifth week			
Monday	37:33 to 38:6	13:12-18	14:27 to 15:4
Tuesday	40:18-31	15:1-15	15:7-19
Wednesday	41:4-14	17:1-9	15:20 to 16:9
Thursday	42:5-16	18:20-33	16:17 to 17:17
Friday	45:11-17	22:1-18	17:17 to 18:5
Sixth week			
Monday	48:17 to 49:4	27:1-41	19:16-25
Tuesday	49:6-10	31:3-16	21:3-21
Wednesday	58:1-11	43:26-31	21:23 to 22:4
Thursday	65: 8:16	46:1-7	23:15 to 24:5
Friday	66:20-24	49:33 to 50:26	31:8-31

CHAPTER FOUR

The Triodion

FROM LAZARUS SATURDAY
THROUGH GREAT AND HOLY WEEK

The Lenten liturgy shows a marked inflexion in its progression toward Pascha with the coming of Great and Holy Week. Thus far, we had followed the Master in his teaching and healing mission through the Palestinian countryside. Now our faith and our hope look toward the rock of Golgotha and the sepulcher which could not keep the author of life. For the next few days, the action will take place around Bethany, the Mount of Olives, and Jerusalem. Our Gospel readings follow the topographical order indicated by the Evangelists. A Palestinian origin for the choice and the distribution of the lessons is most probable, as may be surmised from the relations of ancient pilgrims and from allusions to local usages in the catecheses of St. Cyril of Jerusalem. As a whole, our lectionaries enable us to follow the sequence of events as "filmed on location."

We shall outline, by way of introduction, the events which preceded the resurrection of Lazarus, the entrance of our Lord into Jerusalem, and the days of the Passion. Having attended the feast of the Dedication, a winter celebration, Jesus, threatened by fanatics who charged him with violations of the Sabbath laws and who nearly stoned him, withdrew to Transjordan with his disciples (John 10:22-40). After an undetermined number of days (or weeks) he decided to

71

ascend once more to Jerusalem, in spite of the objections of the disciples, fully aware that the hostility of the Jewish leaders was closing upon them. Jesus' friends at Bethany, a village on the eastern slope of the Mount of Olives, apparently knew of his coming. "Mary and Martha," writes St. John, "sent for him, saying that their brother Lazarus, whom he loved, was sick." Having heard the news, Jesus "abode two more days where he was." On his arrival in Bethany, he found that Lazarus had died and had been buried four days already (John 11:1-17).

The two women have been introduced to us on the Saturday of the Acathist, fifth in Lent. The lesson of that day blocked together two distinct episodes: first, a supper in the house of Martha, a very active housewife, and of her sister Mary, who sat admiringly at the feet of the Master; second, a blessing upon Jesus and his mother by an unknown woman in a crowd: "Blessed is the womb that bore thee and the breasts which thou hast sucked!"[1] A gloss of the Gospel according to St. John (11:2) identifies Mary with "the woman who anointed the Lord and wiped his feet with her hair, whose brother Lazarus was sick," the reference being to John 12:1-8, paralleled by Matthew 26:6-13, and Mark 14:3-9. The episode related by Luke 7:36-50, and which is read for the commemoration of St. Mary of Egypt on the fifth Sunday, takes place in a different context.

Mary of Bethany has been frequently identified, especially in the medieval West, with the sinning woman of Luke 7, and with Mary of Magdala, to whom Jesus appeared after the Resurrection. Now it is true that Luke's account of the anointing of Jesus' feet is very similar to the narratives of Matthew, Mark and John. The Pharisee of Luke 7 happens to bear the same name as Simon, the leper of Bethany, but can hardly be the same person (Mt. 26:6). Mary, sister of Martha and Lazarus, is nowhere branded as a public sinner. As for Mary of Magdala, St. Luke (8:2) mentions that Jesus had delivered her from seven devils, and that she had followed the Master with several other Galilaean women. She was present at the Crucifixion, and was the first to see the Risen Lord at the tomb in the garden. She may well have been the same person as Mary of Bethany. The imbroglio has never been unravelled definitively. Eastern commentators have generally recognized in the above episodes distinct persons called Mary, a rather common name, without trying much to identify them.

Lazarus Saturday. The Epistle at the Divine Liturgy is unspecific and shows no particular relation to the resurrection of Lazarus. We hear instead the conclusion of the Epistle to the Hebrews (12:28 to 13:8). "Having received an unshakeable kingdom, let us offer to God an acceptable worship with reverence and awe, for God is a consuming fire ... Jesus Christ the same yesterday and today and for ever."

The Gospel is St. John's account of the resurrection of Lazarus (John 11:1-45), a pericope rich in concrete notations. It presents the facts in strict order, from the time when Jesus heard of Lazarus' illness to the circumstances of the miracle and the impression it made on the Jews; it records the words of Jesus and of the two sisters without any amplification. No commentary is necessary here, nor even desirable; the text is clear, and the relation of what happened calls for no justification. We need only present the following observations. There are several records of resurrections in the Gospels. Jesus is reported to have raised the son of a widow of Nain in Lower Galilee (Lk. 7:11-18), and the daughter of Jairus (Lk. 8:41-42, 47-56). There had been Old Testament precedents; cf. the stories of Elijah and Elisha; the apostles would be credited with similar "signs," τέρατα. What makes the resurrection of Lazarus unique is that it comes up as a preface to the Resurrection of Christ and to our future participation in divine immortality, on "the last Day," said Martha (verse 24). The belief in a general resurrection originated in the interpretation which some scribes gave of miscellaneous passages of Scripture, chiefly from the prophetic and poetic books. But what was thus far a theological speculation not unanimously endorsed was going to be confirmed as a fact, the experience of which, however, depends ultimately on an unconditional faith in Christ. "Whosoever lives and believes in me shall never die. Believest thou this?" (John 11:26).

The challenge to Martha is a challenge to all Christians. We had better give up miserable attempts at explaining the miracle: apparent death, lethargic sleep, or the like; "Lazarus smells already," objects Martha when Jesus orders the sepulcher to be opened (John 11:39). Obviously, we are disturbed, as Martha was, because of our instinctive aversion for death and its sequels. Instead of focusing on a "non-creature," on death "the wage of sin" (Rom. 6-23), we should rather, as Christians, raise our sights to the new order of things which the Resurrection of Christ has ushered in. The triumph of death is not for ever. We look for the resurrection of the dead, and the life of the world to come. Yet those whom Christ has brought to life in this world remained subject to its limitations; they still had to die, no matter how we may understand the miracle of their resurrection, and in this, their case differs radically from the Resurrection of Christ, for Christ "being raised from the dead, dies no more; death has no more power over him. In his dying, he died to sin, once for all, ἐφάπαξ; but in that he lives, he lives to God" (Rom. 6:9-10).[2] His Resurrection marks the dawn of a new creation; though we are still in the old world, we are called to live and grow in the new.

The course of our liturgical readings tends to syncopate the succession of events between the miracle at Bethany and the entrance of Our Lord into Jerusalem. In reality, the Fourth Gospel supposes a certain interval; after the resurrection of Lazarus, another attempt on the life of Jesus was made by mobsters aroused by the Jewish leaders. Escaping from their hands, Jesus sought refuge in Ephraim, presumably et-Tayibeh, a village some thirteen miles north-east of Jerusalem (John 11:45-54). The next episode would be the return of Jesus and his disciples to the capital, where they would enter to the acclamations of the crowd, but to the dismay of the leaders.

The Entrance of Our Lord into Jerusalem. Three Old Testament lessons are read at the vigil Vespers. The first one is the oracular blessing of Jacob on his son Judah (Gen. 49:1-2, 8-12). A Messiah shall be born from among his descendents. "The scepter shall not depart from Judah nor the ruler's staff from between his feet" (Gen. 49:10).[3] The land-scape of the southern tribe, with its rich vineyards and its highland pastures for flocks of sheep and goats provides a colorful setting for the message of the prophets and of the Gospel narratives. "Judah binds his foal to the vine, his ass's colt to the vine stock . . . he washes his garment in wine, his clothes in the blood of the grapes" (Gen. 49:11). The symbolism is ambivalent. Isaiah would write in another key the idyllic blessing on Judah, for the messianic triumph has its counterpart in God's vengeance over his enemies: "I shall crush them in my wrath, trample them in my anger. Their blood shall squirt upon my garment and I will stain all my raiment, for the day of vengeance is in my heart and the year of my redeemed is come" (Is. 63:1-4). This passage of Isaiah, through typological transference, was applied by the Fathers to Christ in his Passion, as he was left alone "to tread the wine-press, and of the people there was none with me" (cf. Apoc. 7:14; 14:19; 19:15).

The two other lessons are from the Lesser Prophets: Zephaniah 3:14-19 and Zechariah 9:9-15. Zephaniah was a contemporary of Josias King of Judah, whose religious reform he fostered by his preaching, shortly before Jeremiah and the final years of national independence. The third lesson is taken from the latter part of the canonical Book of Zechariah, to whom a number of prophecies of uncertain date were attributed by the late post-exilic compiler. The theme of both oracles is messianic. Zephaniah announces the glorious entrance of Yahweh into Zion, in an indefinite future: "The King of Israel, in the midst of thee" (Zephaniah 3:17), to save and gather the people of the redeemed.

Similar prospects are found in Zechariah, with some qualification concerning the messianic triumph which the "daughter of Zion" is to expect; it will be a triumph, but not the triumph of a victorious overlord riding his charger into the capital. The king shall enter adorned with God's favor, bringing salvation to his people, "lowly, riding upon an ass, upon a colt the foal of an ass" (Zech. 9:9). The humble mount of the Messiah that is to come means no denial of his rank; we would be wrong in thinking that asses or mules are not proper mounts for a king. Jair of Gilead, "who judged Israel twenty years . . . had thirty sons riding on thirty ass's colts, and having thirty cities" (Judg. 10:3-4; see also 13:13-14); Solomon the Magnificent, being led to the spring of Gihon to be anointed king of Israel, rode on King David's own mule (1 Ki. 1:38-44). Horses, at any rate, were a foreign importation from the land of the Hittites[4] and were used exclusively for fighting. The Messiah of the prophets had no use for them; his weapons and his conquests would be of quite another order. It is interesting to note that the psalmist and the prophets had repeatedly warned the Israelites against placing their trust in horses and war chariots (cf. Ps. 20:7, Is. 31:1); we may have an implicit reference to these warnings in Zechariah 9:10. The typological connexion between the prophecy of Zechariah and the Gospels is evident. "All this was done, to fulfill what had been spoken by the prophet" (Mt. 21:4-5; cf. John 12:14-16).

At Matins, a lesson from Matthew (21:1-11) replaces the regular Resurrection Gospel. The Evangelist concentrates on the improvised cortege from Bethphage, a hamlet on the way from Bethany to Jerusalem, at a short distance from the crest of the Mount of Olives.[5] According to the purpose of his Gospel, which aimed at convincing the Jews that Jesus was truly the Messiah announced in the Old Testament, Matthew quotes the prophecy of Zechariah and describes the enthusiasm of the people on the passage of Jesus, as they intone the blessing of Psalm 118:26 on him "who comes in the name of the Lord." The instructions of Jesus to two of the disciples, as we read them in Matthew 21:2-3, summarize the more detailed account of Mark 11:1-7 (cf. Lk. 19:29-35): "Go into the village opposite you and right away you will find an ass with her colt; untie them and bring them to me. If any one says anything to you, you shall say: The lord has need of them."[6] In a like manner, a few days later, Jesus would send two disciples to make preparation for the Passover meal (Mt. 26:17-19; Mk. 14:12-16; Lk. 22:7-13). We are somewhat puzzled by these features of the Gospel narratives. Obviously, some essential data, which the Evangelists regarded as irrelevant, are lacking, and we are not able to interpret the Gospel text with certainty. That Jesus would have "played an act," is a flippant hypothesis which, alas, has been ventured, but ought to be dumped unceremoniously. Jesus seems to have had acquaintances among local people, perhaps some Galilaeans settled in the capital or its suburbs, who would immediately understand who the Master, ὁ διδά-σκαλος, was. Or did the Evangelists, in relating the facts, conform to a pattern of which the prophetic literature and extra-biblical texts offer several examples? We have in mind the story of the anointing of Saul, to whom Samuel offers signs, admittedly quizzical, of the authenticity of his mission: "Thou shalt meet two men . . . who will say to thee, the asses which thou seekest have been found . . . thou shalt come to the plain of Tabor, where three men will meet thee, one carrying three kids; another, three loaves of bread; and another, a wine skin (1 Sam. 10:2-5). If these stylistic similarities between the story of Samuel and the Gospel narrative are not purely fortuitous, we would be in the presence of a clear case of *Formgeschichte*; this, at any rate, does not affect in any way the substance of the facts recorded by the Evangelists. To deny the historicity of the entire episode as it was read in the early Christian community would be a blatant *non sequitur*.

The Epistle of the day (Phil. 4:4-9) echoes the prophecies of the vigil: a rejoicing of the faithful over the coming of the Lord. The perspective, however, has changed. Zephaniah and Zechariah anticipated it in an undetermined but distant future. St. Paul writing to the Philippians from captivity,[7] and eager to ward off any temptation of despair, represents the glorious advent as imminent, through a shortening of perspective common to the Christians of the first generation, whom the departure of those who fell asleep in the Lord would disturb, and soon force to reconsider their expectation. At any rate they lived—and we live—between the times, looking for the life of the world to come. The present tense used by the Apostle is in reality beyond measurement: "The Lord is at hand" (Phil. 4:5), "Maranatha" (1 Cor. 16:22).[8] Watchfulness, then, is the order of the day, a theme developed in the series of parables which St. Matthew intercalated in his Gospel between the Entrance into Jerusalem and the Passion.

In the lesson from the Fourth Gospel which is read at the Divine Liturgy (John 12:1-18), the episode of the entrance of Jesus into the city is reduced to the essentials, within the chronological framework of what had happened during the past few days: the anointing of Jesus' feet by Mary; the hypocritical reaction of Judas, who witnessed the scene; the resolve of the priests to have Jesus "removed"; the procession of the palms;[9] the incomprehension of the disciples who would grasp only later the significance of the event; and the concourse of people emotionally stirred up by the resurrection of Lazarus. All this was to bring the hostility of the Jewish leaders to a head. In their mind, Jesus was already condemned.

The days of the Bridegroom. The services of the first three days in Great and Holy Week are meant as an immediate introduction to the mysteries of the Passion and of the Resurrection.[10] For this last-hour briefing, the Church wishes that we should review the Gospel record in its entirety, especially what Jesus did and said during his last days on earth, prior to the last supper with the Twelve, in the general order in which the Evangelists registered the facts. Once more, their record is not a mere description of what came to pass. Their faith, the faith of the Church, looks to the fulfilment of a divine τέλος, and we may distinguish, but not separate, the historical and the eschatological aspects of the narrative. The latter, which is stressed in the last instructions of Jesus to the disciples, gives to the liturgy of the first three days, the so-called days of the bridegroom, their proper character.

The service during these three days continues the pattern adopted for Great Lent. Matins are properly the "service of the bridegroom," ἀκολουθία τοῦ νυμφίου. On the Matins of the Monday, Tuesday, and Wednesday, the choir sings the following troparion after the threefold Alleluia on the six Psalms: "Behold, the bridegroom comes at midnight, and blessed is the servant whom he shall find watching; and again, unworthy is the servant whom he shall find heedless. Beware therefore, O my soul, do not be weighed down with sleep, lest you be given up to death and lest you be shut out of the kingdom." And the exapostilarion: "Thy bridal chamber I see adorned, O my Savior, and I have no wedding garment that I may enter. O Giver of Light, illumine the vesture of my soul and save me!"[11] Both liturgical compositions are based on the parable of the ten virgins (Mt. 25:1-13), blocked together by the Evangelist with several *logia* stressing the necessity of watchfulness.[12]

The reading of a Gospel lesson is prescribed at Matins. On Monday, it is taken from Matthew (21:18-43). The Evangelist relates how Jesus, who lodged for the night in the house of his friends at Bethany, coming down on Monday morning to the city, looked for some fruit on a fig tree, but finding only leaves, cursed the tree which dried up straightway. The episode strikes us as strange, as it struck Peter, according to St. Mark, who reports that it was not yet the season for figs (Mk. 11:20-21). It is to be interpreted as a symbolic gesture like those reported in the Old Testament prophets, and it belongs to the series of parables which Jesus taught his disciples during these last days of his ministry. The message, under the transparent veil of the parables, castigated the incredulity and the obstinacy of the Jewish leaders, and the sterile teaching of their doctors. God's verdict was pronounced in no uncertain terms: "The kingdom of God shall be taken from you and be given to a people which shall make it bear fruit" (Mt. 21:43).

The lesson for the Matins of Tuesday in Holy Week (Mt. 22:15-23, 39) stages an encounter between Jesus and some disciples of the Pharisees who, along with politicoes of the Herodian party, approached him with an insidious dilemma, "whether or not it was permissible to pay taxes levied for the Roman treasury"—a burning question which Jesus dismissed summarily. He answered in the same way to some Sadducees who tried to embarass him with a problem of casuistry involving the possibility of bodily resurrection, which they denied—no mere academic question a few days after the miracle at Bethany.

In spite of a few points of exegesis which may call for discussion, and of a modicum of allowance for redactional factors, the record is clear. The plots of the Jewish leaders multiply, the snares they lay tighten, and the profile of the Cross sharpens. Jesus knows it, the disciples refuse to accept it, and the Master unfolds before them the divine decree of redemption in a solemn discourse which St. John transcribed in his Gospel and which the Church reads at the Matins of Great and Holy Wednesday (John 12:17-50): "Unless a grain of wheat falls in the ground and dies, it remains alone; but if it dies, it bears much fruit . . . Now my soul is troubled, and what shall I say? Father, save me from this hour! But no, it is for that I have come to this hour. Father, glorify thy name! Then was heard a voice came from heaven: I have glorified it, and I will glorify it again." It was the same mysterious voice which had been heard when Jesus was baptized in the Jordan, and when he conversed with Moses and Elias on Mount Tabor.

At the Hours, the Church prescribes a massive reading of the Gospels, independently from the lessons of the Office: on Monday, at the Third Hour, the first half of Matthew; at the Sixth Hour, the second half; at the Ninth Hour, the first half of Mark. On Tuesday, Third Hour, the second half of Mark; at the Sixth Hour, one third of Luke; at the Ninth, the second third of Luke. On Wednesday, at the Third Hour, the end of Luke; at the Sixth Hour, John, up to the thirteenth chapter; at the Ninth Hour, from the fourteenth chapter to the end.

At the Sixth Hour of the three days, a prophecy from the Old Testament precedes the reading of the Gospel. Ezekiel replaces Isaiah, from which the Lenten lessons were taken. The object of these prophecies, respectively Ezekiel 1:1-20; 1:21 to 2:3; 2:3 to 3:3, is the account of Ezekiel's divine calling from among the exiles on the bank of the river Kebar, an unidentified waterway in southern Mesopotamia.[13] This corresponds to the vision of Isaiah (Is. 6:1-12), which was read on the second Sunday in Lent. In either case we are confronted with the report of a theophany expressed in a redundant imagery, which was suggested, as far as Ezekiel is concerned, by the sight of the Babylonian temples, with their sculptures and fresco-paintings. Four supernatural animals draw the chariot on which the glory of the Transcendent God is carried. They are the equivalent of the Seraphim of Isaiah in the Temple of Jerusalem. It would be futile to attempt a graphic representation of Ezekiel's descriptions, which aim at conveying to his audience that which is essentially above human understanding and imagination. The theophany of Apocalypsis 4:7-8 derives obviously from the vision of Ezekiel, and the four animal figures have become the heraldic symbols of the four Evangelists.

But the didactic function of these lessons is not to be reduced figuratively to express the dogma of God's transcendence. The theophany of the Book of Ezekiel is no static vision. The prophet intends to stress for the benefit of the exiles the independence of God with regard to the Temple of Jerusalem. Yahweh is a spirit, he follows his own people and may be sought by them wherever they are. The Temple which is described in chapters 40 to 44 of Ezekiel is not an edifice of timber and stone; its reality is the reality of a vision which does not belong in the material order. And this brings us a step closer to what seems to have preoccupied the disciples of Jesus during the last week of his life on earth. As they admired the monumental walls of the Temple from the slopes of the Mount of Olives, the Master declared that "there will not be left here one stone upon another, that will not be thrown down" (Mt. 24:2), a prophecy of doom which would be realized some forty years later. And when the Jews had demanded a sign from him, Jesus had answered: "Destroy this Temple and I will raise it up in three days, speaking of the Temple of his body" (John 2:19-21).

The Old Testament lessons at Vespers serve the same didactic purpose as the weekday Lenten readings, with Exodus replacing Genesis, and Job being substituted for Proverbs. The readings from Exodus, respectively 1:1-20; 2:5-10; 2:11-22, constitute the preface to the first Passover. The connection between the Old Testament figure and its fulfilment in the Christian Pascha becomes every day more evident. The substance of these early chapters from Exodus is historically well attested. Jacob and his sons, for whom the tribes of Israel were named, had been received in Egypt by a line of

Pharaohs presumably of Asiatic origin, but a dynastic revolution had radically changed the situation. "There arose a new
king over Egypt, who did not know Joseph" (Ex. 1:1-8).
The Hebrews, from favored, became oppressed, drafted into
gangs of laborers for the royal constructions and submitted
to measures amounting to genocide (Ex. 1:15-22). On Great
and Holy Tuesday, we hear of the birth and infancy of Moses,
saved by an Egyptian princess who rescued him from the
Nile, on whose banks he had been exposed after his birth.
"She called him Moses (Hebr. *Môshéh*), for, she said, I drew
him out of the water" (Ex. 2:10)—a popular etymology:
mâshah, to draw, but more probably an authentic Egyptian
name. The Wednesday lesson relates how Moses, now a
young man, witnessing the inhumane treatment of his own
people at the mercy of their taskmasters, killed an Egyptian
bully, fled for life into the wilderness, and became a refugee
among Midianite tribesmen of the Sinai peninsula. It is there
that one day he would be chosen to be the liberator of Israel,
by Him who spoke from the midst of the Burning Bush (Ex.
3:1-15). The episode, which follows after the text of our
Wednesday lesson, has become, through typological and allegorical exegesis, a popular theme of patristics and of Byzantine hymnography, in a broad variety of applications.[14]

The reading of Exodus is followed by lessons from the
Book of Job or, more precisely, from the prologue of Job,
namely 1:1-12, an introductory narrative in prose, and Satan's
challenge to God: "Does Job fear God for nought? . . . Thou
hast blessed the work of his hands . . . but put forth thy hand
now and touch all that he has, and he will curse thee to thy
face"; 1:13-22: the messengers of woe, Job stricken in his
possessions and in his family; 2:1-10: Job afflicted in his
own flesh, yet persisting in his faith. Fr. Kniazeff notes that
these lessons from Job, which correspond to the lessons from
Proverbs in the preceding weeks, "have a mere didactic value
and do not especially concern sacred history."[15] That is true,
yet there is no absolute parity between the teaching of Proverbs and the teaching of Job. The Book of Proverbs is
a collection of maxims for a wise conduct of human life. The
Book of Job is an oriental tale, and the discussions between

Job and his friends intend to deal with the vexing problem which obsessed the Psalmist as well: Why is it that, contrary to what one would expect from the Providence of a righteous God, it happens that sinners may be prosperous, and virtuous men afflicted without any prospect of redress? On the eve of the Passion, when the Just one—the only Just one—will submit for our sake to the indignity of death, we would incline to find, without allegorizing in the least, a real parallelism between these two figures, types of Christ: Isaiah's Servant of Yahweh, "stricken, smitten of God . . . for the transgression of my people . . . a righteous servant who shall justify many" (Is. 53:4, 8, 11), and Job, "a perfect and upright man," who offers sacrifices for his sons and daughters, "lest they might have sinned and cursed God in their hearts" (Job 1:5). Responding to the patriarchal prayer of Job, we hear from the Gospel of John the sacerdotal prayer of Jesus for his own disciples, "that they may be one even as we are one" (John 17:11).

The Vespers service of each of the days of the bridegroom includes the celebration of the Liturgy of the Presanctified, for which a Gospel lesson is provided, following the Old Testament readings. On Monday, we read the so-called eschatological discourse according to St. Matthew (24:3-35). The description of the cataclysm which would engulf the universe is intermixed with predictions of the proximate destruction of Jerusalem, and the two themes are not always easily distinguished from each other. This is partly imputable to the apocalyptic pattern of style followed by the Evangelist, but a deeper reason for this may be that Jesus, who could prophesy the imminent collapse of the Jewish nation and the ruin of its capital, still was not given to know, according to his human nature, the day and the hour when the figure of this world would pass away (Mt. 24:36); in that day, the "Son of Man" would appear in power and have his angels "gather his elect from the four winds, from one end of heaven to the other." We had already heard St. Luke's version of the eschatological discourse on the Saturday preceding the Sunday of the Last Judgment.

Our ignorance of the time of the Parousia makes it urgent

for us to be on our guard. This is the theme of the parables which Jesus taught his disciples on the days preceding the fateful night in the garden of Gethsemane, when they could not even watch one hour with him. St. Matthew has grouped them together as he developed the theme of watchfulness, which is the object of the Gospel lesson for the Liturgy of the Presanctified on Great Tuesday (Mt. 24:36 to 26:2). We read the parable of the intendant reveling with his worthy associates in the absence of the master, who returns unexpectedly; the parable of the ten virgins; and the parable of the talents for which the depositors will have to give account. The liturgical section for Tuesday ends with the description of the Last Judgment and the last announcement of the Crucifixion.

The Gospel for the Presanctified Liturgy of Holy Wednesday is also from Matthew (26:6-16). It relates the anointing of Jesus' feet during the supper at Bethany; we heard St. John's record of the same episode on Palm Sunday, and the deal of the priests with Judas: thirty pieces of silver, the price of his betraying Jesus. At this point, we enter the drama of the Passion.

In some Orthodox churches, the Matins of Great and Holy Wednesday is replaced by the ἀκολουθία τοῦ ἁγίου ἐλαίου, a communal form of the anointing of the sick, which otherwise is performed for the benefit of individual persons. The ritual prescribes the reading of seven Epistles and seven Gospels, with prayers and verses expressing the meaning of the sevenfold anointing.[16]

Great and Holy Thursday. The liturgical service of the three major days of Holy Week is centered entirely on the events of the Passion and of the death of Christ as recorded by the Evangelists. It could hardly be otherwise. A modicum of comments should suffice here; all we need is to listen to the Holy Gospel, which confronts us with the facts: what Jesus said, did, suffered. The significance of these facts is revealed to us by the sober remarks of the Evangelists and the discourses of Jesus which they transcribed. That a measure of editing took place in this process of transcription cannot be denied,

but this does not mean that the Gospel as it was announced
in the early Church and as we have received it cannot be relied
upon. The key to what we might call the theology of the
Passion is found in the lessons from the Apostolic writings and
the Old Testament readings which inspired our liturgists and
hymnographers. The raw facts are thus framed in the general
economy of salvation, both in prospect and retrospect. It will
be noticed that the liturgical sections of the Gospel frequently
repeat the same episodes or overlap over each other.

On Great and Holy Thursday, the Gospel lesson at Matins
(Lk. 33:1-40) is a summary of what happened from Palm
Sunday to Thursday night according to St. Luke, who seems
to depend less on Mark and shows some affinity with John's
arrangement. The order of pericopes is as follows: the satanic
complot of the priests with Judas, who offers to deliver Jesus
into their hands, quietly, lest the people be aroused; the prepa-
rations for the Passover meal, the description of which includes
the institution of the Christian Eucharist; after the meal, the
conversation of Jesus with the Twelve, in which he shows himself aware of being betrayed, dismisses an incongruous question on "Who is the greatest?", predicts that Peter is going to
deny him publicly, and warns his disciples about the general
hostility they will have to face; then they all rise and Jesus,
followed by the little company, descends from Zion and, crossing the Cedron, enters the garden of Gethsemane on the lower
slopes of the Mount of Olives. St. Luke's incidental remark,
"as he was wont," together with other clues in the Gospels
and in the Book of Acts, would substantiate the hypothesis
according to which Jesus had in Jerusalem and its suburbs a
number of anonymous acquaintances who, after the Resurrection, formed the nucleus of the first Christian community.

At the First Hour, the Church reads from the Book of
Jeremiah (Jer. 11:18-23; 12:1-5, 9-11, 14-15). Jeremiah has
always been regarded as a figure of Christ on account of the
persecutions he endured. In the prologue of the canonical
book which bears his name, he is introduced as "the son of
Hilkiah (*Hilqiyyahu*), of the priests that are in Anathoth,"
a Levitic town in the territory of Benjamin (Jos. 1:28), a
couple of miles north-east of Jerusalem. Abiathar, who had

escaped the massacre of the priests of Nob (1 Sam. 22:20)[17] and served with Zadok under David, had been assigned by Solomon to forced residence in his family estate at Anathoth, following the abortive attempt to anoint Adoniyah as successor to David (1 Ki. 2:26). Looked upon with suspicion both by the clergy of the royal sanctuary and by the men of Anathoth, Jeremiah could compare himself to "a lamb, or an ox, that is brought to the slaughter" (Jer. 11:19), a verse which echoes the poem of the Servant of Yahweh in Isaiah (Is. 53:7), and whose typical application was not lost on the authors of the New Testament (cf. Acts 8:32). And the call of the prophet for the vindication of justice against evil pastors "who have destroyed my vineyard, trodden my inheritance under foot, and made my choice portion a desolate wilderness" (Jer. 12:10), reminiscent of Isaiah's song of the vineyard (Is. 5:1-7), foreshadows our Lord's denunciation of the relentless hatred of the priests who would have no rest until he was crucified.

Three Old Testament lessons follow the singing of *O Gladsome Light* at Vespers, namely Ex. 1-19; Job 38:1-23 and 42:1-5; and Is. 50:4-11). The reason for the choice of these passages is not immediately apparent. We had begun to read from Exodus and from Job on the Monday in Holy Week, but the lessons for Great Thursday follow after an interval for which there is no convincing explanation. There is a certain parallelism between the lesson from Exodus and the lesson from Job, and we offer tentatively the following considerations. The reading of Exodus stages the encampment of the Hebrews at the foot of Mount Sinai. They received from the mouth of Moses the promise of Yahweh that he would make them "a kingdom of priests and a holy nation" (Ex. 19:6). These prophetic words would not be realized among the Israelites according to the flesh, but among the multitude of the redeemed "from every nation, from all tribes and peoples and tongues," who would offer to God "a spiritual sacrifice" in union with their head, Christ the Priest (1 Pet. 2:5). Such utterances are beyond the understanding of natural man and can be perceived only in the mystical encounter of the creature with the unapproachable God: it is in the midst of the theophany on the mountain that "Moses spake, and God answered him with a voice" (Ex. 19:19), and it is from the midst of the whirlwind that God answered Job, after convincing him of his helplessness in front of the secrets of nature. How then could he possibly have understood the ways of God's justice and Providence? This brought to an end Job's futile discussions with his friends, and we hear him confess humbly that "now my eye seeth thee, therefore I abhor myself and repent in dust and ashes" (Job 42:5-6). For it is through humility and repentance that the perception of spiritual things is restored to sinful men, and that they shall be able to overcome the scandal of the Cross, which scattered the disciples. The third Vespers lesson, from the Book of Isaiah (50:4-11), places us in front of the image of Christ scourged and derided, as foreshadowed by the Suffering Servant of Yahweh: "I gave my back to the smiters and my cheeks to them that pulled my beard. I hid not my face from shame and spitting."

The Gospel lesson at the liturgy of St. Basil, which is combined with the service of Vespers, groups together passages from the Synoptics and from the Fourth Gospel covering salient episodes of Passion week: Jesus' final announcement of the Crucifixion: "You know that after two days is the feast of the Passover, and the Son of Man is betrayed to be crucified" (Mt. 26:1-2). In the Upper Room (John 13:1-17), Jesus washes the feet of the disciples in the course of, or after, the meal, δείπνου γινομένου, *coena facta.* "I have given you an example, that you should do as I have done to you," a direct answer to the indecent strife which had arisen among the disciples, "Which one of them should be accounted the greatest?" (cf. Lk. 22:24, which was read at Matins); the washing of the feet has been retained as a pious ceremony in a number of Christian churches or communities. The verses sung in the Latin Church on that occasion, "I gave you a new commandment," *mandatum novum* (John 13:34), are the origin of the English locution *Maundy Thursday.* The following portion of the Gospel reading is Matthew's account of the institution of the Eucharist and the singing of the paschal *Hallel, viz.* Psalms 113-118; then St. Matthew describes how Jesus and his disciples descended from Zion on their way to Gethsemane, how Jesus predicted that "all shall be offended because of me this night, for it is written, I shall smite the shepherd and the sheep of the flock shall be scattered (Zech. 13:7) . . . and thou, Peter, shalt deny me thrice," and how, "sorrowful unto death," Jesus prayed prostrate in the garden, "O my Father, if it is possible, let this cup pass from me; yet, not as I will, but as thou wilt" (Mt. 26:21-39). Luke, 22:43-45, is the only one to mention the Angel who comforts Jesus in his agony, while the Apostles, overcome with grief, sleep. Shifting back to Matthew 26:40 to 27:2, we hear of the arrest of Jesus in the garden, of Peter's denial and bitter tears of repentance, of the interrogatory of Jesus by the Sanhedrin, and of his arraignment before Pilate.

The institution of the Lord's supper, Κυριακόν δεῖπνον, *dominica coena*, is properly the mystery of Great and Holy Thursday.[18] The Epistle of the Divine Liturgy is taken from St. Paul (1 Cor. 11:23-32), who gives his version of the event, paralleled by the Synoptics (Mt. 26:26-29; Mk. 14:22-25; Lk. 22:14-20). The Apostle introduces his own account with reference to some abusive practices which had prevailed at Corinth, where the eucharistic celebration followed a meal taken in the church: "Each one goes ahead with his own meal; one is hungry, and the other is drunk" (1 Cor. 11-20). St. Paul speaks with authority, the authority of *his* Gospel, which he "received from the Lord"; his description concords substantially with that of the Evangelists, and it is this common tradition which the anaphorae of the various churches have followed, each one with its own wording. The essential elements stand above discussion; the institution of the Eucharist stresses the sacrificial character of the Passion and the Death of Christ. The sacrifice was offered by Christ the Priest for the first and the last time in his earthly life. Now is the time of the Church; the Eucharist will be celebrated to the end of time, not as a commemorative ceremony, but inasmuch as he, our Priest, offers himself on our behalf through the hands of his priests, "till He come" (1 Cor. 11:26).

Great and Holy Friday. The order of the liturgical serv-

ice, hymnography and Scripture readings is centered exclusively on the Crucifixion. Matins, commonly called the Service of the Twelve Passion Gospels, is usually anticipated on
Thursday evening. The Royal Hours are served on the Friday
morning with their psalms and lessons. No Divine Liturgy
nor the Office of the Presanctified is served at the conclusion
of Vespers, which ends with the procession and veneration
of the ἐπιτάφιον, *plashchanitsa*, the "winding sheet," and
with Small Compline, which consist of the Lamentations of
the Theotokos and a canon by Simon the Logothete (frequently omitted in Greek churches).

The narratives of the four Gospels on the Passion have
been arranged so as to give the impression of a continuous relation in chronological-topographical order; a certain amount
of duplication or overlapping was of course unavoidable.
Parts of this New Testament material have already been used
in the previous days. *The first Gospel* is the full text of the
farewell discourse of Jesus to his disciples in the Upper
Room, as recorded by St. John (13:31 to 18:1). *The second
Gospel* (John 18:2-28) describes the arrest of Jesus in the
garden of Gethsemane by a band of men and the Temple
guards sent by the priests and led by Judas; Jesus is brought
to Annas, who sends him to Caiaphas the High Priest; in the
courtyard of Caiaphas' residence, Peter denies his master, not
much later than an hour after he had cut off Malchus' ear in
the garden, and straightway, the cock crows, as Jesus had
predicted; Caiaphas, after a summary interrogation, has Jesus
sent under guard to the judgment hall, εἰς τό πραιτώριον,
to be arraigned before the Roman Procurator. *The third
Gospel* (Mt. 26:57-75): another version of the scene in the
High-Priest's palace. *The fourth Gospel* (John 18:28 to
19:16): the circumstantial account of Jesus' appearance before Pilate, skeptical of a kingdom "which is not of this
world," not hostile *a priori*, but afraid of political reper-
cussions; fearful lest the mob would get out of hand, he
"delivers Jesus unto them to be crucified." *The fifth Gospel*
(Mt. 27:3-32): St. Matthew's rendering of the same episodes,
beginning with the suicide of Judas, who casts into the
Temple's treasure the thirty *denarii*, price of his treason, but

the priests decline to receive the blood-stained money and purchase with it a burial ground for strangers. "Thus was fulfilled that which was spoken by Jeremiah the prophet: And they took the thirty pieces of silver, the price of him that was appraised . . . and gave them for the potter's field."[19] The lesson ends with the spectacle of Jesus, mocked and crowned with thorns, and being helped by Simon of Cyrene, whom the soldiers compel to bear his cross. *The sixth Gospel* (Mk. 15:16-32): the crown of thorns; Simon of Cyrene identified as "the father of Alexander and Rufus," presumably well-known in the first Christian community; the lots cast upon Jesus' garments (cf. John 19:23-24, with a reference to Ps. 22:18); the title on the cross, "King of the Jews," and the Crucified derided by the passersby, the priests and the scribes. *The seventh and eighth Gospels*, parallel accounts according to Matthew 27:33-54 and Luke 23:32-49. St. Matthew mentions the two criminals who had been crucified with Jesus, while St. Luke quotes the prayer of the repentant thief, whom a tradition calls Dysmas: "Lord, remember me when thou comest in thy kingdom." We hear the cry of distress of Jesus, "*Eli, Eli, lamma sabachtani?* that is to say, 'My God, my God, why hast thou forsaken me?',", the very cry of the suffering just in Psalm 22:1. Having refused a sponge filled with vinegar (cf. Ps. 69:21, a "Passion Psalm") Jesus expires. *The ninth Gospel* (John 19:25-37): the last words of Jesus to Mary and John the disciple; the sponge of vinegar, Jesus' death; the soldiers breaking the legs of the thieves who had been crucified, lest the bodies still be hanging from the crosses on the high holy days;[20] one of the soldiers, Longinus according to an apocryphal tradition, thrusting his spear into the side of the inanimate body of Jesus, "and forthwith blood and water gushed out. Thus was the Scripture fulfilled, 'a bone of him shall not be broken' (Ex. 12-46), and, 'they shall look on him whom they have pierced' (Zech. 12:10)." *The tenth and eleventh Gospels* (Mk. 15:43-47 and John 19:38-42): Joseph of Arimathaea obtains from Pilate the permission to take away the body of Jesus; with Nicodemus, the Pharisee "who at the first came to Jesus by night" (cf. John 3:2), he wraps the body in linen cloth, and

lays it into his own new rock-cut tomb, at the entrance of
which they roll a heavy stone—a feature well attested by
archaeology. *The twelfth Gospel* (Mt. 27:62-66): in view
of Jesus' prophecy that he would rise up after three days (cf.
Mt. 16:21), the Jewish leaders, lest the body be stolen by the
disciples, request from Pilate to have the sepulcher watched;
the answer, with an intended sarcasm: "Have a guard; make
it all as safe as you know how! And so they went, securing
the sepulcher, sealing the stone, and posting guards."

The unusual frequency of the stereotype, "And this happened in fulfilment of what had been said by the prophet,"
in the Gospel narratives of the Passion should not be ascribed
to an artificial allegorism nor construed as an abstract theory
of the unity of divine Revelation; it denotes rather the conviction that God sovereignly directs historical events through
which he speaks to successive generations of men, and this
conviction is formally expressed by the teachings of the earliest Christian community. It is this divinely inspired Tradition
which the allegorists followed—admittedly to excess—and after them the liturgists and hymnographers of the Byzantine
Church.

The selection of psalms and scriptural lessons for the
Royal Hours[21] of Good Friday in our Byzantine liturgy rests
for the most part on the above principle. A number of the
standard psalms at the Hours through the liturgical year have
been retained, thus Psalm 5, "Give ears to my words, O Lord,"
a morning prayer, at the First Hour; Psalm 51 (LXX 50),
"Have mercy upon me, O God," David's prayer of repentance, at the Third Hour; Psalm 91 (LXX 90), "He that
dwelleth in the secret place of the Most High," singing of
God's infallible protection by day and by night, at the Sixth
Hour;[22] Psalm 86 (LXX 85), "Bow thine ear, O Lord, hear
me!", a psalm of entreaty in days of trial, at the Ninth Hour.
But other psalms were expressly chosen for their typological
connection with Passion events, as evidenced by the New
Testament writers' explicit references, and for the fact that
some of their verses inspired the very words of Jesus himself.
Thus, at the First Hour, Psalm 2, "Why do the heathen

rage?", with its proclamation of the divinity of the Messiah: "Thou art my Son, this day have I begotten thee," quoted by Acts 13:33 and Hebrews 1:5; also at the First Hour, Psalm 22 (LXX 21), "My God, my God, why hast thou forsaken me?", the anguished question of the Crucified to his Father; several verses of this psalm are quoted in the Passion Gospels: "He trusted in the Lord that he would deliver him; so let him deliver him now!", cf. the impious comments of the priests and elders deriding Jesus hanging from the Cross (cf. Mt. 27: 42); "They part my garments among them and cast lots upon vesture" (cf. Mt. 27:35). At the Ninth Hour, Psalm 69 (LXX 68), another "Passion Psalm," "I have become a stranger unto my brethren ... the zeal of thine house has eaten me up, and the reproaches of them that reproach thee have fallen upon me" (cf. John 2:17); "They gave me gall for my meat, and in my thirst they gave me vinegar to drink" (cf. Mt. 27:34).

Three lessons are provided for each of the Hours, a Prophecy, an Epistle, and a Gospel. The former two show eventually a certain thematic correspondance. The Gospel sections stand independently from the Prophecies and Epistles. Most of them had already been used at Matins, but cut differently. At the First Hour, the Prophecy is from Zechariah (11:10-13). The theme is the substitution of a new economy for the exclusive privilege of Israel, now revoked. Yahweh is going to withdraw his hand and permit men to vent their enmity against their neighbors. The prophet will be the executor of that judgment. Armed with two staffs inscribed with symbolic names, "Grace" and "Union," which he breaks asunder, he will unleash the nations and break the unity of Israel and Judah; the evil shepherds who have led the people astray are invited—ironically—to pay the prophet his salary, "a goodly price that I was prized at of them," thirty shekels of silver, which he throws into the Temple's treasury. The entire passage is admittedly obscure and the versions do little to clarify it; our rendering tries to follow the argument according to the Hebrew text. But it is most probable that the compiler of our lectionary has singled out the four verses of

the oracle chiefly on account of the nominal reference made
by the Evangelist (cf. Mt. 27:9-10).

Zechariah's evil shepherds, three of them being "cut off
in one month," possibly an allusion to the succession of polit-
ically appointed High Priests of dubious legitimacy, had way-
laid the people. In a sense, they were the types of St. Paul's
adversaries, whom he describes in the Epistle to the Galatians,
from which the second lesson of the First Hour is taken (Gal.
6:14-18): self-appointed guides of some early Christian communities who would constrain pagan converts to be circumcised "that they may glory in your flesh" (Gal. 6:12-13), in
order to ward off the fanaticism of Jewish leaders by an unworthy capitulation. "But God forbid," exclaims the Apostle,
"that I should glory, save in the cross of Our Lord Jesus
Christ, by whom the world is crucified unto me, and I to the
world." For the former dispensation of grace is over, and
we have entered a new age, through the Passion and Resurrection of Christ.

The Gospel lesson of the First Hour (Mt. 27:1-56) runs
from the arraignment of Jesus before Pilate to the confession
of the centurion who supervised the execution: "Truly this
was the Son of God," and to the pathetic group of women
who had followed Jesus and the disciples from their Galilaean villages.

At the Third Hour, we hear the prophecy of Isaiah
(50:4-11) which has been read already at Vespers of Great
and Holy Thursday, the third Servant Song (see above). The
lesson from the Apostle (Rom. 5:6-11) spells out the theology underlying the drama envisioned by the prophet: not a
sordid episode of men's brutality, but the fact that the Passion
and the Death of Christ were the price paid for setting us at
peace with God. "If, while we were enemies, we were reconciled to God by the death of his Son, how much more, now
that we are reconciled, shall we be saved by his life." The
Gospel reading at the Third Hour (Mk. 15:16-41) parallels
what was read at the First Hour, from the crown of thorns to
the women witnessing the Crucifixion.

The first lesson at the Sixth Hour (Is. 52:13 to 53:12)
could be entitled: "The Passion according to Isaiah"—an

Evangelist rather than a prophet, wrote St. Jerome. A sort
of dialogue takes place between Yahweh and the people.
Yahweh proclaims the future triumph of his Servant, bought
at the price of incredible sufferings, and the fruits of his
labours: "He shall make many righteous, and their iniquities
he shall carry . . . I will make him share the booty of the
mighty because he has stripped himself unto death . . . he who
bore the sins of many and who intercedes for the trans-
gressors" (53:11-12). What the people saw was the spectacle of "a man of sorrows . . . stricken, smitten of God and
afflicted . . . brought as a lamb to the slaughter . . . cut off
from the land of the living . . . He was given a grave with
the wicked, among the haughty" (53:3, 4, 7-9). But the
sepulcher would be made glorious one day,[23] when the prophecy would be accomplished and when Christ would rise victorious from death. The Epistle to the Hebrews (2:11-18),
which is read as the second lesson, states the implications
of the mystery dimly perceived by Isaiah: Christ and those
whom he came to save share in the same humanity; his victory is ours, it is not the victory of angels, for he took on
himself "not their nature, but the seed of Abraham," to
liberate all who were, through sin, in bondage to death. The
Gospel reading is the same as the eighth reading at Matins
(Lk. 23:32-49), from the Crucifixion to the last cry of Jesus,
"Father, into thy hands I commend my spirit" (cf. Ps. 31:5),
and the confession of the centurion: "Truly this was a righteous man."

We repeat at the Ninth Hour the lesson already read on
Great and Holy Thursday at the First Hour (Jer. 11:18 to
12:5). The persecution of Jeremiah by the men of Anathoth
had made him a traditional figure of Christ relentlessly pur-
sued by the hatred of the priests and of the leaders of the
Jews. The lesson from the Apostle (Hebr. 10:19-31) states
by contrast the certainty of our direct access to God through
our High Priest—the leitmotiv of the entire Epistle—with a
warning against the ever-present danger of spiritual regress
and apostasy, "for it is a frightful thing to fall into the hands
of the Living God." The Gospel section (John 18-28 to

19:37) had already been used at Matins, as the fourth and ninth Gospel lessons.

The Old Testament readings at Vespers develop, each one in its own way, the paradox inherent in God's dealings with men. The first lesson stages Moses standing in Yahweh's presence in the solitude of the Sinai mountain-top (Ex. 33:11-23). They converse "face to face, as a man speaks to his companion," yet Moses cannot see the face of God, "for there shall no man see me and live." Moses had prayed that he might behold the Glory, *kâbhôd*, which is the radiance of God's own being. And the Lord said: "There is a place by me where thou shalt stand upon the rock. And when my Glory passes by, I will put thee in a cleft of the rock and cover thee with my hand until I have passed by." This episode of Exodus was to become the foundation of the theology of the Eastern Fathers, of St. Gregory of Nyssa in his *Life of Moses*, and after them, of the main stream of Orthodox spirituality. The vision of God's essence belongs to God alone, the Triune God, in whose life we are called to participate through his vital and life-giving activity. The following lesson (Job 42:12-16) offers a popular illustration of the same paradox. The debate of Job with his friends on the problem of God's justice is closed; God remains incomprehensible to humans; he is free, and we know he is never unjust. Thus the epilogue of the book comes as the exact antithesis of the prologue: instead of the calamities which bore down on the holy man, and which had brought him to the brink of blasphemy, a vision of Edenic blessedness. The paradox involved in the tale of Job, how to justify the suffering of the innocent, had already been stated by the Deutero-Isaiah in the fourth Servant Song, which was read at the Sixth Hour, and which we hear once more at Vespers. One verse (54:1) was added to the previous reading (Is. 52:13 to 53:12); after the gruesome picture of the prophecy, it suddenly calls for rejoicing: "Sing, O barren . . . break forth into singing . . . for the children of the lonely one will be more than the children of the wedded wife." Christian tradition has interpreted these words as a prophetic anticipation of the mystery of the Church and the Synagogue. Already St. Paul has stated the paradox in clear terms and shown that it finds its transcendent resolution in the event of Good Friday. This is the very essence of his teaching as we hear it in the Vespers lesson from 1 Corinthians 1:18 to 2:2: "We preach Christ crucified, unto the Jews a stumbling block and unto the Greeks a folly, but unto those who are called, both Jews and Greeks, the power of God and the wisdom of God." The series of vesperal readings for Good Friday concludes with a composite lesson from the Passion Gospels. It consists of three sections from Matthew, namely 27:1-38, from the arraignment before Pilate to the crucifixion; 27:39-54, from the crucifixion to the cosmic portents of the death of Christ; and 27:55-61, the preparation of the body for burial. In the intervals between the three sections occur a reading from Luke: the prayer of Dysmas, "Lord remember me in thy kingdom" (Lk. 23:39-43), and a reading from John: the breaking of the legs of the two thieves and the spear thrust into Jesus' side (John 19:31-37), these last two episodes occuring only in Luke and John respectively.

Great and Holy Saturday. Christ rests in the tomb, and the millstone was rolled before the entrance. His followers wait anxiously over the Sabbath. In our churches we prostrate ourselves before the winding sheet. Rays of hope pierce through all that darkness, a timid hope that he will rise from the tomb as he said he would, a hope that the expectation of centuries will not be thwarted, but find its consummation. The distinctive feature of the Matins for Great and Holy Saturday, anticipated to Friday evening, is the chanting of Passion verses borrowed or adapted from Scripture and placed in the mouth of Christ himself, in alternation with the 175 verses of Psalm 119 (LXX 118), the encomium of the Law which he came to fulfil, being obedient unto death. Arranged in three *staseis*, these verses are followed by a canon. After the Great Doxology and the troparia, the theme of the general resurrection is sounded by the inspired voice of Ezekiel (37:1-14), who prophesies how the life-giving Spirit will raise those in the tombs and breathe into them a new life. The Jerusalem folklore was quick in identifying Ezekiel's valley of dry bones with the Cedron valley east of the city. As a matter of fact, it had been used for burial

purposes well before the Hellenistic period, when the eastern
slopes below Gethsemane, down to the village of Selwân, began to fill with tombstones and monuments, some of which
may have drawn the attention of Christ (cf. Mt. 23:29 and
Lk. 11:47).[24] A precise localization of Ezekiel's anonymous
valley is immaterial to our present purpose. The prophecy is
addressed to the exiles as a figure of the hoped-for resurrection
of the nation: "I shall place you in your own land" (Ezek.
37:14). We read this as an Old Testament image of the resurrection on the last day, of which the forthcoming Resurrection
of Christ, "the first-born of the dead" (Col. 12:18), is the
first act. Some of the terms used by the prophet, in verses 9 and
13-14, call for an explanation. The text reads: "Thus says the
Lord: Come from the four winds, O Breath, and breathe upon
these slain that they may live . . . I have opened your graves,
O my people, and brought you out of your graves, and I shall
put my spirit in you and you shall live." The original Hebrew
uses the same word *rûah* for "wind" (the material element),
and "spirit," cf. the Greek πνεῦμα and the Latin *spiritus*. The
prophecy of the dry bones is the prologue for the mystery of
the entire day and is followed by a reading from the Apostle
(1 Cor. 5:6-8 and Gal. 2:13-14) stating in clear terms that
"Christ our Passover is sacrificed for us" and that "he has redeemed us from the curse of the Law . . . that the blessing of
Abraham might come on the Gentiles through Jesus Christ."
The Gospel lesson repeats the twelfth Gospel of Good Friday:
the guards posted at the sepulcher (Mt. 27:62-66).

  The Hours on the morning of Great and Holy Saturday
are read without solemnity, the First Hour in the narthex.
Vespers begins in principle "at the tenth hour of the day," *viz.*
at four o'clock P.M.,[25] and is followed by the Liturgy of St.
Basil. After the entrance with the Gospel, fifteen Old Testament lessons are read, which bring to our attention the entire
development of the economy of salvation. It is as if the Church
wished that we should review, on the eve of Pascha, all that
has come to pass from the beginning of the world, in the same
manner that Christ, on the evening of his Resurrection, meeting two disciples on the road to Emmaus "expounded unto
them in all the Scriptures the things concerning himself" (Lk.

24:27). The catechesis on Great and Holy Saturday is a last hour preparation for Pascha. It does not follow the order of the books, nor of the chapters and verses,[26] but focuses on the correspondance of the Old Testament figures with their actual realization, and anticipates the consummation of this age and the advent of the new aeon of which the Resurrection is the initial event. Several of the lessons were definitely chosen in order to show forth the typological relation of Old Testament events and traditions to the mystery of the Resurrection, Pascha and the Eucharist; these are the third lesson, the fourth, fifth and sixth, the eighth, the tenth and the twelfth. The others open prospects on the kingdom that is to come, of which the Church is a potential stage, and they have been regarded as pre-baptismal instructions to the catechumens, as the seventh, ninth, eleventh, thirteenth and fourteenth lessons.[27]

A rapid survey of the fifteen lessons will suffice for entering into the spirit of the liturgy. *The first lesson* (Gen. 1:1-13) has been read on the first Monday of Lent. The primaeval chaos imagined by the Hebrews and the lifelessness of the first three days of Creation are symmetrical with the death of nature which signalled the death of Christ, till he would rise from the tomb on the third day. *The second lesson* (Is. 60:1-16) is an ardent prayer for light after the darkness which had covered the world. It will shine over the New Jerusalem, "the city of the Lord, the Zion of the Holy One of Israel," where the people of the redeemed shall flock together; not the light of the first creation, but the uncreated light, to which we sing in our Paschal hymn. *The third lesson* (Ex. 12:1-11): Old Testament prescriptions for the sacrifice of the paschal lamb, a type of the sacrifice of Christ, and for the ritual meal which Jesus would observe with the Twelve for the last time, for by now the figures recede from the reality of the Christian Eucharist. *The fourth lesson* is the entire Book of Jonah, a figure of the entombment and the Resurrection, authenticated by Jesus himself, who quoted the popular *midrash* to the Pharisees requesting a sign from him. "There shall be no sign given to this evil and adulterous generation, but the sign of Jonas; for as Jonas was three days and three nights in the belly of the whale, so shall the Son of Man be three days and three nights in the heart of the earth . . . and behold, a greater than Jonas is here" (Mt. 12:39-41; cf. Lk. 11:29-32).[28] *The fifth lesson* (Jos. 5:10-15) refers to an episode of the conquest of Palestine by the Hebrews: Under the leadership of Joshua, they had crossed the Jordan and entered the Promised Land. Encamped at Gilgal, in the vicinity of Jericho, they kept the first Passover celebrated in Canaan, at the appointed date. The author of Joshua notes that the manna, with which they had been miraculously sustained during their march through the desert, ceased the following day, and from then on "they did eat of the fruit of the land." The meaning is clear: just as the Israelites entered a new phase of their national existence, so does the Resurrection of Christ and the Christian Eucharist over his body and blood belong in a new order of things which transcends the merely historical. *The sixth lesson* (Ex. 13:20 to 15:19): the departure from Egypt, the miraculous crossing of the Red Sea by the Israelites, and the canticle of Miriam. The symbolism is akin to that of the fifth lesson,[29] with a lyrical stress on the liberation from bondage wrought by the act of God. *The seventh lesson* (Zeph. 3:8-15): an anticipation of the messianic kingdom, the Zion of the future; "The Lord in thy midst, thou shalt not see evil any more." *The eighth lesson* (1 Ki. 17:8-24): a miraculous resurrection, typifying the Resurrection of Christ. It is part of the deeds of Elijah (Elias), the ninth-century B.C. wonderworker called by Yahweh to counteract the mass defection of the Israelites to the religion of Baal, whom his devotees credited with the fertility of the land and the preservation of life.[30] Sent by God to the parts of Sarepta among worshipers of Baal, in the midst of a severe drought, Elijah saved a poor widow from famine, "for thus says the Lord: the jar of flour shall not be spent, nor shall the jug of oil fail, until the day that the Lord sends rain upon the earth"; it came to pass that the son of that widow fell sick and died: "there was no breath left in him." But Yahweh heard the voice of Elijah praying: "O Lord my God, let this child's soul come into him again . . . and the soul of the child came into him again, and he revived." Yahweh, not Baal, is the Lord of life. *The ninth lesson* (Is. 61:10-11 to 62:5): Now the Church raises her sight to the future glory; the oracle offers, without any transposition necessary, a vision extending far beyond history. "As the earth brings forth her bud . . . so the Lord God will cause righteousness and praise to spring forth before all nations." The reborn Israel shall be unto the Lord a crown of glory, a royal diadem, and not the crown of thorns. "As the bridegroom rejoices over the bride, so shall thy God rejoice over thee." What had been a prophetic vision will, through the Cross and the Resurrection, become a reality. *The tenth lesson* (Gen. 22:1-18), another type of the Passion of Christ: the sacrifice of Isaac, firstborn of Abraham, on Mount Moriah. It has been read already at the Liturgy of the Presanctified, on the fifth Friday of Lent. *The eleventh lesson* (Is. 61:1-9). Jesus had inaugurated his public ministry by reading this lesson in the synagogue of Nazareth (Lk. 4:16-21)[31]: "The Spirit of the Lord is upon me, for the Lord has anointed me to bring good tidings to the afflicted, to dress the wounds of those with a broken heart, to proclaim liberty to the captives, and to those who are bound, the opening of their prison . . . And closing the book, he said: Today this Scripture has been fulfilled in your hearing." Only his sacrifice would make effective this program of liberation. *The twelfth lesson* (2 Ki. 4:8-37), Elisha and the resurrection of the son of the Shunammite. This episode practically duplicates the resurrection of the son of the widow of Sarepta, object of the eighth lesson, plus some accessory features; as a matter of fact, the cycle of Elisha is for a large part a secondary amplification of the story of Elijah; the present narrative shows forth an overload of details, but makes the same point as the Elijah story and bears the same relation to the Resurrection of Christ. *The thirteenth lesson* (Is. 63:11 to 64:5) is a psalm commemorating Yahweh's high feats in favor of his people, beginning with the miraculous crossing of the sea; it ends with a prayer to God, that he would contain his anger toward repentant sinners, "for thou, O Lord, art our father!" *The fourteenth lesson* (Jer. 31:31-34, LXX 38:31-34) is the prophet's insistent reminder that the new pact with the house of Israel and the house of Judah shall not be written, like the Sinaitic alliance, on tables of stone, "but I, says the Lord, shall put my Law within their own being and write it upon their

heart." *The fifteenth lesson* (Dan. 3:1-88), is the canticle of
the three Hebrews in Nabuchodonosor's fiery furnace, and
their call upon all creatures to join in their hymn of praise.

The Epistle at the Liturgy of St. Basil (Rom. 6:3-11) re-
capitulates the teaching of the Lenten season in two points:
"Know you not that as many of us as were baptized into Jesus
Christ were baptized into his death? . . . As Christ was raised
up from the dead . . . even so also should we walk in newness
of life,"[32] and "Christ being raised from the dead dies no
more, death has no more power over him, so we must regard
ourselves dead to sin and alive to God in Christ Jesus."

The long vigil is over. The priests remove their dark vest-
ments and put on light-colored ones.[33] The Gospel (Mt. 28:1-
20) follows Mary of Magdala and "the other Mary"[34] walking to the sepulcher, in the early dawn. Suddenly the earth
quakes; an angel rolls the millstone away from the entrance;
the guards, overcome with fright, become as dead men; the
angel addresses the women: "Fear not! I know you seek Jesus
the Crucified; he is not here, he is risen, as he said." And the
women went to bring the news to the apostles, and, behold,
Jesus appeared to them. It was the Gospel that would be
preached to all the world.

CHAPTER FIVE ❋❋❋❋❋❋❋❋ # The Pente-costarion

The Church shifts during the paschal night from the Triodion to another liturgical book, the Pentecostarion, the directives of which we shall follow from Pascha to the Sunday after Pentecost, the Sunday of All Saints. The book is so called for the fifty days which were adumbrated in the Temple worship of the Hebrews by the interval between Passover and the "Feast of Weeks," *Shabû'oth* (seven times seven days plus one). Except for spare readings from the Old Testament on the vigils of the Ascension and Pentecost, or some feast days listed in the Menaion, the Byzantine lectionary will from now on use exclusively the New Testament.

Two observations are necessary for a correct understanding of the Gospel narratives of the Resurrection. First, it was granted to no one to see Jesus rise from the dead. Many had seen him dying on the Cross; Joseph and Nicodemus laid him in the tomb; but there was no human witness of the Resurrection itself. On the dawn of the third day, Jesus appeared to the women and manifested himself on repeated occasions to several persons, to Cleophas and his companion on the road to Emmaus, to Simon Peter and to John, to Thomas the doubter, to James, to the eleven as a group, to "above five hundred brethren at once, of whom the greater part remain unto this present time, though some are fallen asleep" (1 Cor. 15:6); after an interval of some six years, he appeared to St. Paul himself on the road to Damascus (Acts 9:3-9; 22:6-10; 26:13-15). Secondly, these apparitions as recorded by the Evangelists show

forth numerous discrepancies as to number, order and circumstances. These discrepancies stem from the variety of the testimonies which the Evangelists incorporated in their respective
Gospels without attempting to harmonize differences—har-
monization is always suspect![1] In the mosaic of traditions, one
affirmation stands out: Jesus, and no other, appeared to many
witnesses, not as a ghost, an apparition without substance, but
as they had known him during their common peregrinations
along the dusty roads of Palestine or on the shores of the lake.
This does not force anyone's assent to the truth of the Revelation; yet our faith is sure, though its object be inevident. An
apodictic demonstration of ordinary human occurrences is not
a requirement *sine qua non* of every judicial or historical pro-
cedure; all the more would it be presumptuous to demand such
a demonstration of what happened in the secret of the tomb
sealed by the Jews, and which is not to be grasped nor even
imagined by a created mind. Christian liturgy does not concern itself with defending the faith against its deriders or detractors, but with fostering a full acquiescence to the mystery
on the part of the worshipers. This will be made clear by a
survey of the lectionary for Pascha, Bright Week, and the entire paschal season.

Pascha and Bright Week. We have left the women, Mary
of Magdala and "the other Mary," at the tomb, which they
found empty. "Jesus is not here, he is risen," the angel said.
In our churches, the Book of Acts is being read before the
winding sheet, which soon will be removed. On Saturday
night, late, toward 11:30 P.M., the Nocturn is served. The
hymns of the canon revolve around the tomb of the Noble
Joseph, where they had laid the body of Jesus, but the tomb
could not contain him. In a matter of minutes, the obsession
with the Passion and the Cross yields to the realization that
Christ, in truth, is risen from the dead, ἀληθῶς ἀνέστη,
voistinu voskrese; the initial verses of Psalm 68 (LXX 67)
"Let God arise, and his enemies be scattered," will be heard
again and again during the paschal season and be the theme of
the hymnography. The Hebrews understood this psalm as a
fervent appeal to God, that he would override the evil designs

of the enemies of Israel as he had done in the past. It is now transposed to a new order of reality transcending nature and history, since Christ, through his Resurrection, has defeated the last enemy of mankind: death, the non-creature introduced into the world by sin.

In the course of the procession a station is prescribed, according to the Greek usage, "at the appointed place," and the major celebrant reads a Gospel lesson, either Matthew 28:1-20, as in the Great Saturday liturgy, or the shorter account of Mark 16:1-8, the second in the cycle of the eleven Matins Gospels. On re-entering the church, the Resurrection canon is sung, followed by the Liturgy of St. John Chrysostom.[2]

The Epistle is from the Book of Acts (1:1-8): "He showed himself alive to the apostles, being seen of them forty days and speaking of the things that pertain to the kingdom of God," in order that, "once the Holy Spirit would come upon them, they be witnesses to him, both in Jerusalem and in all Judaea, and in Samaria, and unto the uttermost parts of the earth." The Gospel is the Prologue of John (1:1-17), which sets in evidence the theme of the economy of grace and the prospect of the new life in Christ, rather than the Resurrection itself. We enter a new age, the age of the Church, a new world. St. John's ἐν ἀρχῇ, "In the beginning," corresponds to the first word of Genesis, berêshith, and reaches, beyond the work of Creation, to the very life of the Triune God, which we are called to share, as the eternally begotten Son shares in our humanity. According to a common usage in the Church, the Gospel is read successively in several languages, as a reminder that the Word will spread among peoples of all nations, tribes and tongues, and that the title of the Cross was inscribed in Hebrew, Latin, and Greek (John 19:20). The Gospel lesson at Vespers, Ἑσπερινός τῆς ἀγάπης, (John 20:19-25), brings us back to the paschal events: the apparition to the disciples gathered behind closed doors "for fear of the Jews" —Thomas the doubter was not with them at that time—and the sending of the Apostles in the power of the Holy Spirit.

The Acts of the Apostles provide all the Epistles of the Pentecostarion. The birth and prime growth of the Church are the subject-matter of the book, according to the plan outlined in the prologue.[3] The starting point of the movement of expansion is Holy Zion, where the prophecies of the Old Testament were fulfilled. The Church rose with Christ from the sepulcher where death was once defeated. Pascha is conceived not merely as the supreme miracle, but as the first moment of the kingdom that is come; our annual celebration is not just a summit from which we would coast down, but it sounds an effective call to never-ending renewal and continuous growth. This may not have been the primary reason for the Church to adopt the Acts of the Apostles for the Epistles of the paschal season; the place of the Book as the first apostolic writing in the New Testament canon was probably the determining factor, but this does not exclude that a due consideration should be given to content-related factors. The reading of the Epistles follows the order of the Book, except for the necessary cuts of the pericopes to proper size, and for the few days or feasts having proper lessons *de tempore*, which, as a matter of fact, are also taken from Acts.

The Gospel lessons for all the days of Bright Week continue the theme of St. John's prologue. The figure of the Baptist and his role as the forerunner are set in bold relief by the Evangelist, who quotes the Baptist's own words: "I am not the Christ . . . I am the voice of one crying in the wilderness: Make straight the ways of the Lord, as said the prophet Isaias (Is. 40:3) . . . I baptize with water, but among you stands one whom you know not, he who comes after me" (John 1:18-28), read on Bright Monday. Exceptionally, we read from Luke on Bright Tuesday (Lk. 24:12-35), the meeting of the Risen Lord with two disciples on the Emmaus road, "on the first day of the week," says the Evangelist. This would be on Sunday evening, or are we to understand, the first day following Pascha? At any rate, the calendar of our liturgist, in assigning this Gospel to the liturgy of Bright Tuesday, seems off schedule: St. Luke expressly notes that when Jesus vanished from the sight of the two disciples after their supper in the village, "they rose that same hour" and returned to Jerusalem, at the latest on Monday evening. We resume on Bright Wednesday the series of testimonies by John the Baptist who, at the sight of Jesus and two disciples, exclaimed prophetically:

"Behold the lamb of God," thus accrediting him not only to the bystanders, but in a special way to the apostles whom he was presently to call (John 1:35-51). The interview by night of Jesus and Nicodemus, he who one day would join Joseph of Arimathaea to prepare the body of the Crucified for burial, is read on Bright Thursday (John 3:1-15). Jesus had foretold that "the Son of Man would be lifted up, that whosoever believes in him should not perish, but have eternal life, for God so loved the world, that he gave his only begotten Son." There is an obvious correspondence between this prophetic announcement and the catechesis to the disciples of Emmaus, who were "slow of heart to believe all that the prophets had spoken; ought not Christ to have suffered these things and to enter in his glory?" (Lk. 24:25-26). The lesson on Bright Friday is the episode of Jesus chasing the money-changers and the merchants from the Temple, as he came to Jerusalem for the Passover (John 2:12-22).[4] There may be a relation between the quotation from Psalm 69:9, "Zeal for thy house will consume me," which the disciples remembered after the Resurrection, and Jesus' own prophecy, much quoted by his accusers: "Destroy this Temple, and in three days I will raise it up . . . but he spoke of the temple of his body." On Bright Saturday, we hear John's last testimony as he was baptizing at Aenon near Salem (John 3:22-33). Seeing Jesus and his disciples approaching, on their way from Galilee to Judaea through the road of the Jordan valley, he declared once more: "I am not the Christ, but I was sent before him." We are given to understand that the baptism of John had been a mere preparation for Christian baptism. The relation of this lesson to the paschal administration of baptism is clear; it is not immaterial that the Western Church called Bright Saturday and the following Sunday respectively *sabbatum* and *dominica in albis*, when the newly baptized Christians laid aside the white robes which they had donned after baptismal immersion.

The Sundays and weeks of Pascha. In a sense all the Sundays of the year are Sundays of Pascha, for they are set apart from all other days to commemorate the Resurrection of Our Lord. Sunday is called in Slavonic the "Day of Resurrection,"

Voskreseniye; in Greek and in Latin, "The Day of the Lord," Κυριακόν, *Dominica*. The cycle of the eleven Matins Gospels, Εὐαγγέλια ἑωθινά, read every week at the Sunday vigil, extends the celebration of Pascha to the entire year, together with the cycle of the Resurrection hymns in the eight tones, which also runs through the year. The Matins Gospels are read from the royal doors of the iconostasis, a ceremonial rubric which may have its origin in the Church of Jerusalem. The *Peregrinatio Etheriae* mentions the usage of reading the Gospel at Sunday Matins already in the fourth century,[5] and in our days the Hagiotaphites chant the Gospel of the Orthros not from the ambon of the basilica, but from the Sepulcher at the center of the Anastasis, as if the celebrant, standing at the entrance of the sepulcher, would turn to the faithful and announce, like the angel to the women: "You came to seek Jesus, but he is not here, he is risen."

The successive appearances of the Risen Lord are the subject of the eleven Matin Gospels. We have heard most of them during Holy Week and Bright Week. A mere listing will suffice here: (1) Apparition in Galilee and universal mission of the Apostles (Mt. 28:16-20). (2) The tomb found empty by Mary of Magdala, Mary mother of James, and Salome (Mk. 16:1-8). (3) Apparitions of Christ to Mary of Magdala, two disciples away from Jerusalem and the Eleven; the conclusion of Mark and the Ascension (Mk. 16:9-20). (4) The tomb found empty by the women and by Peter (Lk. 24:1-12). (5) Apparition to two disciples on the road to Emmaus (Lk. 24:12-35). (6) Apparition to the Eleven and their order of mission (Lk. 24:36-53). (7) The tomb found empty by Mary of Magdala and by Peter and John (John 20:1-10). (8) Apparition to Mary Magdalen alone (John 20:11-18). (9) Apparition to the Eleven and to Thomas (John 20:19-31). (10) Apparition to Peter and his companions at the Lake of Tiberias (John 21:11-14). (11) Jesus challenges Peter's protestation of love and dismisses questions concerning John (John 21:15-25). The regular cycle of the Resurrection Gospels begins with the first Sunday after Pentecost (All Saints). The schedule of the Resurrection Gospels for the Sundays of Pascha follows a slightly different order. Fr. Kniazeff esteems that

the office of the Sunday Matins with their Gospel readings
may have set the pattern for those festal Matins which rate a
Gospel lesson.[6]

The lessons from the Gospel according to St. John on
weekday and Saturday liturgies are read in the order of the
text save for minor cuts and appropriate spacing. No specific
relation, therefore, should be sought between these readings
and the paschal mystery in its essence. The lessons for the
Sunday Liturgy, also drawn from the Fourth Gospel, are "proper." The Sundays of Pascha are commonly named for the episodes recorded in the assigned Gospel sections: Thomas'
Sunday, second of Pascha, when the doubter, who had chal-
lenged the reality of the Resurrection, was invited by Jesus,
after eight days, to see and touch the sacred wounds; but
"Blessed are those who have not seen, and yet believe" (John
20:19-31); the Sunday of the myrrh-bearers, third of Pascha,
whose Gospel, by exception, is drawn from Mark (15:43 to
16:8). On the fourth Sunday of Pascha, we read the account
of the paralytic healed by Jesus at the pool of Bethzatha (John
5:1-15). The text reports the event in its minute circumstances
and transcribes the dialogue most vividly. The pool, located
close to the Sheep Gate, had five porticoes, στοάς, viz. two
adjacent quadrangular basins, the dividing pier between them
forming the fifth portico. Recent excavations have shown that
this architectural ensemble was probably the monumental elaboration of natural (or rock-cut) cavities gathering under-
ground water credited with supernatural powers. We may
have here one example of a pre-Christian sanctuary sacred
to Asklepios and continuing as such until the Byzantine period.
The Jewish populace of Jerusalem had its own interpretation:
an angel moved the water of the pool, and this was the favorable time for the immersion of patients (John 5:4). With the
advent of Christianity as the state religion, it was consecrated
officially as a sanctuary commemorating the miracle of the
paralytic healed by Jesus.[7] The list of Sundays of Pascha continues with the Sunday of the Samaritan woman who conversed
with Jesus at the well of Jacob,[8] fifth of Pascha (John 4:5-42),
and the Sunday of the blind man who, being cured by Jesus,

confessed his faith in "the Son of Man" and worshiped him, sixth of Pascha (John 9:1-38).

The pericopes read on the second and third Sunday are immediately related to the Resurrection; the others refer to miracles performed by Jesus during the three years of his public life. The common denominator is that these miracles demand from the beneficiaries a formal act of faith in Jesus, the Christ, that he may heal the body and forgive sins. The miracles of the apostles related in the Book of Acts—"Who believes in me will do the works I do and greater still" (John 14:12)—suppose the same conditions of faith in the divine power which is Jesus' own. Before the Resurrection, he was for believers the long-expected Messiah; he is now the Risen Lord.

These Gospel readings present no particular difficulty, except for those among us who have ruled out in advance the possibility of whatever is not, or many not be explained rationally and derogates from what is commonly regarded as the course of nature. To undertake convincing them is labor lost.

The liturgy of the twenty-fifth day after the Resurrection, "Mid-Pentecost," on the fourth Wednesday of Pascha, does not conform to the pattern of the other weekdays with their continuous chain of Epistles from Acts and Gospel readings from John. The lesson of Acts (14:6-18), which at first sight seems a-typical, is in a sense closely related to the Gospel (John 7:14-30). St. Paul and his companion Barnabas had to flee from Iconium where they had met with the violent opposition of part of the population, and they sought refuge in other Lycaonian towns. At Lystra, a Roman colony and the birthplace of Timothy, they healed a man "who was a cripple from birth and who had never walked." The miracle divided public opinion still more; the two missionaries were the target of over-enthusiastic worship of some heathen who believed that the gods had come to town: Barnabas was Zeus and Paul was Hermes, "because he did the talking"; on the other hand a mob of rowdies stoned them, leaving Paul half-dead. This episode may be regarded as the counterpart of the scene described in the chapter of John from which the Gospel lesson is taken. "Some said of Jesus, This is the prophet; others said, This is the Christ"; but his adversaries sought to lay their hands on

him (John 7:30, 40-44). His healing lame and blind people
on the Sabbath had been taken as a pretext by his opponents,
and it may not be pure coincidence that the Church bids us to
read this Gospel on the week following the Sunday of the
Paralytic.

However, the choice of the Gospel lesson for Mid-Pentecost raises a problem which, to my knowledge, has not been
completely solved.[9] The scene, according to John 7:14, took
place "about the middle of the Feast of Huts, σκηνοπηγία
(verse 2). On Pentecost Sunday, we read the continuation of
the same episode with the formal notation, "on the last day of
the feast" (John 7:37). How did that pericope describing in-
cidents dated by the Evangelist of the days of the σκηνοπηγία
come to be assigned for reading during the season of Pentecost?
We would incline to seek the solution of the antinomy in the
history of the Jewish festivals.

The Law of Moses prescribed that all male Israelites should
"feast" the Lord three times a year (Ex. 23:14-17; cf. 34:23;
Deut. 16:16), which meant, after the centralization of the cult,
"ascending" to Jerusalem.[10] The three legal festivals were:
Passover, in *Nisân* (the first month of spring), originally the
rejoicing of shepherds on the increase of their flocks and the
offering of the first ears of grain ripening in the fields, re-
interpreted as a memorial of the liberation from Egypt: the
paschal lamb and the unleavened bread. The Feast of Weeks,
Shabbû'oth, fifty days after the paschal offering of the first
sheaf, came in conclusion of the harvest; the feast doubled as
a memorial of the giving of the Law on Mount Sinai and a
renewal of the Covenant, but there is no mention of this in the
Torah, and only indirect clues in the Biblical writings. The
Feast of Huts, *Sukkoth*, σκηνοπηγία,[11] the joyous in-gather-
ing of all the summer fruits, was kept in *Tishri*, the seventh
month, counting from the moon of *Nisân*; the name of the feast
is derived from the huts of branches and of foliage erected in
the vineyards during the grape harvest,[12] and re-interpreted in
reference to the shelters of the Israelites during their wander-
ings through the desert.

Radical Old Testament criticism has regarded the transposition of primitive rural celebrations into commemorations

of major historical events as a late innovation on the part of the post-exilic leaders and the rabbis of the Jewish diaspora. This is a gratuitous assumption, which underrates or overlooks a number of clues suggesting a definite connection between the Feast of Weeks as agricultural celebration and as the memorial of the Sinaitic Covenant.

On the other hand, we observe a gradual decline of the Feast of Weeks, correlative with the growing popularity of the autumnal feast of *Sukkoth*. This shift is particularly notice-able in the time of the post-exilic reconstruction, when the cal-endar and the *ordo* of the cluster of holidays of the month of Tishri were determined once and for all: *Rosh-hashanah*, New Year,[13] on the first day of the month; *Yom Kippur*, the Day of Atonement, on the tenth; *Sukkoth* proper, on the fifteenth and the following seven days; *Simhat Torah*, the "rejoicing at the Law," on the ninth day of *Sukkoth*, a feast presumably detached from the Jewish Pentecost, of which it seems to have been a normal feature. In Hellenistic Palestine, due to the eclipse of the Feast of Weeks, the three popular festivals were Passover, *Sukkoth*, and the winter feast of the *Hanukkah*, τὰ ἐγκαίνια, *encaenia* (cf. John 10:22; τὰ φῶτα in Josephus); it com-memorates the rededication of the Temple by Judas Maca-bee, three years after its profanation by the Syrians (168-165 B.C.).[14]

The evolution of the Temple worship may throw some light on our problem, namely the reason for the choice of Gos-pel texts relative to the feast of *Sukkoth* as liturgical readings for Pentecost and Mid-Pentecost. It looks as if the compilers of the Byzantine lectionary had restored to its original context the commemoration of the Sinaitic Covenant, which the Feast of Weeks had lost and which corresponds to our Christian Pentecost. Only the Spirit has now breathed life on the stone tables of the Sinai, and the legal covenant with Israel has made way for the universality of the Gospel. In-stead of the water of Siloam which the priests brought in procession to the Temple on the first day of *Sukkoth* at the singing of the Gradual Psalms, we drink of the living waters promised to the Samaritan woman (John 4:14), and our light is no longer that of the candelabra of the *Hanukkah*, but the light of Christ himself, the uncreated light (John 8:12).

The Ascension of Our Lord. Forty days after the Resurrection, on Thursday of the sixth week of Pascha, Christ was "taken up into heaven" ἀνελήφθη (Mk. 16:19), ἀνεφέρετο εἰς τόν οὐρανόν (Lk. 24:51).[15] As with the Resurrection, the liturgy of this feast does not merely abide by the account of the (indescribable) event, and we are not left standing here in wonderment. We look forward to a renewal in the Holy Spirit and, beyond the earthly stage of the Church, toward the second Advent in glory.

This orientation is traced by the Old Testament readings for the vigil Vespers: Isaiah 2:1-3, a vision of the nations gathered together on Yahweh's mountain. The Jews in the time of Christ expected that the prophecy would find its realization in an indefinite future, but well within history. We believe that the Church is the initial phase of a divine plan reaching beyond the limits of time. The second lesson is from the latter part of the Book of Isaiah (62:10 to 63:9). The triumph of the Messiah was purchased at the price of a superhuman struggle against evil: "I have trodden the wine press alone, and from the people no one was standing with me. I trod them in my anger, and their blood has spilled on my raiment," a passage used by the Latin Church in her services of the Passion. The Septuagint and the Vulgate have used for 63:9 a text different from the standard Hebrew, which is manifestly corrupted. Our reading is definitely messianic: "Not a messenger nor an angel shall save them, οὐ πρέσβυς οὐδὲ ἄγγελος, but he himself, ἀλλ' αὐτός."[16] The third lesson is a prophecy of Zechariah (14:1, 4, 8-11). On the Day of the Lord, the Mount of Olives shall be split from east to west, and live waters shall flow out of Jerusalem, "half of them to the Eastern Sea, and half of them to the Western Sea," so as to encompass the entire world, a transparent symbol of the universality of salvation.

The universal mission of the Church, Jesus' last instruction to his disciples, the Ascension and the sitting at the right hand of God (Mk. 16:19-20) are the subject of the Gospel lesson at Matins. At the Divine Liturgy, the prologue of the Book of Acts (1:1-12) and the epilogue of the Third Gospel (Lk. 24:36-53) accentuate still more the implications of the mystery for the future. As we stand with the apostles on the summit of the Mount of Olives,[17] dazzled by the luminous cloud that took Jesus from human sight—an element of the Old Testament theophanies—we are instructed to look ahead, for "this Jesus who was taken up, will come in the same way as we saw him go to heaven," and we are to be his witnesses to the end of time. And the Gospel stresses the reality of the event: it is not a phantom which the apostles saw ascending into heaven, but the Risen Lord whom they beheld, with whom they had shared meals, whose last words of instruction they had received, similar to the catechesis on the road to Emmaus.

On the Sunday after the Ascension, seventh of Pascha, the tenth Gospel of the regular cycle is read at Matins. The Epistle at the Divine Liturgy (Acts 20:16-18, 28-36), St. Paul's farewell to the elders of the church at Ephesus, is an a-typical lesson of the chain of readings for the offices of the Pentecostarion, and the Gospel (John 14:27 to 15:7) is a fragment of the discourse of Christ to the apostles after the last evening in the Upper Room: "Abide in me, and I in you . . . I am the vine, you are the branches . . . As the branch cannot bear fruit of itself . . . no more can you, except you abide in me."

Pentecost, that is, the fiftieth day after the Resurrection, Πεντηκοστή, corresponding to the Jewish Feast of Weeks, *Shabbû'oth*. However, the typology of the Old Testament readings for the vigil Vespers is not derived from texts relative to the Jewish festival; it is entirely oriented toward the forthcoming effusion of the Holy Spirit, who will bring life to the body of the Church, even as it brought life to the Law of Moses. Thus, a first lesson (Num. 11:16-17, 22-29), describes how "Yahweh came in the cloud and took of the spirit that was upon Moses" and gave it to the seventy elders whom Moses had chosen to be his coadjutors, and how, "when the spirit rested upon them, they prophesied and did not cease." The application to the disciples is transparent, and there is even the hint of a general effusion of spiritual charisms: upon learn-

ing that two of the elected elders, who had remained in the
camp, also prophesied, Moses exclaimed: "Would God that
all the Lord's people be prophets!"

The prophecy of Joel (2:23-32),[18] which is read as the
second lesson, announces a general effusion of the Spirit in
the advent of the messianic era. It would be realized on the
day of Pentecost, when the Holy Spirit descended in a visible
form upon the Apostles, and St. Peter, addressing the crowd,
made the words of Joel the text of his discourse (cf. Acts 2:17
ff.): "I will pour out my Spirit upon all flesh, and your sons
and daughters shall prophesy, your old men shall dream
dreams, and young men shall see visions."

This spirit is the same spirit of which we hear in the third
lesson (Ezek. 36:24-28). It will be bestowed upon the elect:
"I shall take you from among the heathen and gather you out
of all countries ... A new heart will I give you, and a new
spirit will I give you." The home to which Israel shall be
brought is a spiritual land, not the earthly land which Yahweh
gave to the fathers. This open-ended eschatological perspective finds its accomplishment in the universal outpouring of
the Spirit on the redeemed. Here begins the mission of the
Christian Church.

The lesson at Matins is a part of the ninth Resurrection
Gospel in the series of the ἑωθινά. It relates the apparition
of the Risen Lord to the apostles on the evening following the
Resurrection, Thomas being absent. Our attention is drawn
to verses 21-23, which define the special mission of the
apostles, to whom Jesus imparts the Holy Spirit, no longer a
term for an impersonal virtue, but the third person of the
Trinity, proceeding from the Father. St. John's record of the
logion is rhythmic, as were many prophetic or sybilline oracles:
"Receive ye the Holy Ghost. — Whose sins you shall remit,
remitted they are to them. — Whose sins you retain, retained
they are." A similar passage on the remission of sins occurs in
Matthew 16:19-20; the context is St. Peter's confession of
Christ at Caesarea Philippi, and the formal promise made to
Peter, "the Rock," that the Church will be built on him, "and
the gates of hell shall not prevail." The ecclesial implications
of these texts cannot possibly be set aside.[19] The Holy Spirit

will be present in the Church during her long vigil to the
Second Advent and be her driving force in the task of saving sinners.

The text of the Epistle (Acts 2:1-11) is capital. The event
of Pentecost is presented in the apparel of a Theophany: "A
sound from heaven, like a mighty gust of wind ... divided
tongues of fire," μεριζόμεναι γλῶσσαι ὡσεὶ πυρός,
alighting on each of the apostles, who were filled with the
Holy Spirit and started to speak in "other tongues," ἑτέραις
γλώσσαις, to the wonderment of the bystanders, who heard
the mighty works of God being proclaimed in their own
idioms. Any commentary would be out of place here. We
only wish to remark that the gift of tongues among the early
Christians and repeatedly in later Christianity, has been dan-
gerously misinterpreted, in spite of St. Paul's guarded teaching
on the relative value of charisms in view of the common use-
fulness to the Church, cf. 1 Cor. 14:1-9. The insistence of the
text of Acts is clearly on the universal intelligibility of the
Gospel as it was proclaimed for the first time to the mosaic
of populations which, since the advent of Hellenism in Palestine, had become a characteristic of the city of Jerusalem.

The pericope of the Fourth Gospel which is read at the
Divine Liturgy (John 7:37-52 and 8:12) is an anticipation of
the mystery of Pentecost, inasmuch as the Evangelist points
clearly to the future development of the Church. It follows
the section which we heard at Mid-Pentecost. We have discussed above the puzzling choice of Gospel passages whose
context, as formally indicated by the Evangelist, is the Jewish
festival of the Tabernacles, *Sukkoth*, and not, as would have
been expected, the "Feast of Weeks." St. John relates how,
"on the last day of the feast, Jesus stood and cried: If any one
thirst, let him come to me and drink. He that believes in me,
out of his bosom shall flow rivers of living water," a water
more excellent indeed than the water of Jacob's well, of which
we read on the fifth Sunday of Pascha. St. John notes expressly the prophetic nature of the logion: "Jesus spoke these words
about the Spirit which those who believed in him were to receive; for the Holy Spirit had not been given because Jesus was
not yet glorified."

The last verse of the Gospel for Pentecost Sunday (John 8:12) had passed from the themes "fire" and "living water" —cf. the Latin hymn *fons vivus, ignis, charitas*—to the theme "light of the world." The Holy Spirit is the principle, not only of holy enthusiasm, but of the knowledge of God, which is no mere brain knowledge, but engaged knowledge,[20] the knowledge that builds, and this is the object of the Scripture lessons for the Monday after Pentecost, the "Day of the Holy Spirit." The Epistle is Ephesians 5:9-19, an appeal to Christians, loud and clear: "Awake, thou that sleepest, arise from the dead, and Christ shall shine unto thee," ἐπιφαύσει ὁ Χριστός. The choice gift of the Spirit is that knowledge which a variant of verse 14 describes as an immediate contact with Christ: "Thou shalt touch Christ," ἐπιψαύσεις τοῦ Χριστοῦ, reminiscent of 1 John 1:1, "that which our hands have touched." The rhythmic structure of Ephesians 5:14 suggests that it is a fragment of one of the earliest hymns of the Church, the spiritual songs, ὡδαί πνευματικαί, to which St. Paul makes allusion in verse 19 (cf. Col. 3:16-17).

The pericope read at the Gospel (Mt. 18:10-20), in the context of the ludicrous debate of the Apostles on "Who is the greatest?", is animated by the spirit of the Sermon on the Mount and formulates the very charter of Christian life in the community of the brethren: "When two or three are gathered in my name, there am I in the midst of them." Here is the basic principle on which the Church will be edified, and whose manifold applications we shall follow from day to day in the liturgy of time, until the beginning of next year's Triodion.

CHAPTER SIX

The Weeks After Pentecost

The Sunday of All Saints. The amorphous flight of weeks throughout the year finds its point of reference in the centrality of Pascha. Sunday is the Day of the Resurrection, *Voskreseniye*, and two liturgical cycles, that of the Resurrection Gospels, and the Oktoechos, or "Book of the eight tones," somehow extend the paschal mystery to the weeks after Pentecost, linking the current year with the next over the coming months, till the Church opens once more the book of the Triodion.

At the same time, the outpouring of the Holy Spirit on the first Pentecost Sunday signalled the birth of the universal Church, and it is appropriate that we should devote the first Sunday of the season to the commemoration of the Saints whom the Church has borne to the kingdom. At Great Vespers, at the Sunday vigil, we hear God's call to the nations. They shall come together and stand witness to Him who from eternity has been the Revealer, Law-giver and Redeemer, for thus says the Lord, "who has made a path in the sea, a road through the mighty waters: I shall make a way in the wilderness, and rivers to flow in the steppe" (Is. 43:9-14).

The two other lessons are drawn from the Book of Wisdom. We learn of the peace which awaits the souls of the righteous when the trials of this life will be over, for the just are in God's hand; having been refined like gold in the crucible, they shall, on the day of visitation, "flare and fly like sparks in the rushes" (Wisdom 3:1-9). It is clear that the Book of Wisdom, in using these images, aims far beyond the horizon

119

of the prophets, when they proclaimed nothing more than the triumph of Israel upon enemies which would be destroyed by fire like stubble (Is. 1:3, LXX; Zech. 12:6; Malachi 4:1). The text is priceless, because it affirms unambiguously that man survives physical death, and also because immortality is not conceived here as an impersonal property of the human soul: immaterial and therefore, according to Plato, incorruptible in its essence. The Sage makes it plain that the status of those who "have slept in" is a provisional status, calling for the metamorphosis of the resurrection on the Last Day.

It is from this vantage point of the Last Day that the third lesson considers human destiny (Wisdom 5:15-23 and 6:1-3). The righteous have nothing to fear. The Sage never tires of repeating that they are safe in the hand of God. On the day of retribution, they will receive from him "a royal crown and a diadem of beauty." But against the impious, God will arm himself and muster all creation. The traditional symbols of the prophets are used for describing his armor: "justice his breastplate, impartial judgment his helmet, holiness his shield, and a sharp sword his vengeance." Later St. Paul will describe the spiritual armor of the Christian in similar terms (Eph. 6:10-16). The picture of the final cataclysm draws on the apocalyptic literature and on memories from the past history of Israel: bolts of thunder, shafts of lightning, hailstones hurled from heaven as on the Canaanites at the ascent of Bethoron (Jos. 10-11); the waves of the sea shall close upon the godless as upon the chariots of Pharaoh (Ex. 14:26-30), and the rivers shall engulf them, like the torrent Kishon sweeping away the slain of Sisera's army (Judges 5:21). The first three verses of chapter 6 are added to the apocalyptic vision. The Sage appeals to kings, who have been given a greater responsibility than their subjects. He reminds them that their sovereignty comes from the Most High, who shall probe their acts and scrutinize their intentions. The call, "Listen, O kings, and understand!" echoes in the verses which we sing at Great Compline, "God is with us; understand, you nations, and submit yourselves, for God is with us" (cf. Is. 8:9 ff., LXX). It is perhaps due to this similarity that the liturgist included these verses from chapter 6 of Wisdom in the Vespers lesson. But it is also possible, though it cannot be proved, that he wished to emphasize that the entire fragment is not merely an apt illustration of the doctrine of moral retribution—virtue rewarded and vice punished—but an expression of the divine economy of Creation headed toward the advent of the kingdom. The triumph of the saints will be more than a sum of personal victories; it will be a cosmic triumph.

The Apostle reading is the latter part of the encomium of faith in the Epistle to the Hebrews (11:32 to 12:2). The list of Old Testament heroes of the faith from Abraham to Moses and the prophets had been read on the Sunday before the Nativity of Our Lord, which is devoted to the "Holy Fathers," and on Orthodoxy Sunday, first in Lent. Today, the emphasis is on the "better thing" which has been prepared for the New Testament Saints. The "Fathers" of the Old Testament, before and under the Law, whom we commemorate for their heroic faith, could not enter upon the promised inheritance, for only through Christ was the new dispensation of grace made possible. They had to wait until his Resurrection, "that they might not attain perfection but with us" in the Church, ἵνα μή χωρίς ἡμῶν τελειωθῶσιν (11:40). Together with all the saints, and "seeing that we are compassed about with so great a cloud of witnesses" the multitude which no man could number (Apoc. 7:9),[1] we shall "run with perseverance the race that is set before us, looking unto Jesus, the author and finisher of our faith."

It is again the theme of faith which is proposed to us in the composite Gospel lesson from Matthew 10:32-33; 10:37-38; and 19:27-30: faith, not merely a personal emotion, but faith confessed before men as circumstances may demand, not only through words, but through deeds. St. Peter's profession of faith would not save him, but rather his obedience and the surrendering of his life, as the supreme testimony which all saints can bear to Christ. This means self-denial, and it means that we shall take up our cross and follow after him who "for the joy that was set before him endured the cross and despised the shame," as we read at the end of the Epistle. The last verses of the Gospel lesson answer Peter's direct question, "We have forsaken all and followed thee; what shall we have there-

for?" Jesus answered: "A hundredfold, and to inherit everlasting life," in the new order in which we shall have a share
with all the saints of all times.

The New Testament lectionary. We may be brief on the
mechanics of the Byzantine lectionary for the time after Pentecost. The Old Testament is not read and no Scripture lessons
are designated for the Sunday vigil except the Resurrection
Gospels. The lectionary is organized on the principle of the
lectio continua, which however is not observed with the same
rigor as in the liturgies of some oriental churches. The preceding chapters have already acquainted us with the distribution
of the New Testament lessons in three series: the course of
Sunday readings, Κυριακοδρόμιον; the Saturday readings;
and the week-day readings, each of the three series following
the general order of the text in the canonical books. The spacing of the Sunday Gospel readings is particularly noticeable as
one skips, so to speak, over several chapters from one Sunday
to the following without being able, most of the time, to account with probability for the choice of each lesson in particular. The basic lectionary provides for thirty-two Sundays, beginning with the Sunday of All Saints, first after Pentecost,
and running through to Zacchaeus Sunday, last before the Lenten Triodion of the following year.[2]

Since the dates of Easter and the paschal cycle, namely the
Lenten Triodion and the Pentecostarion, are not determined
on the basis of the solar calendar, the number of weeks from
Pentecost to the following Triodion varies from year to year;
on the one hand, we have to reckon with Sundays in excess of
the basic thirty-two which have been provided for; on the other
hand, lessons designated for Sundays which are pre-empted
by some major feast, as for instance the Nativity or the Theophany, remain at our disposal. This calls for an adjustment
of the calendar with the paschal cycle, and the way in which
this adjustment is done in the various *Typica* or liturgical cal-
endars of the Orthodox churches is far from uniform. It is
neither our plan nor within our competence to examine here
the complicated rules set to solve this problem.

The course of Sunday readings from Matthew runs from

the second to the seventeenth Sunday after Pentecost; Luke is read from the eighteenth Sunday onward.[3] The corresponding Sunday Epistles are drawn from Romans, Corinthians, Galatians, Ephesians, Colossians, and the first Epistle to Timothy. On Saturdays, the Gospels are from Matthew and Luke; the first letter to the Thessalonians is added after Colossians. On weekdays, the Gospel lessons are from Matthew, from the Monday after Pentecost to the eleventh week; Mark, twelfth to sixteenth week; Luke, seventeenth to twenty-ninth week; and again Mark. The Epistles to the Philippians, the second to the Thessalonians, Titus, Hebrews, and the General Epistles, are added, in the order of the canon, to the Epistle readings used on Saturdays and Sundays. The Book of Revelation (Apocalypse), traces of which are eventually found in Byzantine hymnology, is not read in the Divine Liturgy nor other services, in contrast with the Latin practice.

We have repeatedly pointed out the consequences of the reading of Scripture in continuous sequence in our liturgical worship. It is obvious that a course of lessons which follows the order of the Old and New Testament writings cannot yield to the changing mood of the seasons and the feasts of the liturgical year, for which "proper" lessons had to be provided. Furthermore, whereas the human authors or compilers of most of the Biblical Scriptures were fairly systematic in their writings and their use of sources—whatever their system was—, we have seen that some Old Testament Books are mere collections of prophetic oracles or of miscellaneous sayings more or less skillfully put together, like the cubes of a ruined mosaic, lest they get irretrievably lost.

The compilers of the lectionaries, unable or unwilling as they were to appraise critically the composition or genesis of the inspired books, could do nothing else but follow the order of the text as given, for better or for worse, and to make the cuts and adjustments they deemed necessary in order to provide for readable units. Note also that the division of the text in chapters and verses is a late feature of our Bibles, posterior to the elaboration of our lectionaries. Liturgical sections do not necessarily correspond to biblical chapters, and it happens that two unrelated passages are blocked together in the same lesson, or conversely that one episode, or discourse, or poetic fragment, is cut in two in the lectionary; this, of course, is logically questionable, and often confusing.

Three factors preserve the work of our liturgists from the relativism of a purely academic approach to the Scriptures: first, the ultimate decisiveness of their biblical faith; secondly, their belief in the organic unity of the Old and the New Testament; and thirdly, their typological interpretation of the prophetic and historical books of the Old Testament, which could authorize itself on the example of the Evangelists and apostolic writers and of the expositions by the Church Fathers. The application of the typological method is of course evident in the case of "proper" lessons, like those of major services or of the feasts listed in the Menaion; it also saves the reading of "common" lessons throughout the year from representing a routine exercise having no definable objective. The above observations bear primarily on the current liturgical readings from the Old Testament, but secondarily and proportionally on the "common" lessons from the New Testament. The Epistle and Gospel readings for the weeks after Pentecost are unspecific and amount to a general course of instruction, whose purpose is to acquaint Christians with the revealed doctrine of the Evangelists and of the apostolic writings. The sequence of those lessons reflects necessarily the composition and the internal logic of the books of the New Testament canon.

There is no lack of good introductions to the literature of the New Testament at all levels[4] and these could advantageously be consulted as a general preparation to reading and hearing the liturgical lessons. The following notes are offered as a mere reminder for previously informed persons. The Gospels present us with a factual account of the "Christ event," reflecting the image which the first generation of Christians had formed of the Master, and the earliest preaching, essentially a straightforward proclamation, κήρυγμα, of the good news. The substance of the message is the same in the four Gospels, but the approach is different, whether we consider the Synoptics or the Gospel according to St. John.

St. Mark, a witness to the catechesis of St. Peter of whom he was a disciple, writes down the raw facts in an unsophisticated, unsystematic way. A loose chronological sequence leaves a considerable leeway for ordering the single episodes and logia which the Evangelist records as he had heard them. He is overwhelmed by the continuous scandal of a Messiah disowned and rebuked by his own, persecuted and crucified by the leaders of his people, but ultimately vindicated by his triumphal Resurrection.

In contrast, St. Matthew presents the same facts in a carefully elaborated framework, grouping his material in large logical units, even when some fragments had to be shifted from whatever seemed to have been their historical context, in order to fit them into his categories. The unifying factor is the Evangelist's conviction that the episodes of the life of Christ had been foretold by the prophets or had their prototypes in the Scriptures of the Old Testament. St. Matthew who, according to tradition, had composed his Gospel in Aramaic language as a collection of *logia* pronounced by Christ, was addressing himself to local Christians issued from Judaism, who needed to be confirmed in their faith or armed against objections from their former coreligionists.

St. Luke, a Greek writing for Greeks, anxious to describe the progress of the Christian missionary adventure, is also systematic, but not after the manner of Matthew. He distributes his material so as to indicate a geographic progression. The Gospel is announced first in Galilee, the neighboring district of the Lake of Gennesaret, and the Decapolis. St. Luke restyles episodes common to Mark and Matthew in order to render them more intelligible to his foreign readers; he shows Jesus and his disciples "ascending" to Jerusalem after their ministry in Galilee, for it is in Jerusalem that everything will be decided: the Cross, the Tomb, the Resurrection. The Gospel will be proclaimed "in his name, among all nations, beginning at Jerusalem" (Lk. 24:47). Thus the ordering of the third Gospel differs noticeably from the logical arrangement of St. Matthew the bureaucrat; it is the report of a traveller, and it is continued throughout the Book of Acts, from Jerusalem to Rome.

St. John, the eagle-eyed, stands apart from the other Evangelists as he interprets for his contemporaries the inscrutable depths of Jesus' teachings and of the Christian mystery. His typological remarks are inspired by theological, rather than polemical or apologetic interest. This is not to say that he soars above the contigencies of history, nor that he is unconcerned with the "historical Jesus." Perhaps not enough attention has been paid by modern exegetes to the fact that the Fourth Gospel abounds in concrete notations, apparently of little or no theological importance, but simply "because that is how it happened."

The principal objectives and developments of St. Paul's so-called "Great Epistles," namely Romans, Corinthians, even Galatians and Ephesians, can be defined and followed without too much difficulty, and it is generally easy to identify in a general way the adversaries he had to face: overt or covert trouble-makers, Judaizers, leaders of cliques, dissolute characters, gnostics and ideologues, who threatened the faith or the purity of the Church. Such people are of all times. The diversity of subjects treated in private letters to individual correspondants, like Timothy, Titus, or Philemon,[5] and in the Catholic Epistles, from Peter to Jude, makes it difficult to characterize them profitably in a few words. Even more than was the case with the everyday Gospels of the lectionary, we will have to be content with listening to the lessons from the apostolic writings as they are read at the Liturgy, and let the text speak for itself.

The Sundays of Matthew. We shall survey briefly the Gospel lessons of the Sundays after Pentecost without taking into account the interruptions or modifications of the regular course of readings brought about by the occurrence of major feasts or movable Sundays. We do not have to consider here the series of the Epistles, nor of the weekday and Saturday Gospels, which follow the principle of the *lectio continua*, and whose choice is not determined according to content. The list of Gospel readings for the Sundays of Matthew shows a remarkable correspondence with the Evangelist's classification of his source-material in broad categories according to subject-matter. We have no way of ascertaining whether the liturgists were fully aware of the parallelism of their selections with the categories of St. Matthew.

The record of the traditions relative to the birth, childhood, and early years of Christ in the obscurity of Nazareth does not concern us presently. It shall find its normal place in the lessons of the Christmas season in the Menaion, cf. chapter VII. Our lectionary for the weeks after Pentecost starts on the Sunday after All Saints[6] with readings drawn from Matthew's account of Jesus' activity in Galilee and the district of the lake. We hear the first call to the Apostles: Simon, Peter and Andrew, James and John, with whom Jesus would inaugurate his preaching and healing mission (Mt. 4:18-23), second Sunday after Pentecost. Verses from the Sermon on the Mount are read on the third Sunday (Mt. 6:22-33). Then follows, week after week, the catalogue of miracles confirming at every step the evangelization of the countryside.

The occasional jumping from the lesson of one Sunday to that of the next over various events recorded by the Evangelist makes particularly striking the correspondence of the liturgical sections and the systematic articulation of Matthew, while some incidental material is being skipped; the series of miracles performed by Jesus, to the dismay of the Pharisees and their scribes, who never forgave his doing good on the Sabbath, is all the more impressive: healing the servant of a centurion in Capernaum, fourth Sunday (Mt. 8:5-13); exorcizing the Gergezene lunatics, fifth Sunday (Mt. 8:28 to 9:1); the paralytic healed and absolved of his sins, sixth Sunday (Mt. 9:1-8); the healing of two blind men and of a mute possessed by the devil, seventh Sunday (Mt. 9:27-35); the miraculous feeding of a crowd of five thousand persons on five loaves of bread and two fishes, eighth Sunday (Mt. 14:14-22); the miraculous walking of Jesus on the lake, while Peter sinks for lack of faith, ninth Sunday (Mt. 14:22-34). Note here the emphasis on the indispensable requirement of faith, which was implicit or, more often, explicitly mentioned in the readings of all the preceding weeks. The series of the Galilaean miracles closes on the tenth Sunday, with the healing of a boy tormented by a very mean devil, of the kind that cannot be expelled "but by prayer and fasting"; the lesson ends on Jesus' prediction of his Passion and of the Resurrection (Mt. 17:14-23).[7]

The lectionary passes now to the parables of Jesus, which St. Matthew groups without much regard to the circumstances in which they had been pronounced, whether in the early phase of Jesus' public life or on the eve of the Passion, as his spiritual testament. Thus we hear the parable of the merciless servant whose debt the king had cancelled, but who would pressure his fellow servants into paying to the last penny what they owed him, eleventh Sunday (Mt. 18:23-35); the episode of the rich young man who would not part from his possessions, and the lesson which Jesus gave to his disciples on that occasion, that "it is easier for a camel to go through the eye of a needle than for a rich man to enter into the kingdom of God, twelfth Sunday (Mt. 19:16-26); the parable of the vine-grower and the wicked workers who beat and stone their master's servants and kill his heir, a transparent allusion to the death of Christ and the revocation of the Jews' privilege under the Old Covenant, for "did you never read in the Scriptures: the stone which the builders rejected, the same became the head of the corner," thirteenth Sunday (Mt. 21:33-42); the parable of the invitation to the wedding feast rudely declined by those who had been first called, fourteenth Sunday (Mt. 22:1-14); Jesus answering the captious question of a lawyer, "What is the greatest commandment?" and confounding a group of Pharisees with a question of his own, sure to expose their bad faith, fifteenth Sunday (Mt. 22:35-46); the parable of the talents, sixteenth Sunday (Mt. 25:14-30).

The series of the Sundays of Matthew ends with the episode of the Canaanite woman of the region of Tyre and Sidon whose daughter was healed by Jesus on account of the mother's faith, seventeenth Sunday (Mt. 15:21-28). It is certainly not at its place in the lectionary. It should have been listed between the lessons of the ninth and the tenth Sundays, as one of the miracles performed in answer to outstanding acts of faith. There is no obvious reason for this anomaly, which a thorough comparative study of early Christian liturgies might, or again might not, explain conclusively. This Gospel lesson is eventually repeated, according to the Greek usage, on the last

Sunday before the Publican and Pharisee Sunday. The lec-
tionary for the Sundays after Pentecost does not include St.
Matthew's account of the Passion and Resurrection of Our
Lord which, quite naturally, is read during Great and Holy
Week and the Paschal season, just as the narratives of the
Nativity of Christ and his early years are reserved for the
feasts of the winter months.

The Sundays of Luke. They run, subject to the same res-
ervations as the Sundays of Matthew, from the eighteenth to
the thirty-second Sunday after Pentecost. The sequence of
Gospel readings, save one exception, concords with St. Luke's
arrangement of his material in geographic order. However
the correspondence of the lectionary with the divisions of the
Third Gospel is not as evident as in the case of the Sundays of
Matthew.

From the eighteenth to the twenty-fourth Sunday, first to
seventh of Luke, the action is in Galilee and the neighboring
districts. We hear of the miraculous catch of fish on the Lake
of Gennesaret, when Simon Peter and his companions, who
had toiled in vain all the night, let down their nets on Jesus'
word (Lk. 5:1-11, read on the eighteenth Sunday, first of
Luke). The Gospel of the nineteenth Sunday, second of Luke,
finds Galilaean crowds at the feet of the Master, "in the plain"
(KJ), or "on a level place" (RSV), ἐπί τόπου πεδινοῦ, as
he descended from the mountain after a night of prayer. His
discourse as reported by St. Luke corresponds to the Sermon
on the Mount in the Gospel according to St. Matthew.[8] The
fragment which we read (Lk. 6:31-36) is the Christian "Gold-
en Rule": "As you wish that men would do to you, do so to
them . . . love your enemies . . . and you will be children of the
Most High, for he is kind (even) to the ungrateful and to the
evil ones." On the twentieth Sunday, third of Luke, we read
of the resurrection of a widow's son at Nain, a village in Lower Galilee, close to Mount Tabor (Lk. 7:11-16). The parable
of the sower and of the seed which falls on a diversity of soils
with unequal results belongs also to the Galilaean ministry,
twenty-first Sunday, fourth of Luke (Lk. 8:5-15). But the
parable of the rich man and the poor Lazarus (Lk. 16:19-31),
which we read on the twenty-second Sunday, fifth of Luke, is

obviously not at its place. The sudden jump of the lectionary from the eighth chapter of the Gospel to chapter 16 is already suspect; the parable belongs among miscellaneous fragments which St. Luke has borrowed from Matthew or drawn from his own sources and has included in the second great division of his Gospel, namely the account of the journey from Galilee to Judaea and ultimately to Jerusalem along the north-south furrow of the Jordan Valley. We come back to Luke's Galilaean file with an episode which took place "in the country of the Gadarenes," meaning the inhabitants of the Transjordanian ridge overlooking the eastern shore of the lake.' A man possessed of a "legion" of demons was delivered by Jesus, and a herd of swines into which the devils were permitted to enter, ran down the cliffs and drowned in the lake, twenty-second Sunday, sixth of Luke (Lk. 8:26-39). Another version of the same incident is given by St. Matthew, 8:28 ff., which we read on the fifth Sunday after Pentecost.

Beginning with the twenty-fifth Sunday after Pentecost, eighth of Luke, we leave behind the now familiar landscape of Galilee and the shores of the lake, passing to the second great division of the third Gospel. We are heading south, down the valley. There is of course a good deal of schematization in this presentation. We may deduce from incidental remarks of the Evangelists, and we know for sure from the precise notations of St. John that Christ "ascended" to Jerusalem on several well-recorded instances and that he varied his itinerary according to circumstances, even passing through Samaria, a district inimical to the Jews. But St. Luke makes abstraction of these journeys up and down and tends to represent the travelling of Jesus and his disciples as a continuous, unified journey toward Judaea and Jerusalem, where the drama of our redemption would reach its climax. Luke's geography, in this section of his Gospel, is conventional and theological, rather than realistic. In addition to episodes explicitly dated and localized, Luke has incorporated a number of fragments drawn from sources common to the other Evangelists, or from his own sources, which are not related to a particular time or a particular place. For these reasons, the section of the Gospel of Luke extending from 10:51 to the end

of chapter 19, out of which our Sunday lessons from the twenty-fifth to the thirty-first Sunday after Pentecost are taken,
appears less homogeneous than the Galilaean section. It remains, however, that the outcome of the entire drama looms
every day more threatening over the horizon, as the enemies
of Christ press for a definitive solution: to have him removed.
We have no way of knowing whether our liturgists have been
especially interested in the method of composition of St. Luke
and his geographic schemes. We feel nevertheless that these
should be outlined here, as we proceed from week to week
toward the time of next year's Triodion.

The first half of the Gospel lesson for the twenty-fifth
Sunday, eighth of Luke (Lk. 10:25-28), corresponds to Matthew 22:35 ff., which we have read on the fifteenth Sunday
after Pentecost: Jesus' answer to the catch-question asked by a
scribe: "What is the greatest commandment?" The logion
belongs certainly in the series of late discourses and parables
pronounced by Christ shortly before his Passion. The second
half, proper to Luke (10:29-37), is the parable of the Good
Samaritan, Jesus incisive answer to the inquisitive lawyer who
asked: "But after all, who is my neighbor?" The parable, of
course, could have been pronounced anywhere, but the scenario,
the man "going down from Jerusalem to Jericho," invites us to
classify it among the late pericopes of Jesus' teachings. The
parable was understood, beginning in the fourth century, as
an allegory, and gave rise, especially in the West, to extrava-
gant commentaries: the half-way inn was the Church; the two
denarii paid in advance to the inn-keeper for taking care of the
wounded traveller, the Old and the New Testament, etc. Even
in our days, guides are apt to show to uncritical tourists the inn
of the Good Samaritan—a ruined mediaeval khan—and point
to the reddish color of the soil which caused that section of
the road to be named in Arabic "the Ascent of the Blood."
The insecurity of the region had made necessary the establishment of a military post under Byzantine and Latin domination,
and the toponym "Ascent of the Blood" recalls the Old Testament *Ma'alat adummim.*[10]

The pericope which we hear on the twenty-sixth Sunday
after Pentecost, ninth of Luke (12:16-21), belongs to the

same group of late parables as that of the good Samaritan, even though the verses which follow are in the manner of the Sermon on the Mount. The Evangelist sketches a big, fat landowner intent upon enlarging his already considerable barns and cellars, and who has no other ambition but to "take his ease, eat, drink, and be merry" for many years. The occasion for the parable is the request made to Christ by "one of the crowd," that the Master would help him solve a knotty problem of inheritance. The point is made clear in verse 15, a formal warning to all: a man's life does not consist in the abundance of his possessions. Like this parable, the text of the lesson for the twenty-seventh Sunday, tenth of Luke, is proper to the Evangelist (Lk. 13:10-17). One more miraculous healing! The patient: a woman infirm for eighteen years, who was "bent over and could not straighten herself"; the diagnosis: a case of possession by an evil spirit, whom Jesus put to flight by laying his hands on the patient, and "immediately she was made straight and glorified God." Now this happened on the Sabbath, and that was too much for the ruler of the synagogue, all the more in the face of an enthusiastic crowd. The parable of the guests invited to a great supper, and their flimsy excuses for not attending, comes next, on the twenty-eighth Sunday, Luke's eleventh (Lk. 14:16-24, parallel to Mt. 22:1 ff., which was read on the fourteenth Sunday). It belongs clearly in the Jerusalem context. The cutting edge of the story, namely the transfer of the Covenant privileges from the Jews, who had been called first, to God's new people, is sharper in Luke than in Matthew, who has surcharged the parable with accessory features.

The healing of ten lepers, of whom only one turned back to thank his benefactor after having presented himself to the priest as the Law required (Lk. 17:11-19, read on the twenty-ninth Sunday, twelfth of Luke), took place, not "through the midst of Samaria and Galilee," as the King James version has it, but rather along the border of Samaria, which Jesus and his disciples wanted to avoid, and Galilee, from which they came, so as to reach the valley of the Jordan by the shortest way, and descend southward in the direction of Jericho, from whence they would go up to Jerusalem."[11] The episode, which is proper to Luke, makes it plain that the economy of salvation extends beyond ethnic borders: the grateful ex-leper was a Samaritan! It happens that the Epistle for that Sunday, Colossians 3:4-11, contains St. Paul's formal declaration that in Christ "there is neither Greek nor Jew . . . for He is all and in all." It may have been the intention of the liturgist to pair together this Epistle and this Gospel. It can be neither proved nor disproved. Any such coincidence, if unintentional, would rest on the unity of the divine economy, expressed both in the Gospel and in the Apostolic writings.

We have heard on the twelfth Sunday after Pentecost St. Matthew's version of the logion on the counsel of Christian perfection, in integral fulfilment of the legal precepts. It appears in almost identical form in Luke 18:18-27, which we read on the thirtieth Sunday, thirteenth of Luke. The pericope is undetermined as to time and place, but figures in both Gospels among other records of the latter phase of Jesus' ministry. At the same time, both Evangelists agree the location and the principal circumstances of the miracle performed in the outskirts of Jericho, of which we read on the thirty-first Sunday, Luke's fourteenth (Lk. 18:35-43; cf. Mt. 20:29 ff, not used in the lectionary). St. Luke relates the healing of a blind beggar; St. Matthew speaks of two blind men. In either story, these people appeal loudly to the "Son of David," and Jesus is moved of compassion. Once more the miracle is his answer to an act of faith.

Zacchaeus Sunday. In theory, this is the thirty-second Sunday after Pentecost, the fifteenth of Luke, unless it has been necessary to provide for additional Sundays in order to fill the gap between the last Sunday of the Κυριακοδρόμιον and the beginning of the Lenten Triodion. The story (Lk. 19:1-10), is deceptively simple: no miracle, if we understand by "miracle" a happening different from the usual course of nature; it is a healing, but a spiritual healing, in the secrecy of a human heart; it had already taken place when Jesus appeared. Zacchaeus, a Publican of high rank but of short stature, wished to see Jesus—like the Greeks who, a few weeks later, approached Philip, that he would introduce them properly (John 12:21); no mere curiosity, but the obscure feeling that he who

was about to pass through the streets of Jericho was alone able
to straighten up whatever is devious in the soul of a man, and
deviousness there had been in Zacchaeus' life: publicans were
a notorious lot. We had better not feel too proud of our self-
proclaimed integrity, after twenty centuries of Christianity!
Zacchaeus' change of heart was complete, and expressed with
the same naive exuberance which had made this worthy government official climb a tree, just like the Jericho street young-
sters, in order to see better. It takes a "man of desire" to do
such things and to say: "The half of my goods I give to the
poor, and if I have defrauded anyone of anything, I restore it
fourfold."[12] And Jesus said to him: "This day is salvation come
to Zacchaeus' house, for he also is a son of Abraham."

The story of Zacchaeus marks a strategic turn in the Gospel
according to St. Luke, who had divided his "Life of Jesus" into
four parts: the early years, the Galilaean ministry, the journey
southward, and the Great and Holy Week. Jericho is a landmark, for it is from thence that Jesus and the apostles will go
up to Jerusalem. We have noted earlier that the Evangelist had
deliberately omitted to report occasional journeys to and fro,
for he was not interested in offering a detailed time-table. The
next pericopes, after the parable of the pounds, Μνᾶς (Lk.
19:11-28), will find Jesus and his followers on the way to
Bethany and Bethphage, on the eve of the triumphal entrance
into Jerusalem. Our lectionary had followed them from week
to week, and we approach another paschal cycle. Next comes
the time of one more Lenten Triodion.

CHAPTER SEVEN

The Festal Menaion

The choice of Scripture readings for the feasts of the Menaion is determined by their subject-matter and their rank. We might have organized this chapter in a logical order such as, (1) Feasts of Our Lord, (2) Feasts of the Mother of God, (3) Feasts of the Saints. Such a division, however, would have obscured an important truth, namely that the feasts in honor of the Virgin are never without an organic dependence on the "Christ-event," from which alone they derive their significance. The Logos, prior to his being born a man, or after the Resurrection, is always at the center of the Christian drama: "He is in our midst, He is and He shall be." An independent Marian theology, or an independent worship not consistently rooted in the Christological dogma but rather developed for themselves are late elaborations of a "Baroque" type of Christianity, even though some of their features appear already in the Middle Ages as expressions of a sincere but ill-advised devotion. We shall therefore follow the order of the Menaion with regard to the major feasts of our Lord and of the Theotokos,[1] after which we shall briefly comment on a few characteristic selections from Scripture for the feasts of the saints.

The festal calendar begins on the first day of September, which opens the Church year. The entry in the Greek Menaion reads: Ἀρχὴ τῆς Ἰνδίκτου ἤτοι τοῦ νέου ἐκκλησιαστικοῦ ἔτους, "beginning of the Indiction and also of the new ecclesiastical year."[2] This date is unfamiliar to us, accustomed as we are to celebrating New Year on the first of January. It originates in a mode of computation common throughout the Near and Middle East, the civil year of the Hellenistic kingdoms, derived from the agricultural cycle in Mediterranean lands. It has otherwise no particular significance, nor is any solemnity attached to the first day of the Church year. The sole purpose of Scripture lessons at Vespers and at the Divine Liturgy is to remind Christians that they should enter the season in a spirit of faith, prayer and dedication.

The prophecy of Isaiah 61:1-9, at Great Vespers, is precisely the liturgical section of the Hebrew Bible which Jesus read in the synagogue of Nazareth on the first day of what is called his public life: "The Spirit of the Lord is upon me, because the Lord has appointed me to bring good tidings to the poor," and it is fitting that these prophetic words as quoted by St. Luke (4:18-19) be read again at the first Liturgy of the year, following St. Paul's exhortation to Timothy on the duty of constant watchfulness (1 Tim. 2:1-7). The second reading at Vespers is a montage of verses from Leviticus (26:3-12, 14-17, 19-20, 22-24, 33, 40-42), confronting the Christian, as it did confront the Israelites of old, with an inescapable choice: either faithfulness unto salvation, or revolt unto perdition. The decision should be our daily concern, and the way is laid before us by the Sage, a way leading to the blessed end of the faithful, not measured by the number of years of their life on earth (Wisdom 4:7-15), third lesson at Vespers.

The Birth of the Theotokos. The first great feast of the ecclesiastical year is the feast of the Birth of the Theotokos, on September 8. The date is obviously conventional: nine months are counted since she is said to have been conceived by St. Ann, a date celebrated under the title "Immaculate Conception of the Blessed Virgin" in the Roman Church, on December 8. There is no scriptural nor historical record of the birth of Mary. The feast constitutes the normal introduction to the series of feasts of the Incarnation, from Christmas to the feast of the Meeting of Our Lord Jesus Christ, on February 2.

There is more than a chronological priority of the birth of Mary over the various episodes relative to the Incarnation. What we commemorate is not merely a chain of natural events, but rather the gradual unfolding of God's design in the world of men. For the time being, the future Incarnation is a matter of faith and hope: Jesus has not appeared yet on the stage of history. The spotlight is on Mary, born, raised, and destined to be the Theotokos. We have become so used to this title that we do not react any more, but just take it for granted. The Hapgood translation of the services has been criticized for using the expression "Birth-Giver of God," which indeed sounds awkward; it adds nothing real to "Mother of God," which is the literal translation of Theotokos, yet it forces us to concentrate on the humanly incredible affirmation that the eternally-begotten, "One of the Holy Trinity," was born of a woman and became one of us, consubstantial with man, as he is consubstantial with the Father. The last major feast of the Church year, namely the Κοίμησις, "the sleeping-in of the Theotokos," on August 15, is similarly related to the mystery of Christ: Mary, his and our mother, having fulfilled her destiny on earth and shown forth in her person the prospect of salvation to all mankind, will be reunited with her Son, who rose from the dead and ascended to glory.

The Scripture readings for the Marian feasts fall into two categories. Some lessons are common to several feasts, the object of which they fit equally well, provided that some allowance is made for minor contextual differences, for instance: the account of Mary's visit to Elizabeth, and Mary's canticle, the *Magnificat* (Lk. 1:38-49),[3] or the episode of Martha and Mary combined in a single lesson with the blessing on those "that hear the word of God and keep it" (Lk. 10:38-42; 11:27-28). Other lessons are proper to feasts commemorating specific events recorded in the Gospels or foreshadowed in Old Testament prophecies and types.

As we have indicated above, the canonical Scriptures leave us totally ignorant of the circumstances of Mary's birth and of the names and condition of her parents. This silence is one of the principal reasons for the proliferation of apocryphal writings which aimed at satisfying the insatiable curiosity of the faithful, and especially of the pilgrim journeying to the Holy Land. The doctrinal orthodoxy of that literature is often as questionable as its good taste or historical value. It is possible in several instances to give a tentative account of the process by which anonymous authors have devised the detailed information avidly sought by the faithful. One example may illustrate this.

The names of Joachim and Anna, "the righteous ancestors of our Lord," are those which the apocrypha give them. Joachim is not mentioned in the New Testament, neither in the genealogy according to St. Luke nor in the genealogy according to St. Matthew, unless we accept the hazardous identification of Jechonias (Mt. 1:11-12) with Joachim, on the theory that Jechonias is a plausible Greek transcription of Jehoiakim or Jehoiakin, kings of Judah (2 Ki. 23:34 and 24:6); if so, we would have here a hint of the royal ancestry of Jesus, "son of David."

As for St. Ann, Mary's mother, she bears the same name as the mother of Samuel (1 Sam. 1:20), and it is not immaterial that Mary's canticle, "My soul magnifies the Lord" (Lk. 1:46-55), shows an inspiration similar to that of the canticle of Hannah (1 Sam. 2:1-11), to the extent that some of their verses are almost identical in form and substance. According to the apocrypha, Joachim and Anna lived in seclusion away from the capital.[4] The story is an amplification of the theme, frequent in the Scriptures, of the miraculous conception of women deemed barren, such as Sarah giving birth to Isaac in her old age (Gen. 21:1-3) or Elizabeth to John the Baptist. Note that Joachim, like Zacharias, John's father, is in priestly orders, and the disgrace of being deprived of posterity affected Aaronic priests in a singular way. St. Luke writes of Elizabeth that "she hid herself five months" after she had conceived (Lk. 1:24), presumably waiting until the fact of her pregnancy could no longer be doubted and the opprobrium of her sterility manifestly lifted from upon her. The fact that our hymnographers have often exploited apocryphal stories needs not disturb us. Checking on their historicity was of no concern to them.

As much as we should like to know the circumstances of Mary's birth, they are not essential. The point is rather the indispensable role of the Virgin in the mystery of the Incarnation, as the full title of the feast indicates: "The birth of our Most Holy Lady the Theotokos," and as the Scripture readings at Vespers clearly demonstrate. These lessons do multiple duty:

Jacob's dream (Gen. 28:10-17), and the call of wisdom to her
banquet (Prov. 9:1-11) are read again at the vigil of the Sleeping-in of the Theotokos and at the Vespers of the Feast of the
Protection. The lesson from Ezekiel, a description of the eastern gate of the Temple (Ezek. 43:27 to 44:4), is also read at
the vigil of the Entry of the Theotokos into the Temple. The
thematic propriety of these pieces demands some explanation.

The first records how Jacob, at that time a young man, at
odds with his twin brother whom he had cheated more than is
tolerable, was on his way to the country of their Aramaean
kin-folk, to find a suitable bride from their clan. Stopping for
the night in a desert place, he saw in dream "a ladder set up on
the earth, and the top of it reached heaven, and behold, the
angels of God ascending and descending on it." "Surely God
is in this place," exclaimed Jacob waking up from his sleep,
"and I knew it not . . . How dreadful is this place! This is none
other but the house of God,[5] and this is the gate of heaven."
We are given to understand that Jacob was favored with the
revelation of a twofold chain of communication between heav-
en and earth, between God and his chosen ones, through the
ministry of the angels. The reality signified by the type is the
revelation of a new economy of salvation which has come to
all mankind through the intercession of the Son of God. Before
the Incarnation, there was a promise and a hope; after the Incarnation, an actual reality. From now on, man is no longer
in danger of passing out in the void of an impossible dream.
His desire is firmly anchored in the earth of men. He whom
Isaiah hailed as "the angel of the great counsel," μεγάλης
βουλῆς ἄγγελος (Is. 9:6, LXX), will transfer our prayers
and vows "unto the altar on high, from which we shall be
filled with all heavenly blessing."[6] The initial fact of the new
dispensation is the birth of Mary, without whom God's
will would have remained unfulfilled. Therefore we sing:
"Through her, things on earth are joined with heaven," and
"Hail, heavenly ladder upon which God descended! Hail,
bridge leading those on earth to heaven!"[7]

The typological connection of the second reading at Vespers with the mystery of the Incarnation is equally consistent.
We shift from Bethel and the dream of Jacob to Zion and to

Ezekiel's vision of the Temple of the future, now that the Temple of Solomon had been destroyed by the armies of Nabuchodonosor (Ezek. 43:27 to 44:4). It is all over with a bankrupt monarchy. Yahweh himself shall reign over the land, "from the place of his throne." The eastern gate of the sanctuary shall remain for ever closed, "because the Lord, the God of Israel, has entered by it." It is the gate of the *nâsi*, the "Exalted one," not an earthly prince, not an earthly Highness, who would govern in the name of God, as it was understood in postexilic Jerusalem,[8] but He whom the prophet expects and heralds, whose features, however, he fails to see distinctly in the twilight of the age: Christ himself. The symbolism of the gate is twofold: the gate is the judicial seat of the ruler, and it is the gateway through which the monarch makes his solemn entrance. Our hymnographers have mostly retained the latter on "Lord, I have cried": "Born herself of a barren mother, the Theotokos bore in her flesh the God of all, in a fashion surpassing nature, from a womb without seed. She is the only gateway of the only begotten Son of God who passed through the gate, yet kept it closed." And St. Andrew of Crete: "O, undefiled Theotokos, who hast borne the light-giver and the cause of the life of men, thou art revealed as the treasure of our life and the gateway of the unapproachable Light."[9]

The third lesson is from Proverbs (9:1-11). It may be useful to remember at this point that the manner in which the Wisdom Books are used for the feasts of the Theotokos is noticeably different from the way they are read during the Triodion and Great Lent. The purpose of lessons from Proverbs as a preparation for Pascha is primarily didactic. Human wisdom, of which divine Wisdom is the source and the model, is expressed in down-to-earth maxims which teach us to behave as responsible creatures of God, potentially delivered from the bondage of sin. The vigil lessons for the feasts of the Theotokos consider divine Wisdom as an active attribute of God, the uncreated principle of universal harmony, a creative and ordering foreknowledge of all things. Seen from that angle, Wisdom belongs in the Logos theology, rather than in ethics. This is not to say that we see in the Virgin an Incarnation of divine Wisdom, nor does the Church wish to develop a sophi-

ology on another foundation but Christ; but precisely because
it was eternally foreordained that the Logos would be made
flesh in Mary are we reminded of her unique place in the plan
of salvation wrought by divine Wisdom. This is therefore how
we may understand the lesson from Proverbs 9:1-11, as a call
to the banquet prepared in her house of seven pillars, the fear
of the Lord being the condition for partaking of her food and
of the wine she has mixed; thus shall men be made wise, not
according to the world, which scorns Christian wisdom as folly.
Mary's obedience opened for us the banquet hall, and her own
birth marked the turning point in the history of human salvation. Thus the Roman Church hails her as "Throne of Wisdom," *Sedes Sapientiae*, and she is so invoked after the opening
prayer at academic exercises. The Acathist (third stasis),
sings: "Hail, receptacle of God's Wisdom, private chamber of
the Providence! Hail, thou who showest philosophers to be
unwise, who makest speechmakers speechless!"

The Gospel reading at Matins is the account of Mary's visit
to Elizabeth in the house of Zacharias the priest, and her hymn
of praise and thanksgiving as she exclaimed exultantly: "My
soul magnifies the Lord" (Lk. 1:39-49, 56). The emphasis is
on her participation in the mystery of the Incarnation, whose
paradoxical aspects are the object of the Epistle at the Divine
Liturgy: on the one hand, the *kenosis*, since "Christ Jesus, being in the form of God, took upon himself the form of a servant, obedient unto death, even the death of the cross"; on the
other hand, "the exaltation of his name above every name, that
every tongue should confess that Jesus Christ is Lord, to the
glory of God the Father" (Phil. 2:5-11). The Gospel (Lk.
10:38-42; 11:27-28) juxtaposes the episode of Jesus' reception
in the house of Martha and Mary, and the blessing of an anonymous woman on the Theotokos, for having borne him who
passed, healing and teaching, through the crowds. In both instances, we are indirectly reminded of the role of the Virgin as
the maidservant of the Lord: she is both Martha and Mary, she
who cared for the infant and who gave attention to the needs
of humble folks at Cana, and she "who kept all these things in
her heart" (Lk. 2:19). Blessed is her womb who bore the

Savior, and blessed are "they that hear the word of God and keep it!"

The Universal Exaltation of the Precious and Life-Giving Cross, "Ὕψωσις (September 14). The association of the words "feast" and "Cross" is a paradox: the Cross, to the Jews a stumbling block, to the Greeks a folly; yet "to those who are called, the power and the wisdom of God" (1 Cor. 1:23-24). We commemorate the Passion and the Crucifixion not as ugly episodes inspired by a sordid politicking, but as the voluntary sacrifice of the Son of God who became man to save us. Therefore the liturgy of the Cross is not a lamentation over a dead hero, the wailing of devotees working themselves up to a paroxysm of frenzy, but the memorial of an event of cosmic significance, reaching beyond the limits of history.[10] The Cross stands while the world rolls, *Crux stat dum volvitur orbis,* proclaims the motto of the Carthusian hermits. We see in the cross a reason for hope, and the Resurrection makes this hope to become the unshakeable assurance of our Christian faith.

The date of September 14 assigned to the feast of the Exaltation has its roots in history. It recalls, according to traditions preserved in the Church of Jerusalem, the discovery of the Cross by St. Helen and the solemn dedication of the sanctuary of the Resurrection, built by order of Emperor Constantine and completed in 335. It commemorates also the triumphal elevation of the Cross in the Great Church, *Haghia Sophia* of the Imperial Capital, in 629, celebrating the victory of Heraclius over the Persians, who had carried away the precious trophy after their conquest of Jerusalem in 614.[11] Thus the feast of the Exaltation is, in a sense, a votive celebration.

The setting of the feast of the Veneration or Adoration of the Holy Cross on the third Sunday of Lent, σταυροπρο-σκύνησις, is different. It shares in austerity of the Great Fast. Its purpose is to re-assure the Christians against any temptation of despondency and despair, as they wonder whether repentance in dust and ashes will be acceptable to God, and whether the tomb which received the body of the dead Christ will ever release its prey. But the entire liturgy of the Ὕψωσις is a triumphal paean to victory through the Cross, an exultant proclamation of the new life experienced by the Christians.

The liturgical observance is structured after the manner of the major feasts: at the Vespers of the vigil, readings from the Old Testament. The forefathers had looked toward a salvation foreshadowed in the figures of past ages; now the mystery shines bright in our eyes, as we listen to the New Testament readings of the day. Their brightness floods even the Sundays before and after the Exaltation of the Cross, whose liturgical readings are added to those of the regular course of Epistles and Gospels.

The Vespers lessons draw on the historical books of the Old Testament, the Wisdom writings, and the prophets. The first lesson is Exodus 15:22 to 16:1. It recalls an episode of the march of the Israelites toward the Sinai, after their miraculous crossing of the sea and the defeat of their Egyptian pursuers. They camped at Marah, according to etymology the "bitter" fountain of waters, which Moses cured by dipping a rod of a certain wood which the Lord revealed to him. This miraculous wood is none else, typologically, than the wood of the life-giving Cross, and its symbolism is re-enacted in the ritual of the Theophany, when the officiating priest dips the cross into the water to be sanctified. The second lesson at Vespers, from Proverbs 3:11-18, extolls wisdom, "a tree of life to them that lay hold of her, and blessed is every one that retains her!" The inference, kept implicit, has the rigor of a syllogism: the Cross is the tree of life, wisdom is unto life, therefore the Cross is Wisdom—that Wisdom which the world knows not. The third reading, from the latter part of the Book of Isaiah (60:11-16), transports us into the world of the New Jerusalem, the new order of a new age, when "the glory of Lebanon," its crown of trees, "shall beautify the place of my sanctuary," a reminiscence of the cedar panels of Solomon's Temple and a vision we are at pain to reconcile with that of the strife-torn lands of the Near East, to which peace is slow to come.

These are but variations on the theme of the tree of life in the garden of Eden. The Old Testament prefiguration of the Holy Cross dominates the entire cycle of poetry and iconography of the Orthodox world, and also of the ancient and me-diaeval Western church. I am thinking presently of the hymns

composed by Venantius Fortunatus, a sixth-century Italian from
the Veneto, educated in the Byzantine tradition, who became
abbot of a Gallo-Roman community and later bishop of Poiti-
ers. These hymns are used in the liturgy of the Latin Churches
for the feasts and in the votive offices of the Holy Cross. In the
days of Eden, the Creator had marked the tree from which the
Cross would be made and whose virtue would heal the wounds
inflicted upon mankind by the lethal fruit of the tree which induced Adam and Eve into disobedience.[12] Equally suggestive
are the legends, the icons and the frescoes of the monastery of
the Holy Cross, Deir el-Musallabeh, in the south-west suburbs
of Jerusalem, an eleventh-century Georgian foundation, now
under care of the Hagiotaphites.[13]

For all its life-giving virtue, the Cross remains the Cross.
Its imminence prostrated the Savior in the garden of Gethsemane. The explosive joy of Pascha and the assurance of restored life should not make us forget the bitterness of the
Passion. Thus the first antiphon of the Divine Liturgy is the
cry of despair which Jesus appropriated as he suffered in his
human soul the final horror of being abandoned by his Father:
"My God, my God, why hast thou forsaken me?" (Ps. 22, LXX
21; Mt. 27:46). Yet the feast resolves into triumph, for God's
reign has come through the Cross,[14] the Cross of the Savior and
the cross which he exhorts us to take up after him.

This double aspect of the Cross is the burden of the New
Testament readings at Matins and at the Divine Liturgy. The
lesson at Matins is from the Gospel according to St. John
(12:28-36). Jesus announces his forthcoming death after the
loud Hosannahs of the crowd as he rode into Jerusalem; then
he was acclaimed as the Messiah, and a voice from heaven bare
witness to him, as it did when he was baptized in the Jordan
and when he was transfigured on Mount Tabor. "This voice
came not for my sake, but for your sake, and I, if I be lifted up
from the earth, will draw all men unto me." The logion, obscure for the crowd, did point to a double lifting-up: on the
Cross unto death, and from the Tomb unto glorification and
universal domination.

The Gospel at the Liturgy is a cento of verses from John
(19:6-11, 13:20, 25-28, 30-35). It describes the events of the

Passion: the evil counsel of the priests and elders, the arraignment before Pilate, the ascent to the rock of Golgotha, the
crucifixion and the death of Jesus in the presence of his mother
and of the beloved disciple. "He that saw it bears record, and
his record is true." The selection, deliberately skipping intermediate verses and stripped to the bare facts, defies any words
of commentary, seeing that the drama of the Cross can be nothing else but scandal or folly to the unbeliever.

It has been observed that whereas the services of the Lenten
Triodion view the Crucifixion as the central event of Great and
Holy Week, the feast of the Exaltation considers rather the
repercussion of the mystery on the life of the Church and of
individual Christians.[15] This is particularly noticeable from the
New Testament readings prescribed for the Sunday before and
the Sunday after the Cross. Thus the Apostle: "Far from it
that I should glory, except in the Cross of Christ" (Gal. 6:14),
and "I myself was crucified with him and I live, yet not I, but
Christ lives in me" (Gal. 2:20). And the Gospel readings:
Christ would be lifted up "like Moses lifted up the bronze ser-
pent in the wilderness, that whosoever believes in him would
not perish but have eternal life" (John 3:14-15, quoting Numbers 21:9); hence the conclusion: all would-be followers of
Christ must take up their cross (Mk. 8:34).

The Entry of the Theotokos into the Temple (November
21). What means this date? The interval of seventy-four days
since the feast of the Birth of the Theotokos approximates the
period of segregation prescribed by the Law of Moses for a
woman who gives birth to a daughter (Lev. 12:5). But symbolic dates, as a rule, do not admit of approximations; moreover, the concern of our liturgists was not with the "churching"
of St. Ann. The date of the feast seems to have been originally
that of the dedication of a sixth-century church known in
Jerusalem as the Νέα,[16] in which case the feast of the Entry
would have the character of a votive celebration commemorating what is commonly called in the West the "Presentation of
the Virgin Mary."

The hymns of the feast draw heavily on the Protevangelion
of James,[17] a second-century apocryphal Gospel of Egyptian

origin, which relates how, at the age of three, Mary was brought by Joachim and Ann to the Temple in fulfilment of a vow, and how she was attended by angels in the Holy of Holies. The story impressed the pilgrims who, in the streets of Jerusalem, were shown the place of her birth and even the house where "she learned the letters." The iconographers and hymnographers thrived on such source material, but at the same time they knew how to detect, under the artificialities of the legend, the not uncertain features of a mystery which would soon be revealed in its fulness.

The scriptural readings of the Byzantine liturgy are oriented in that direction. The first two lessons of the vigil Vespers (Ex. 40:1-5, 9-10, 16, 34-35, and 1 Ki. 7:51, 8:1, 3-7, 9-11) are proper to the feast. They are closely interrelated and constitute the Old Testament background of the Epistle reading at the Divine Liturgy (Hebr. 9:1-7). We begin with the description of the building and furnishing of the Tabernacle of Moses, and of the Temple in Jerusalem: the portable sanctuary, ôhél, σκηνή, which Moses had built in the desert according to the instructions of God himself, and the "house" of stones and mortar which Solomon erected in his capital, to be the permanent abode of Yahweh in the midst of the chosen nation. A tradition preserved by the priests identified the rocky hilltop on which the Temple was built with Mount Moriah, where Abraham's faith had been put to test when he was ordered to offer Isaac in sacrifice (2 Chron. 3:1; cf. Gen. 22:1-14).

These liturgical selections aim less at a graphic description of the sanctuaries than at their theological significance. However it is not immaterial that the plan of the Temple: the vestibule, êlâm or ûlâm; the great hall, hêkal; and the Holy of Holies, debîr, survives in the three divisions of our church buildings: the narthex, the body of the Church—the "nave" in western parlance—, and the sanctuary.[18] Particularly important in this architectural succession is a belief in the continuity of the divine revelation; the God of Moses is the same as the God of the patriarchs, and he who resided between the Cherubim of the Temple is the one whom we adore in the Trinity of Persons.

The mysterious presence of God in the sanctuaries of the Hebrews was materialized in a sacred object, the Ark of the

Covenant, and manifested by a theophany: the "glory," *kâbôd*, δόξα, that filled the Tabernacle and the House of the Lord, making of the structures erected by human hands the dwelling of the Transcendent, inaccessible to the profane. This was signified in Ezekiel's description of the eastern gate of the Temple, read as the third lesson of Vespers (Ezek. 43:27 to 44:4) and which we have already heard for the Birth of the Theotokos.

The Ark of the Covenant, in the midst of the Holy of Holies, had been, so to speak, the sacrament of God's invisible presence among his people. When the Temple of Solomon was destroyed by the Babylonians, the sanctuary rebuilt by the returning exiles remained empty; the Ark was no longer there. The forced spiritualization of the cult which depended no longer on figures would hasten the advent of the reality described in the Epistle to the Hebrews (9:1-7), as we read at the Divine Liturgy. Whereas the High Priest of the Jews entered the sanctuary once a year to offer the blood of expiation for himself and for the sins of the people, Christ himself would once and for all enter the Tabernacle on high with his own blood, for he is our High Priest.[19] Mary, who made this possible through her dedication and of her own free will, is therefore properly acclaimed as the "Tabernacle of God and the Logos . . . the Ark gilded by the Spirit" (Akathist, stasis 4) or "the Ark of the Covenant," *arca foederis* (in the *Litaniae Lauretanae* of the Roman Church). The Gospel readings, due to the absence of scriptural references to the specific object of the feast, are the same as those designated for the feast of the Birth of the Theotokos except that they have been interchanged: what was read at Matins is now read at the Divine Liturgy and *vice versa*.

The Nativity of Our Lord (December 25). The season of the great winter festivals,[20] *viz*. the Nativity and the Theophany, begins with two preparatory Sundays which modify the regular course of the Sundays after Pentecost. The Scriptures for the Sunday of the Forefathers, second before Christmas, stress the passage of the old Law to the new order, from the life of the "old man" to the new life in Christ, as we read from the

Epistle of the Divine Liturgy (Col. 3:4-11). The Gospel (Lk. 14:16-24) is the parable of those who had rudely declined the invitation to the banquet of the king and were replaced by men and women from all lands and all walks of life—obviously an allusion to the rejection of the Jews as a privileged ethnic body, and to the open Covenant of the Gospel. The Sunday preceding Christmas commemorates the ancestors of Christ. The Epistle is the encomium of the Old Testament saints who were saved through faith (Hebr. 11:9-10, 17-32, 32-34) and the Gospel is the first chapter of Matthew: "The Book of the generation of Jesus Christ the son of David, the son of Abraham." He is the eternally begotten Son of God, but the feast we are about to celebrate is that of his birth according to the flesh.

A brief description of the Office of the Nativity will help us to understand the distribution of the scriptural readings. The feast begins on December 24 with the Royal Hours,[21] for each of which an Old Testament lesson from the prophetical books is provided, followed by a reading from the Apostle and a Gospel lesson. Some of these readings are repeated at Vespers, and the service of Vespers concludes with the Liturgy of St. Basil. The all-night vigil consists of Great Compline and Matins, and the festal Liturgy is that of St. John Chrysostom.[22] A similar order will be observed for the feast of the Theophany (January 6). In fact, the Nativity as an independent celebration was split from a primitive Theophany, or Epiphany. The distinction of the two feasts seems to have originated in Jerusalem and, of course, Bethleem. Epiphanius spoke of the Epiphanies (in the plural), and in 385 Pope Siricius mentioned the *Natalicia* (again a plural). St. John Chrysostom preaching at Antioch (ca. 386-388) declared that the December feast was held in the West since the beginning. The double celebration, *viz.* of the Nativity in December and of the Theophany in January, prevailed in the "Great Church" at the end of the fourth or early in the fifth century.

1. Prophecies and Old Testament lessons. The prophecies and Old Testament lessons read at the Hours and at Vespers are messianic oracles and types, the realization of which is the object of the feast. The lesson at the First Hour, repeated at

Vespers, is from Micah, the villager-prophet from Moresheth-Gath in the rolling foothills of Judah, contemporary of Isaiah's early years (Micah 5:2-4). It contains the text which the scribes would quote to the spies of Herod, who inquired where the King-Messiah would be born (Mt. 2:5-6). The answer: In Bethleem Ephrata, out of which shall rise "He that is to be ruler in Israel." Obviously the prophet envisioned a descendent of David the Bethleemite, who would inaugurate an era of peace and glory after the tribulations of the nation threatened by its enemies.[23]

A lesson from Baruch, Jeremiah's secretary,[24] is read at the Third Hour and at Vespers (3:36 to 4:4). It is not, strictly speaking, a prophecy, but rather a fragment from a wisdom writing, extolling God's gift to mankind: "This is our God, and no other shall be compared with him. He has grasped the whole way of knowledge and imparted it to Jacob his servant and to Israel his beloved. Afterward he was seen on earth and conversed with men."[25] There is little doubt that this last verse was regarded by our liturgists as a literal allusion to the Incarnation.

We read the following prophecies from Isaiah: 7:10 to 8:4, 9-10, at the Sixth Hour and Vespers; 9:6-7 at the Ninth Hour and Vespers; 11:1-10 at Vespers only. They are all excerpted from the so-called "Book of Immanuel," which seems to have been an originally self-standing unit, authentically Isaian and an essential part of the collection of inspired writings gathered to form our canonical book. The first of these prophecies is a short-range one. Part of it was read on the Friday in the second week of Lent. The people of Jerusalem, whose vices and impiety the prophets had repeatedly castigated, were the target of their neighbors from the north: the schismatic kingdom of Israel and the Syrians of Damascus. Isaiah was sent to them with a message of comfort and, in order to authenticate his mission, he offered to King Ahaz of Judah a prophetic sign: "Behold, the virgin shall conceive and bear a son and shall call (or, according to the Greek: thou shalt call) his name Immanuel." The Hebrew for "virgin," 'almah means simply a young woman, virgin or not. The Greek of the Septuagint, ἡ παρθένος, "the virgin," reflects an ancient tradition of Jewish origin for the interpretation of *hâ-'almah*. St. Matthew interprets the text as a direct prophecy of the virgin birth of Christ, and is followed by the unanimous Christian tradition.[26] Before the child is capable of discernment, Judah will have been relieved from immediate danger. Isaiah's announcement of the birth of his own son, to whom he gave a symbolic name: *Maher-shalal-hash-baz*, "Speedy spoil, quick booty," follows a similar pattern: "before he can say Father or Mother, the riches of Damascus and Samaria shall be taken away before the king of Assyria, for God is with us" (Is. 8:3-4, 10).[27]

The prophecy of the Ninth Hour, repeated at Vespers (9:6-7), recites the royal protocol of the mysterious Immanuel. We heard part of it on the third Monday of Lent at the Sixth Hour. The titles of Immanuel compare with the throne-names of Near Eastern monarchs, and an ancient tradition reproduced in the Septuagint goes even further, when he is described as the "Angel of the Great Counsel" (verse 6). The historical context has changed: Samaria and Damascus are no longer to be feared; they have been conquered by the Assyrians. But the Assyrian hordes now threaten Judah directly. There was little hope that the situation would much improve during the coming years, even though Sennacherib, called back by some trouble brewing in his capital, had to call off his operations against Jerusalem. In this the people could take immediate comfort, but the prophecy of the royal child of the divine names is definitely a long-range prophecy, to be realized in God's good time, unknown to the Judaeans and to the prophet himself, "for the zeal of the Lord of Hosts will perform this."

The above prophecies of Micah, Baruch, and Isaiah are repeated at Vespers. To these are added the following: Genesis 1:1-13, describing the creation and the first three days of the world, "in the beginning," *berêshith*. It is significant that the Gospel according to St. John begins with the same words, ἐν ἀρχῇ, "In the beginning was the Logos," the Logos who today becomes flesh under our eyes. Then we read a selection of verses from the oracles of Balaam (Nu. 24:2-3, 5-9, 17-18). The context is as follows: the Israelites, after their devious march from the Sinai under the leadership of Moses and Joshua, had overrun the sheikhdoms of Transjordan and

THE FESTAL MENAION 151

camped in the 'Araboth Moab, by the north-eastern shore of
the Dead Sea. Balak, a Transjordanian chieftain, in the face of
the Israelite invasion, sent for Balaam, a rather dubious wiz-
ard, and bribed him, that he would pronounce a curse against
the Israelites. But how could one curse those whom God had
blessed? What Balaam uttered was a benediction and a prophecy. Jacob-Israel shall be firmly established in the land and
prosper under a dynasty which Yahweh himself shall raise up,
for "there shall come a star out of Jacob, and a scepter shall rise
out of Israel and shall smite the corners of Moab and destroy
the children of Seth." The allusion to the wars of the Davidic
kings is transparent, no matter which date is assigned to the
poems by literary criticism. Christian tradition did not over-
look the messianic intent of the story: Jesus Christ, the son of
David according to the flesh, is that star which Balaam saw
rising on the horizon. Another oracle of Isaiah, not read at the
Hours (11:1-10), accentuates still more the futuristic trend of
the Immanuel prophecy of the wonderful names. The peace
and justice of the Messiah to be born "of the stem of Jesse,"
David's father, are idealized and transposed in a higher key:
"The wolf shall dwell with the lamb, and the leopard shall lie
down with the kid, the calf and the lion cub and the fatling together, and a little child shall lead them." The primaeval excellence of the Creation described in the opening verses of
Genesis will be restored as the fruit of the labors of him who
today is born a man, and by the breathing of the Spirit. The
prophecies at Vespers conclude with Daniel (2:31-36, 44-45):
Nabuchodonosor's dream of the idol of gold, silver, brass and
iron, having feet of clay, *viz.* the empires about to be defeated
and the rise of the kingdom which shall never be destroyed.
Once more, the prospect is transhistorical and points to the
kingdom of Christ, "which is not of this world." This is no
idle vision, though, for "the dream is certain, and the interpretation thereof is sure" (Dan. 2:45).

2. *New Testament readings.* It may be useful to remember
here that the apostolic writings were generally composed before the Gospels, although they appear in the reverse order in
our printed Bibles. The Apostles reflected on facts which

were common knowledge in their days and which would be
put in writing at a slightly later date. These facts speak for
themselves. The Gospel readings for the feast of the Nativity
call for a minimum of commentary. The various episodes are
assigned to the Royal Hours in the following order: at the
First Hour, the doubt that beset St. Joseph when Mary "was
found with child of the Holy Ghost" and the quotation from
Isaiah's first prophecy of the Immanuel (Mt. 1:18-25); this
lesson is repeated at Matins. At the Third Hour, St. Luke's
account of the Nativity; it records the decree of Caesar Augus-
tus, the journey of Joseph and Mary from Nazareth to Bethleem, the birth of Jesus, the choir of angels singing in the night,
and the adoration of the shepherds (Lk. 2:1-20). At the Sixth
Hour, Matthew's relation of the birth of Christ, the Magi, a
reference to Micah's prophecy on Bethleem Ephrata (Mt. 2:1-
12). At the Ninth Hour, the flight of the Holy Family to
Egypt, the mass murder of the infants of Bethleem by order of
Herod, "that it might be fulfilled that which was spoken by
Jeremiah the prophet, saying: In Ramah there was a voice
heard, lamentation and weeping and great mourning, Rachel
weeping for her children, and would not be comforted, because
they are not,"[28] and the return to Nazareth after the death of
the tyrant, in fulfilment of a prophetic saying of Hosea: "Out
of Egypt have I called my son" (Mt. 2:13-23, cf. Hosea 11:1).

 The theology of the Nativity is developed in the Apostolic
writings. At the Royal Hours, they are taken from the letter to
the Galatians, the "Gospel" of St. Paul who insist that he received it from Christ himself, and from the Epistle to the Hebrews. At the First Hour, we hear of God's plan of salvation
for mankind, of the divinity of the Son eternally begotten, today born a man, anointed unto the threefold office of prophet,
priest, and king (Hebr. 1:1-12). At the Third Hour, the new
charter of our salvation: the Law had its time as our pedagogue
to bring us to Christ.[29] But now that Christ is come, "we are no
longer under a schoolmaster ... for as many of you as have
been baptized into Christ have put on Christ," the verse which
we sing at the Divine Liturgy instead of the Trisagion (Gal.
3:23-29). At the Sixth Hour, Christ's uniqueness, foretold in
Psalm 110, for "to which of the angels did God say at any time:

Sit on my right hand, until I make thine enemies my footstool?"
(Hebr. 1:10 to 2:3). At the Ninth Hour, his humanity, which
makes him truly our brother, being tempted like us, that he
might "succour them that are tempted" (Hebr. 2:11-18).

At Vespers (Liturgy of St. Basil), following the Typica,
the Epistle repeats Hebrews 1:1-12, already used at the First
Hour, and Luke 2:1-20, the Gospel of the Third Hour. At the
Liturgy of the Day (St. John Chrysostom), the Epistle states
the mystery of the Incarnation in its bare simplicity: God, in the
fulness of time, "sent forth his Son, made of a woman, made
under the Law, that we might receive the adoption of sons"
(Gal. 4:4-7). The Gospel is Matthew 2:1-12, already read at
the Sixth Hour. Most of the above New Testament readings
are used again on the days immediately connected with the
Christmas celebration: the Synaxis (*Sobor*) of the Theotokos
on December 26, the Sunday after the Nativity, and the
Leave-Taking of the feast.

The Circumcision of Our Lord. The feast of the Circumcision, on the first day of January, does not rank equal to the
Nativity and the Theophany. As a matter of fact, it shares the
day with the Memorial of St. Basil the Great, whose Liturgy
is served instead of that of St. John Chrysostom. The feast has
a rich Old Testament background. The Law of Moses prescribed that every male Israelite should be circumcised on the
eighth day after his birth. This was but the codification of an
age-old usage which was associated, in the narratives of Genesis, with the Covenant sealed between Yahweh and Abraham;
it would from then on be a distinctive mark of the Hebrews.
Accordingly, the first lesson at Vespers is a cento of verses from
Genesis (17:1-7, 9-12, 14). The two other lessons are from
the Book of Proverbs, *viz.* 8:22-30, on the origin of personified
Wisdom, and 10:31 to 11:12, salutary advise of the Sage to
humans. To Israelites, circumcision meant their incorporation
into the people of the Covenant, and this has determined the
New Testament readings for the feast: at Matins, the Gospel
according to St. John (10:9-16), "I am the door"; at the Divine
Liturgy, Colossians 2:8-12, our baptism defined as a circumcision not by human hands, as we are "buried with Christ in

baptism, that we may be raised with him"; and the Gospel
lesson from Luke (2:20-21, 40-52), recording the circumcision of the child, the imposition of the name, Jesus, the growing up in Nazareth, the first pilgrimage to Jerusalem for
Passover, in other words, the silent years of preparation for the
Messianic task.

The Theophany (January 6). The successive episodes originally regarded as one "theophany" in the etymological sense,
viz. a divine manifestation, later singled out as by cleavege, are
commemorated as different feasts: the Nativity, the Circumcision, the Theophany proper, the Ὑπαπαντή or Feast of the
Meeting, all different facets of the central mystery of the Incarnation. In the eastern tradition, the Feast of the Theophany
commemorates the baptism of our Lord in the Jordan, when
the heavens split open, when the Father's voice bore witness to Christ, and when the Spirit in the form of a dove descended upon him. Accessorily, the Theophany is also called
in the Greek lands the "Feast of Lights," ἑορτὴ τῶν φώτων,
as the Church celebrates the enlightenment of the world by the
light of Christ. In contrast with the Orthodox liturgies, the
Latin feast of the "Epiphany" has a threefold objective: the
manifestation of the Son of God to the Gentiles in the
person of the Magi,[30] the baptism in the Jordan, and the
first miracle of Jesus, when he changed water into wine at a
wedding feast, upon the prompting of his mother.

The accord of the Synoptics in describing the baptism of
Christ is matched only by the precision of the narrative and a
sobriety carried to the point of laconism (Mt. 3:13-17; Mk.
1:9-11; Lk. 3:21-22). The fourth Gospel confirms their account by quoting the testimony of the Baptist, whose preaching
of repentance in view of the imminent coming of a Messiah
forms the background on which the baptism of Christ is set in
bold relief. To the factual record, St. Matthew adds a significant remark: it behoved that "all justice be thus accomplished"
(Mt. 3:15), for the baptism of Christ, like the circumcision
and the presentation to the Temple in obedience to the Law, is
part of the kenotic process by which the Savior "emptied" him-

self of the glory that was his ere the world began (John 17:5) and took upon himself the form of a slave (Phil. 2:7).

On the other hand, the circumstances of the baptism of Jesus in the Jordan, unanimously reported by the Evangelists, constitute the factual basis on which the Church would proclaim the revelation of the Holy Trinity. This faith of the Church we profess over against Arian- or Nestorian-flavored speculations according to which the episode of the baptism marks only the time when Jesus would have become conscious of his mission as the Messiah. If an antidote against such rationalizations is needed, we would like to point to the third-century tradition of the Greek monastery of the Prodromos, repeatedly destroyed and rebuilt, on the presumed site of the baptism,[31] close to the ford of Hadjla, where the river is easily accessible to the crowds of pilgrims. We have no illusion as to the acceptability of what we present merely as a clue, unconvincing to *ex professo* sceptics or methodical doubters.

In the eyes of the Church, the mystery of the Incarnation, through the Theophany, enters into the reality of historical events. The old dispensation is left behind and we pass to a new order, the transfer being reflected in the New Testament readings for the Sunday before the Theophany. The opening verses of Mark are read at the Divine Liturgy (Mk. 1:1-8): "The beginning of the Evangel of Jesus Christ the Son of God. As it is written in the prophet, Behold, I send my messenger before thy face, and he shall prepare the way before thee." The action will revolve around John, the baptizer, Jesus, the baptized, and after him all who will be baptized in him and will "put on Christ." And St. Paul, who did more than any other Apostle to make the new dispensation known as a viable, universal reality, charges his disciple Timothy to take over: "Watch thou in all things... I have fought a good fight, I have finished my course, I have kept the faith" (2 Tim. 4:5-8). Now is the time of the Church.

The ordering of the services on the eve and on the day of the Theophany is the same as for the Nativity, with the addition of a double blessing of water, the ἁγιασμός, at the vigil and after the Divine Liturgy. The Scripture readings describe the mystery in its entire development. The Old Testament prophecies and types foretell the future economy of salvation, the lessons from the Apostle introduce John as the last prophet and the Forerunner, the Gospels state the facts.

1. Prophecies and Old Testament lessons. The call to repentance as a preparation for the reign of the Messiah, leitmotiv of John's preaching, echoes the voice of Isaiah denouncing the hypocrisy, impiety, and social evils of his contemporaries. The prophetic message transcends the historical past and extends to the end of time: "Put away the evil of your doings" (Is. 1:16); "Prepare the way of the Lord" (Is. 40:3). The fiery exhortations of Isaiah and the Forerunner have their historical epilogue on the banks of the Jordan as an urgent appeal to a sacramental catharsis, "washing of regeneration and renewal in the Holy Spirit" (Titus 3:5). Appropriately, the prophecies and Old Testament types read at the Royal Hours and at Vespers sound like a biblical anthology on the theme "water." Several of the proper psalms of the Royal Hours were chosen for their poetic similes and their allusions to the ministerial role of water in creation, for example Psalm 29, "The voice of the Lord upon the waters," and Psalm 42, "As the hart longs for living streams." The water of the Theophany is not the inert element abused by sinful men; restored to its pristine purity, raised to another level, it is the sacrament of life. It belongs in the new aeon inaugurated by Christ; it is anticipated in the prophecies and Old Testament types which we read at the Hours and at Vespers.

The Old Testament readings at the Royal Hours are all taken from the Book of Isaiah: early prophecies dating from the eighth century B.C., later oracles, and miscellaneous fragments. The lesson at the First Hour, repeated at the blessing of water (Is. 35:1-10), opens a paradisiac vision, in which the Israelites could find comfort against the drab realities of their national existence, the invasion, and the Babylonian exile.[32] It aims beyond a mere restoration of the historical Israel; the imagery is not of the present age. "Waters shall break out in the wilderness . . . streams in the desert, springs of water in a parched land. A highway shall be there, and it shall be called the way of righteousness." We may see and hear, without un-

due stretch of imagination, the Baptizer standing on the bank
of the river Jordan, and announcing the road that would be
prepared for the Messiah. The prophecy of the Third Hour,
which is read again at Vespers (Is. 1:16-20), is an urgent call
to repentance, both harsh and hopeful: "Put away your
evil doings . . . wash yourselves and make yourselves clean . . .
Though your sins be scarlet, they shall be white as snow; red
as crimson, they shall become as white wool." Isaiah's appeal
echoes the confident prayer of David: "Purge me with hyssop
and I shall be clean; wash me, and I shall be whiter than snow,"
a verse of Psalm 51, which is sung before High Mass on Sundays in the Roman rite as the celebrant sprinkles the faithful
with holy water. This cleansing, life-giving water we are urged
to draw joyfully "from the fountains of salvation," that we
may sing unto the Lord, "for great is the Holy One of Israel
in our midst," as we hear these words proclaimed at the Sixth
Hour and at the Blessing of the Water (Is. 12:3-6). We hear
a similar message at the Ninth Hour and at Vespers (Is. 49:8-
15): "He that has mercy on them shall lead them, even by
springs of water shall he guide them." Salvation is formally
extended to all mankind: "They shall come from far, from the
north, and from the west, and from the Land of Sinim"; the
Covenant with Israel shall burst out of narrow ethnic confines.
"They shall walk on an even path," the very one which the
Baptist would announce, and "neither scorching wind nor
sun shall smite them."[33]

The following sections from the Old Testament are read
at the Great Vespers. The Genesis account of the first three
days of Creation (Gen. 1:1-13), which we heard already at
Christmas, opens the series of Old Testament readings and
make us assist at the organization of the cosmos, when the Spirit
of God hovered over a watery chaos from which all degrees of
life would emerge at the command of God's creative Word.
The second lesson at Vespers is a cento of verses from Exodus
describing the miraculous crossing of the Sea of Reeds by the
Israelites delivered from Egyptian bondage (Ex. 14:15-18,
21-23, 27-29). The third lesson is the episode of Moses curing
the bitter waters of Marah by means of a certain wood which
God had taught him, and the encampment by the waters of

Elim (Ex. 15:22 to 16:1). The miraculous wood used by Moses has been regarded in the patristic and liturgical tradition as a type of the life-giving Cross. Christ himself sanctified the waters of the Jordan, where he descended to be baptized by John. The crossing of the sea by the Israelites had been a decisive event in the history of the nation. The fording of the Jordan, as they were about to enter the Promised Land, marked a further turn in the economy of salvation. In a narrative in which the historical and the marvelous are inextricably mixed, the Book of Joshua relates how the waters of the river were heaped up providentially upstream and how the people "were passed clean over Jordan" (Jos. 3:7-8, 15-17).[34] Some four centuries later, Elijah, the Old Testament figure for John the Baptist, would take his mantle of prophet and whip the surface of the stream, whose waters "would be divided hither and thither," and he walked over with his disciple Elisha, from whom he was taken up in a whirlwind (2 Ki. 5:9-14). This first series of biblical stories ends with the reading of Isaiah 1:16-20, already used at the Third Hour.

A second series of Old Testament readings with a similar soteriological intent begins with the episode of Jacob fording the Jordan westward into Canaan with his wives, his children, and his flocks, eager as he was to have the stream, its meanders, its thickets, as a secure border between his own family and the doubtful kinship of his Aramaean relatives or of his brother Esau (Gen. 32:1-10). Then we read from the Book of Exodus how Moses as an infant was rescued from the waters of the Nile and brought up by the daughter of Pharaoh (Ex. 2:5-10). Jesus as an infant also would find a temporary shelter in Egypt. We read Gideon's omen of the fleece heavy with dew in the midst of a parched land, which has become a favorite theme of patristic commentators, who apply it chiefly to the person of the Theotokos (Judges 6:36-40). Next we read the climactic episode of the triumph of Yahweh over Baal, the rider of clouds, when the sacrifice and prayer of Elijah on the summit of Mount Carmel ended a three-year drought, and when the long-awaited rain brought life and fertility back to the desolate countryside (1 Ki. 18:30-39). Elisha's miracle, when he cured the unpalatable water which alimented the city of Jericho, is the object of the next lesson (2 Ki. 2:19-22), reminiscent of the miracle of Moses at Marah, the relation of which we read at the Ninth Hour. The second series of Old Testament lessons at Vespers closes on the prophecy of Isaiah (49:8-15), read earlier at the Ninth Hour.

Our twentieth-century minds may find some difficulty in relating these Bible stories and prophecies to the central theme of the feast. In fact, they have all a point in common. In addition to the recurring theme "waters," foreshadowing the baptism of regeneration, they imply a radical, "existential" change in the destiny of a people or of an individual, involving an agonizing decision to be taken, an issue of life or death. And so it is with us, for we were buried with Christ in baptism, in which we were also raised with him through faith in the operation of God (Col. 2:12).

2. New Testament readings at the Hours and at Vespers. The lessons from the Old Testament at the Hours and at Vespers contituted the prophetical and typological introduction to the revelation of the New Testament, and it is in the Gospel record and the Apostolic writings that Christians find their rule of faith and life, generation after generation. The testimony of St. Paul on the Baptist and on Jesus (Acts 13:25-33), followed by St. Mark's record of John's preaching in the wilderness (Mk. 3:1-6), are the topic of the First Hour. The episode of Paul meeting the so-called "Christians of St. John," who claimed to have been baptized but had never heard of the Holy Spirit (Acts 19:1-8), and St. Mark's description of John, the ascetic, prophet, Forerunner, and of his baptism of repentance (Mk. 1:1-8), are read at the Third Hour. The fruits of Christian baptism: dying unto sin but living unto God (Rom. 6:3-11), and Mark's laconic record of the baptism of Jesus (1:9-11, continued to verse 15 in the Slavic usage), are the readings for the Sixth Hour. The lessons of the Ninth Hour are taken from the Epistle to Titus: the "washing of regeneration and renewing in the Holy Ghost" (Titus 2:11-14, 3:4-7), and from St. Matthew's straightforward account of the baptism of Christ (3:13-17) or, in Greek usage, from St. Luke (3:1-18).

The Vespers ends with the Liturgy of St. Basil, as on the

feast of the Nativity. The accent of the Epistle (1 Cor. 9:19-27) is on the universality of the offer of salvation: baptism is for all, Jews and Gentiles. The Gospel is according to St. Luke (3:1-18), who is anxious to synchronize the Gospel events with the data of universal history and writes in great detail how, "in the fifteenth year of Tiberius Caesar," and under the government of the tetrarchs ruling the various Palestinian districts, John addressed the crowds assembled in the valley of the Jordan, quoting the prophecy of Isaiah, "Voice of one who shouts in the desert,"[35] urging sinners to conversion, and announcing the coming of him whose baptism is not in water, but "with the Holy Ghost and with fire," even the fire of judgment.

3. Scripture readings at the Blessing of Water. The lessons already used at the First Hour (Is. 35:1-10) and at the Sixth Hour (Is. 12:3-6) are repeated at the ἁγιασμός and completed with another reading from the Book of Isaiah (Is. 55:1-13): a call to those who hunger and thirst to draw near and taste of the real food and water freely offered to all men, who eat meats that satisfy not and drink waters which do not quench their thirst. The offer remains open-ended; the prophet could not specify when it would become effective, for this is the domain of the New Testament, inasmuch as the kingdom, in its inaugural phase, becomes a reality in history while the consummation still lies beyond.

St. Paul, in a passage of the first letter to the Corinthians (10:1-4), which is read at the blessing of water, deduces the potential universality of salvation from the fact that "all our Fathers were baptized unto Moses in the sea," and drank from the spiritual Rock in the wilderness, "and the Rock was Christ."[36] This lesson is followed by the reading of Mark's pericope on the witness of the Holy Spirit in a visible form and the voice of the Father (Mk. 1:9-11), repeated from the Sixth Hour.

4. New Testament readings at Matins, the Divine Liturgy, and the week following the Theophany. The Matin Gospel of the Theophany is Mark 1:9-11, which was read already at the Sixth Hour and at the Blessing of Water. The festal Divine

Liturgy repeats the Apostle's reading (Titus 2:11-14; 3:4-7) and the Gospel section (Mt. 3:13-17) read at the Ninth Hour by the Slavic churches.

The lesson from Acts 19:1-8, read at the Third Royal Hour on the eve of the Theophany, is used again at the Divine Liturgy of the Synaxis (*Sobor*) of John the Baptist. The Gospel reading is from John (1:29-34). This pericope presupposes the factual record of the Synoptics,[37] and places a strong emphasis on the personal testimony of the Baptist: "I knew him not, but He that sent me to baptize with water, the same said unto me: Upon whom thou shalt see the Spirit descending and remaining on him, the same is he who baptizes with the Holy Ghost. And I saw, and bare record that this is God's elect." The Baptizer acted as he was moved by the Spirit, and this against his personal judgment: "It is I who have need to be baptized of Thee, and Thou comest unto me!" (Mt. 3:14). We hear the last echo of the feast on the Sunday after the Theophany, when the Gospel at the Divine Liturgy (Mt. 4:12-17) relates Christ's reaction and utterances upon learning of the arrest of John the Baptist by order of the tetrarch.

The Meeting of Our Lord Jesus Christ (February 2). This is called in the western church the "Purification of the Blessed Virgin Mary," when the time came for her to undergo the ritual prescribed for the mother of a male child forty days after his birth, and to offer the sacrifice for the redeeming of a firstborn. Entering the Temple, mother and child were met by Simeon the elder and Ann the prophetess, who had been secretly warned by the Spirit. Hence the Greek name of the feast, Ὑπαπαντή (from ὑπαπαντάω, to go to meet some one).

The Mosaic observance is linked with an ancient tabu imposed on all women who had given birth to a child: they were barred from participation in the social and religious life of the community. The Law of Moses prescribed a period of segregation for the mother on account of her ritual "impurity," followed by a number of days at home prior to taking her place in society. The rite of purification would be performed forty days after the birth of a son, eighty days after the birth of a daughter. The ritual prescribed the offering of a lamb and a turtle dove or young pigeon, a second dove being substituted for the lamb in the case of a poor family. Such were the observances to which Mary submitted herself when she brought the infant Jesus into the Temple. St. Luke notes that Joseph and Mary made the offering of the poor, a detail which did not escape the attention of the Fathers and the iconographers.

Three lessons from the Old Testament are read at Great Vespers. The first one is an arrangement from Exodus 12:51 to 13:16, Leviticus chapter 12 and Numbers chapter 8. It recalls the tragic slaying of the first-born of the Egyptians by the Angel of Death, which gave to the Hebrews the signal for departure; this episode was regarded in Israel as the basis for the redemption of every first-born by appropriate sacrifices.[38]

The second reading at Vespers is the vision of Isaiah which marked his calling to the prophetic ministry, "in the year that King Uzziah died" (Is. 6:1-12). The connection with the feast of the Meeting seems to rest on the following: the scene took place in the Temple, the Temple of Solomon for Isaiah, the Temple rebuilt by Herod for the presentation of the child Jesus, in either case God's house. Yahweh appears in glory to Isaiah in a vision of the mind. In the Gospel scene, there is no vision but rather the invisible presence of God in the person of the eternally begotten Son, now born a frail infant; not the radiance unbearable of the divinity but the thorough "emptying" of glory, the κένωσις (cf. Phil. 2:7). Bystanders had not been aware of what Isaiah contemplated in the light of the Spirit. Simeon and Ann were alone given to pierce the hidden mystery. St. Luke simply notes that Joseph and Mary marvelled in amazement at what they heard.

The third Vespers lesson (Is. 19:1, 3-5, 12, 16, 19-21) opens the remote prospect of a universal revelation, for "there shall be an altar to the Lord in the midst of Egypt and a pillar at the border thereof to the Lord." This brings us back to Egypt as the personification of the Gentiles, unto whom the light of Christ will shine. From oppressors, the Egyptians had become oppressed, and the Lord himself would deliver them.[39]

The Epistle at the Divine Liturgy (Hebr. 7:1-17) presents us with the comparison frequently brought forth in the feasts of Christ between the Levitic priesthood and the priesthood of Christ, of which Melkisedech, the king-priest of Salem, is the figure. It bears on the theme of the feast of the Meeting in a special way; what it teaches is not only the superiority of the New Testament priesthood over the Old Testament one, but the confrontation of both in the same holy place at a definite moment of history: the mitred and vested Aaronic priest, and the babe in the arms of Simeon, since by the mere fact that the Logos has assumed our human nature, he became our priest "made not after the law of carnal commandment, but after the power of an endless life."

Part of the Gospel scene of the meeting according to St. Luke (2:25-32) is used at Matins, but it is read in full at the Divine Liturgy (2:22-40). It relates how the child was brought by his parents to Jerusalem, mentions the pair of doves of the offering, Simeon coming "by the Spirit" into the Temple, taking the infant in his arms, and intoning the hymn which the Church repeats every day at Vespers: "Now lettest thou thy servant depart in peace," a paean to him who is "the light to lighten the Gentiles[40] and the glory of thy people Israel," at the same time a prophecy of the sword which, one day, would pierce Mary's own soul.[41] "Coming at that instant . . . Ann, the prophetess, daughter of Phanuel of the tribe of Asher, advanced in age, about eighty-four years, . . . and she departed not from the Temple, but served with fastings and prayers night and day, gave thanks likewise unto the Lord, and spake of him to all them that looked for redemption in Jerusalem." St. Luke adds: "When they had performed all things according to the Law of the Lord, they returned to Galilee, to their own city Nazareth. And the child grew and waxed strong in spirit, filled with wisdom, and the grace of God was upon him."

The Annunciation to the Theotokos (March 25). This is the feast of the Incarnation par excellence; the scene which inspired icon painters and the artists of the Renaissance and, at a deeper level, the mystery of Mary's decision, in the secrecy of her heart, to comply with God's request. Her *fiat* is the first recorded fact of the Incarnation of God the Word. The feast stands apart from the other feasts of the Theotokos and of the Christmas-Theophany season. The date is reckoned by counting back nine months from the following Christmas, the nine months of a normal pregnancy. Perhaps such a computation based on common biological observation does indicate on the part of the Church a deliberate intent to keep in close contact with the realities of the Incarnation and to avoid an escape into empty dreams or into the void of docetism. Whether or not, the date thus assigned causes the feast to fall during the Lenten season, Great Week, or Bright Week. The feast of the Annunciation is definitely not like one of the anniversaries conventionally listed in the order of the calendar, and it belongs rather in what we have called earlier the eschatological time. The structure of the office is combined with the liturgy of the Triodion or of the Pentecostarion. Important variations result according to whether it falls on the a-liturgical days or on Saturdays and Sundays in Lent, or otherwise on Easter or during the Paschal season. Furthermore, the Greek ordo differs slightly from the Slav.[42]

The observances are centered on the Gospel according to St. Luke. The first chapter relates the facts in their dramatic simplicity, which has inspired the western devotion of the *Angelus*; three times a day, at the sound of the church bells, Christians are urged to recite the familiar verses: "The Angel of the Lord announced to Mary, and she conceived of the Holy Ghost . . . Behold the handmaid of the Lord, be it done unto me according to thy word . . . And the Word was made flesh, and dwelt among us . . . Hail, Mary, full of grace," χαῖρε κεχαριτωμένη.

The readings at Vespers are the same as for the birth of Mary; there is the same stress on the Incarnation, except that God's design, prefigured in the Old Testament, is one step nearer to its realization: the conception, still a guarded secret, is a fact; the timeless has entered time. Two readings are added to these lessons whenever the feast falls on a Saturday, Sunday, or during Easter week. The first one is the episode of the Burning Bush, from which Yahweh revealed himself in the Sinai desert (Ex. 3:1-8). It announces the entire economy of the Revelation. The son of Mary is truly the Logos who spoke to Moses and who had revealed himself to the patriarchs: "Before Abraham was, I am" (John 8:58).[43] The typology of the

narrative has singularly impressed the Fathers and the hymnographers, who saw in the Burning Bush a figure of the Virgin,
as she passed undefiled through the midst of men devoured by
the fire of their passions, and as her bodily integrity was, in a
manner exceeding all sense, preserved in the ordeal of child-
bearing.

In the following lesson (Prov. 8:22-30), Wisdom speaks
of herself in the first person. The fragment has to be replaced
in the general perspective of the Revelation. We have noted
already the early identification of the Divine Wisdom with the
Christian Logos. In the so-called Wisdom of Solomon, a Book
of the Alexandrian canon, Wisdom is defined as "the effulgence of Light Eternal, flawless mirror of God's energy, icon
of his goodness" (Wisdom 7:26). In today's lesson from
Proverbs, it is on account of the Virgin's part in the eternally
conceived plan of salvation that the Church dares place in her
mouth the very words of Wisdom incarnate: "The Lord possessed me in the beginning of his way, before his works of old.
I was set up from everlasting."

The Christological significance of the Feast of the Annunciation is nowhere more evident than in the Epistle reading at
the Divine Liturgy, one of the numerous passages of Hebrews
on the priestly office of Jesus Christ (Hebr. 2:11-18).[44] Not
angels saved us, but He who through his birth from Mary became one of us, connatural with us as he was eternally connatural with the Father. Tested by men's common sufferings,
knowing the weight of temptation, he qualifies as our inter-
cessor and High Priest, "to make reconciliation for the
people.

The Gospel lessons are from Luke. We read chapter 1:39-
49, 56, at Matins, a lesson used also on the feast of the Birth
of the Theotokos. St. Luke, concerned with dates and with
symptoms as a physician would be, relates how Mary, after her
visitation by the Angel, went to see her cousin Elizabeth, at
that time six months pregnant with John, and how Elizabeth
felt "the babe leaping in her womb for joy."[45] The Evangelist
interprets her words of welcome to Mary as prophetic: "Blessed
art thou among women and blessed is the fruit of thy womb."
And he adds: "Blessed is she that believed," whose decisive

fiat was a cause of our salvation. Luke's account of the Annunciation itself is read at the Divine Liturgy (Lk. 1:24-38): the mission of the angel Gabriel, the moment of hesitation of the Virgin, and her free-will acquiescence. No commentary is necessary here nor would any be relevant.[46]

The Transfiguration of Our Lord (August 6). This is another Theophany: the manifestation of Jesus Christ as the Son of God. At the baptism in the Jordan, a voice from heaven had proclaimed his divinity, and the Spirit, in the form of a dove, had descended upon him. The Theophany on Mount Tabor occurred on the eve of the crisis which would end the long eclipse of his divine nature. On the mountain he appeared irradiated with supernatural light, not the light of the first creation when God said, "Let there be light," but the effulgence of the divinity "before all lights," πρό τῶν φώτων ὑπάρχων.[47] His witnesses were Moses and Elijah (Elias), who both had conversed with God on Mount Sinai, and Peter, James and John, three chosen disciples. Coming down from the mountain top, Jesus announced how he would be betrayed at the hand of men, "and they would kill him, and on the third day he would rise again" (Mt. 17:22-23). The Byzantine hymnographers have not failed to recognize the connection between the Transfiguration and the forthcoming Passion, Tabor and Golgotha: "Before thy Crucifixion, O Lord"—literally "Before thy Cross," πρό τοῦ σταυροῦ σου, Κύριε.[48] Nor is it accidental that the *katavasia* at the end of each canticle of the canon is taken from the office of the Exaltation of the Cross, which we shall celebrate after forty days.

The first two lessons at Vespers take us to Mount Sinai (Ex. 24:12-18 and Ex. 33:11-23; 34:4-6, 8). They relate two episodes of the life of Moses. The former, how he descended from the mountain and how, on the seventh day, God called him from the midst of the cloud which covered the summit to give him "tables of stone, and a Law, and commandments which I have written, that thou mayest teach them." The second passage relates how Moses conversed with God in the Tent of the Covenant, "face to face, as a man speaks to his friend," and sought a confirmation of his mission as a prophet and a leader. In his dismay at the apostasy of part of the people, worshipers of the golden calf, Moses had broken the tables of the Law and now, summoned for a second time on the holy mountain, in the forbidding solitude of the highest peak crowned with an impenetrable cloud and lighted with blinding flashes of fire, he received from God's hand new stone tables inscribed, like the former ones, with the words of the Law. Both narratives[49] betray the inadequacy of the human mind to grasp, and of the human tongue to express, the divine transcendence, and the versions accentuate, rather than clarify, the awkwardness of the Hebrew original. Moses, who is reported to converse with God face to face, is not admitted to the contempation of his "countenance." Yahweh passes before him, and Moses sees him only from the back.[50]

The third Vespers lesson (1 Ki. 3-9, 11-13, 15-16) might be entitled: "Mount Sinai revisited." Elijah, following in the footsteps of Moses, after an exhausting march through the wilderness of the Negeb but sustained by God's miraculous food, arrives at Horeb—another name for the Sinai—and is ordered to ascend the mountain. Not any more than Moses will he be granted to see God's face. The cave in which he passes the night is to shelter him from the "awe-full" approach of the Lord. "Behold, the Lord passed by"; but he was not in the windstorm which shook the mountains, not in the earthquake, not in the fire. Then Elijah heard "a still small voice,"[51] the voice of God giving him his secret order of mission.

We pass now from the types to the actual Gospel record. The Transfiguration of Christ is described in the Synoptics in almost identical terms. Our liturgists have chosen to read Luke at Matins (Lk. 9:28-36) and Matthew at the Divine Liturgy (Mt. 17:1-9). Jesus took with him Peter and the two sons of Zebedee, James and John, and ascended "a high mountain" to pray.[52] There he was transfigured, μετεμορφώθη, before them: "the fashion of his countenance was altered," notes St. Luke (9:29); "his face did shine as the sun and his raiment was white as the light" (Mt. 17:2), "so as no fuller on earth can white them" (Mk. 9:3). And behold, there talked with him two men, which were Moses and Elias, who appeared in glory, and spake of his departure, which he should accomplish in

Jerusalem" (Lk. 9:30-31). A luminous cloud—God's cloud which had surrounded him on Mount Sinai—covered the hilltop, and the dazzled disciples heard a voice out of the cloud: "This is my beloved Son, in whom I am well pleased; hear him!" (Mt. 17:5). The Father had spoken these same words when Jesus was baptized by John, who came "in the spirit and power of Elias" (Lk. 1:17); the crowds which acclaimed Jesus on the Mount of Olives a few days before his death would hear the Father's voice for a third time (John 12:28-30). Early Christians were later to receive the testimony of St. Peter which is read at the Epistle (2 Peter 1:10-19),[53] "This voice, we heard it borne from heaven, for we were with him on the holy mount."

The theology and spirituality of the Orthodox Church have been particularly sensitive to the mystery of the Transfiguration. We need only mention the treatise of St. Gregory of Nyssa entitled "The Life of Moses." The relation of the Book of Exodus is transposed through allegory into an exposition of Christian asceticism and high mysticism. It gave rise to the spirituality of the hesychasts of Mount Athos, expounded and defended in the fourteenth century by St. Gregory Palamas,[54] and to the development of a theology of absolute transcendence, sensed vitally by all the saints, while our iconographers aimed at conveying to us the supernatural brilliance of the "Taboric light." The fact that Latin theology as a whole chose rather to approach the problem of our knowledge of God through the abstract categories of scholasticism explains perhaps why the Feast of the Transfiguration does not enjoy in the western church the preeminence it has in the Orthodox world, whether with regard to liturgical celebration or to popular response.[55]

The Sleeping-in of the Theotokos (August 15). The "Dormition," κοίμησις, of our Lady the Theotokos is the last of the major feasts in the Church year, symmetrical to the commemoration of her birth. It is the last act in the cycle of the Incarnation. Mary, having witnessed the Lord's triumph over death and the rise of the Church, closed her eyes to mortal light, her body was laid in the tomb, and she was re-united to her son.

The Gospel data are close to nil. All we are told is that Jesus, hanging from the Cross at the foot of which Mary stood with John, entrusted his mother to the disciple whom he loved, "and from that hour the disciple took her to his own home" (John 1:26-27).

A tradition has it that John took her to Ephesus. However, Jerusalem claimed right early to have been the place of her death. Neither tradition can be historically substantiated, and St. Epiphanius (d. 403) remained sceptical: "Let any one scan the Scriptures; he will not read that Mary died or did not die; that she was buried or not." The Jerusalem tradition prevailed, favored by the development of the pilgrimage. An apocryphal writing known under the Latin title *Liber transitus Beatae Mariae Virginis*, ἡ κοίμησις τῆς Θεοτόκου, purported to describe the details of her death, her burial at Gethsemane in the presence of the Apostles who had been miraculously summoned to Mary's deathbed, and her translation to heaven by the ministry of angels.[56]

In the second quarter of the fifth century, Juvenal, Bishop of Jerusalem,[57] professed to know where the body of Mary had been laid, and let a new church be built to enshrine the empty sepulcher, close to the fourth-century basilica of Gethsemane. Recent excavations seem to support the authority of this tradition. As in the case of the feasts of the Birth and the Entry of the Theotokos into the Temple, the hymnography of the Byzantine Office makes a lavish use of the apocrypha. St. John Damascene, who composed the second canon of the feast some three centuries after the alleged discovery of the tomb, could hardly do anything else but rely in good faith on the local tradition.

The Orthodox Church remained and remains extremely reserved in her attitude toward a popular devotion feeding on the picturesque details of the *Liber transitus* rather than on the theological significance of the feast. The name κοίμησις, *dormitio*, refers to the peaceful death of the Virgin and suggests nothing extraordinary or supernatural. The term "transfer," μετάστασις, which occurs several times in the canon of the Damascene, indicates scarcely anything more than Mary's departure from this life when, having deposed her mortal body, she passed beyond the boundaries of time and corruption. Rather than the bodily transfer of the Virgin to heaven, the icons show Christ standing near the couch on which she lies, as he embraces her pure soul in the form of a tiny feminine figure.[58]

The title "Assumption of the Blessed Virgin Mary" has generally prevailed in the Roman Church,[59] and the belief of her bodily translation to heaven, crudely expressed in popular circles, became the object of a dogmatic definition in 1950, under the Pontificate of Pius XII. The definition is a corollary of the doctrine of the Immaculate Conception,[60] itself defined in 1854 on the basis of doubtful speculations on the nature of "original sin."

Because of the absence of specific scriptural material, the lessons of our services are bound to be of a general character, and they belong in what we have called earlier "common readings" for the feasts of the Theotokos. As a matter of fact the Office and Liturgy of the Dormition borrow all the lessons appointed for the feast of the Nativity of the Virgin Mary: at Great Vespers, the Genesis account of Jacob's dream (Gen. 28:10-17), Ezekiel's description of the eastern gate of the Temple (43:27 to 44:4) and the call of divine Wisdom to her banquet (Prov. 9:1-11). These Scriptures are appropriated to the commemoration of the death and exaltation of Mary without undue arbitrariness, for she is carried up to heaven on Jacob's ascending ladder, introduced through the gate sealed to all mortals into the heavenly courts, where the feast of divine Wisdom ceases never. At Matins the Church reads the Gospel of the visitatiton to Elizabeth and the *Magnificat* (Lk. 1:39-49, 56); at the Divine Liturgy, the mystery of the obedience unto death to which she associated herself at the foot of the Cross (Phil. 2:5-11), and the Gospel episode of the meal in the house of Martha and Mary, followed by the blessing on all who, like the Theotokos, have heard and kept the Word of God (Lk. 10:38-42; 11:27-28).

Other Marian celebrations through the year[61] make a similar use of common Scripture readings, like the feast of the Protection of the Theotokos (October 1), substituting Hebrews 9:1-7, otherwise read at the feast of the Entry of the Blessed

Virgin into the Temple, for the reading from the Epistle to the Philippians.

The Sanctoral: Elijah and the Prodromos. It is not arbitrarily that we are bracketing together the feasts of Elijah (Elias), July 20, and John the Baptist, June 24. The typological connection between the Old Testament prophet and the Precursor is positively stated by Christ himself. Coming down from the Mount of the Transfiguration, where he had conversed with Moses and Elias, when the disciples asked him "why do the scribes say that first Elijah must come" prior to the advent of the Messiah, he had answered: "Elijah truly shall come first . . . He is come already, but they knew him not." Then the disciples understood that he was speaking of John the Baptist (Mt. 17:10-13).

The scriptural material, Old and New Testament, is abundant, and our liturgists had nothing else to do but reproduce the life-picture of the prophet and of the Precursor as they found it in the Books of Kings and in the Gospels. The Books of Kings, from which the lessons for the Great Vespers of the feast of Elijah (Elias) are drawn, namely 1 Ki. 17:1-23; 1 Ki. 18:1, 17, 41-46 to 19:16; 1 Ki. 19:19-21 and 2 Ki. 2:1, 6-14, represent Elijah as the hero of a *saga* whose object is to relate in the epic mode episodes of the ninth-century struggle of Yahvism against the religion of Baal. The latter, whose worship had been smuggled into the schismatic kingdom of Samaria by foreign queens, enjoyed the favor of the kings and courtiers of the "House of Omri," who were intent upon a political alliance with their northern neighbors. In the south of Palestine, Judah itself, though less open to foreign influences, was not immune, and its prophets never tired of denouncing among indigenous populations conquered but not assimilated, Canaanite practices which the official religion of Yahweh was never able to supplant.

The conflict between the two faiths is not to be taken lightly. On the one hand, Yahweh, the national God of the Israelites, a minority weakened by the apostasy and the deviationism of many; on the other hand, Baal, worshiped under various names throughout the Semitic West, god of the summits

shrouded by clouds, father of the rains which bring fertility to
the earth. Baal's archenemy was Môt, the lord of the nether-
world, who sent death and drought to the land.[62]

Elijah stood alone to meet the challenge of a hostile multitude; it is not immaterial that the miracles he performed in
Yahweh's name took place in Baalist country, for Yahweh is
master of the Universe, and his providence extends beyond
geographical or ethnic limitations. As a matter of fact, the cult
of the prophet-saint has remained extremely popular to this
day among the rural populations of Palestine, Lebanon and
Syria, whether Christians, Moslems or Druses, who call upon
him in time of stress, drought, famine, and in the crises of life.[63]

The first lesson at Great Vespers (1 Ki. 17:1-23) acquaints
us with the calling of Elijah to the prophetic ministry, and his
activity as a wonderworker on the Phoenician shores. Elijah,
from Tisbeh in Gilead, a village of Transjordan, began to announce the drought which was going to desolate Achab's entire
kingdom and the Phoenician seaboard in punishment for their
defection or for their adherence to Baalism. The prophetic
word had always been understood as having the virtue of a
sacrament, not unlike the curse which David pronounced upon
the hills of Gilboa, where the heroes of Israel were slain by the
Philistines: "Neither dew nor rain shall fall upon you!" (2
Sam. 1:21). Elijah went into hiding from the wrath of the
king in the ravine of Kerith, where he was miraculously fed
by ravens. Moses, too, and the Israelites, had been given to
eat manna in their march through the desert, and they had
drunk water from the rock. Forced out of his retreat—the torrent had dried up—Elijah was ordered to "arise and go to
Zarephath, which belongs to Sidon."[64] An uninvited guest in
the house of a poor widow whose meager provision of flour
and oil was coming to an end, he announced, in the power of
Yahweh, that the flour in the jar and the oil in the cruse would
be wonderfully renewed, as long as the sky remained closed.
Thus was the life maintained, and it would be restored when
the prophet, in the name of the Living God, raised from the
dead the son of his hostess.

The second lesson, a selection of verses from the eighteenth
chapter of the first Book of Kings, takes us from the coastal

districts of Phoenicia to the heights of Carmel, a wooded range stretching deep inland, where it divides the fertile Valley of Jizreel, *hâ-'èmeq*, from the plain of Sharon. Its terminal promontory juts out into the sea, equally welcome as a landmark and dreaded for the violence of wind and current by the mariners of Tyre and Sidon. They called it the *Rosh Qadosh*, the cape sacred to Baal, just as the Hellenistic seafarers would give to the *Ras Shaqqa*, some twenty miles south of Tripoli, the name of Θεοῦ πρόσωπον, the "face of God." Tacitus remarks of Mount Carmel that no temple nor divine image had been erected there, only an altar and the awe which high places are wont to inspire: *Nec templum nec simulacrum, ara tantum et reverentia.* Mount Carmel became the theater of Elijah's sacrifice, described with elaborate details by the author of Kings, as a demonstration of the absolute transcendence of Yahweh and of the impotent nothingness of Baal. Baal remained deaf to the supplications of his devotees and to their heathen ritual. But Yahweh answered the lonely prayer of Elijah by sending from heaven the fire which consumed the offering. Note the irony: Baal was defeated on his own grounds and by his own weapons; he who was called the "rider of clouds" could not cast his bolt of lightning on the prepared sacrifice nor was he able to summon the rain. But at the prayer of Elijah there arose from the sea a little cloud,[65] not bigger than a man's hand, the sky darkened, and the long-expected rain began to fall. We read in 1 Kings 19:1-16 the epilogue of the story. Queen Jezebel had sworn to avenge the blood of the priests of Baal whom Elijah had ordered slain at the brook Kishon, at the foot of the holy mountain. Elijah fled for his life into the southern desert. Comforted by an angel, as Hagar had been at the well in the wilderness (Gen. 21:14-19),[66] he reached Mount Horeb after a march of forty days and forty nights, went up the mountain and, like Moses of old, was given God's orders for a prophetic mission.

The object of the third lesson at Vespers (2 Ki. 2:1, 6-14) is Elijah's last miracle, when he whipped the waters of the Jordan with his mantle of prophet and, crossing over with his disciple Elisha, who would become his successor, he was taken up to heaven in a chariot of fire. The typological significance of the scene has inspired the Fathers, hymnographers and icon painters.

The New Testament lessons at Matins and at the Divine Liturgy refer to Elijah inasmuch as he is mentioned in the Epistle of James for the power of his prayer of faith (James 5:10-20) and in the Gospel of St. Luke (Lk. 4:22-30) as a living illustration of the proverb quoted by Jesus to the men of Nazareth, "No prophet is accepted in his own country," seeing that most of Elijah's miracles were made not in the heart of the kingdom, but on the frontier, in regions where Baal seemed to reign uncontested.

John the Baptist. We pass now from the archetype, Elijah, to the Baptist, who appears on the stage of history in the power of the prophet and wonder worker. John belongs in the cycle of the Incarnation, and we have repeatedly evoked his figure while commenting on the Scripture readings of the Theophany. In addition to the Synaxis (*Sobor*) of the Saint, held on January 7, the Menaion devotes two special feasts to the Precursor: the commemoration of his birth (June 24),[67] and of his beheading in the dungeon of Machaerous (August 29).

The feast of the Nativity of St. John brings to memory instances of famous men born to women who had conceived in an advanced age, after years of being childless. The figure of Sarah is evoked at Great Vespers, in a cento of passages from Genesis (17:15-17, 19; 18:11-14; 21:1-8), stressing the significance of the birth of Isaac as an essential link in the chain of providential events. The second reading, a selection of verses from the Book of Judges (13:2-8, 13-14, 17-18, 21), serves the same purpose with a distinctive nuance. Samson also, like Isaac, was born of parents who had long been childless, and his birth is announced by an angel, as will be the birth of John and of Jesus. It is not, however, the personal character of Samson, or the role he would play in the messianic scheme, which supports the typological interpretation. As a matter of fact, Samson is an odd figure, neither saintly nor knightly, but a truculent frontier hero of village brawls rather than of epic battles. It took nothing less than his tragic end, when he buried himself under the ruins of the temple of Dagon with the Philistines, to raise him to heroic stature. What made him to be chosen as a figure of John the Baptist is rather his consecration as a Nazorite "from the womb to the tomb" (Judges 13:7): "No razor would pass on his head, wine and strong beverage he would not drink."[68] The Evangelists, though they do not refer to John as a Nazorite, ascribe to him a similar asceticism (Mk. 1:6; Lk. 1:15), in contrast with the way of life of Jesus, much maligned by his enemies (Mt. 11-18-19; Lk. 7:33-34).

A selection of passages from the latter part of Isaiah anticipates prophetically the messianic function of the Precursor (Is. 40:1-3, 9; 41:17-18; 45:8; 48:20-21; 54:1). To the exiles soon to be repatriated or already resettled in the land, the prophet offers the vision of a future transposed from the restoration of the Davidic kingdom which was the object of their dream to an ideal state of universal peace and justice extended to all nations: mountains shall be leveled, streams of water will flow in the wilderness, the skies shall send dew from above, and justice will fall like rain.[69] It should occur to no one that the message is to be understood in its materiality. John the Baptist would draw his inspiration from it, when he addressed the crowds gathered to hear him and making ready to be baptized of his baptism of repentance: "Voice of him who shouts: In the desert prepare ye the ways of the Lord" (Is. 40:3 and Mt. 3:1-3; Mk. 1:1-4; Lk. 3:3-6).

We are now prepared to hear the Gospel lessons at Matins (Lk. 1:24-25, 57-68, 76, 80), and at the Divine Liturgy (Lk. 1:5-25, 57-68, 76, 80). St. Luke records the facts with his habitual precision and in historical order: the annunciation to Zacharias, his incredulity, his being struck dumb, the conception and the birth of John, the circumcision and the naming of the child, as the power of speech is restored to Zacharias, and finally the prophetic verses of the *Benedictus*, foretelling John's mission as the Precursor of him who would usher in the messianic era.

The Epistle at the Divine Liturgy (Rom. 13:12 to 14:4), states the obligations of the Christian in the new aeon which is dawning and soon will be consummated, for "the night is far spent, the day is at hand," and having "put on" Christ in our baptism, we are bound to a life of faith and loving obedience.

The Beheading of John the Baptist (August 29) is the gory outcome of a multiple drama of immorality. Herod Antipas, tetrarch of Galilee, had taken in adulterous union Herodias, whose consenting husband, Herod Philip, tetrarch of Ituraea and Trachonitis, was Antipas' half brother, both being sons of Herod the Great by different mothers. The first wife of Herod Antipas, a Nabataean princess, fled to her father, King Aretas, to forestall a public humiliation. The affair blew up into a major scandal reported in detail by Flavius Josephus (*Antiquities* XVIII, 5:12). John, whose preaching had attracted crowds of followers and whom Antipas himself held in reverence, knowing, notes St. Mark, "that he was a righteous and holy man," dared openly to rebuke the tetrarch: "It is not lawful for thee to have thy brother's wife." Herod Antipas, in order to silence John, had him arrested and confined in a dungeon of the palace-fortress of Machaerous in Transjordan. On the occasion of a banquet held in the hall of the palace, Salome, Herodias' daughter, danced lasciviously for the company "and pleased Herod." Herodias, bent on vengeance, suggested to her daughter to ask as a favor the head of John. "And she came straightaway unto the king and asked, saying: Give me at once the head of John the Baptist on a platter." Antipas reluctantly ordered a guard to execute the prisoner and bring his head to the girl. The episode has become a classic in art and iconography, and needs no comment.

In the sordid drama of Machaerous, John stood out as the first to bear witness with his blood to the new order he had heralded. It is the vision of this new order inaugurated by Christ himself which the Church would have us remember, as the liturgist chose for the first lesson of Vespers passages from the latter part of Isaiah already read for the Nativity of St. John the Baptist. The second lesson, a selection of verses from Malachi (3:1-2, 5-7, 12, 17 and 4:4-6) announces prophetically the messenger whom Yahweh would send before himself on the eve of "his day." This is most likely what the disciples had in mind when they asked Jesus after the Transfiguration why it was believed that Elias was to come first. Thus does John appear as the forerunner in two ways: pointing to Jesus about to begin his ministry as the Savior, and announcing, in the virtue of Elijah, the second Advent in glory. The third lesson is taken from the Book of Wisdom (4:7, 16-20; 5:1-7). The Sage is heard reflecting on death: Why the death of a righteous and innocent man? Why is justice apparently denied or delayed? These are the very questions we ask today, and the very problem which had baffled Job. Christ, the Risen Lord, has and is the only answer.

We hear at the Divine Liturgy how St. Paul, addressing the Jews at Antioch of Pisidia, quoted John's testimony on the person and the mission of Jesus the Christ (Acts 13:25-33). St. Matthew's account of the beheading of John (Mt. 14:1-13) is read at Matins, and St. Mark's more detailed relation (Mk. 6:14-30) at the Divine Liturgy.[70]

The Saints of the Christian Church. We do not intend to comment on the Scripture readings for the feasts of the saints as we have done so far for the other feasts listed in the Menaion. Only a small number of them have their own Scripture readings. A smaller number still are of such a degree that would call for Scripture lessons at Vespers. The connection between the personality of the saints and the readings of Scripture assigned to their feasts is based on analogies, and the lessons are in most cases unspecific. The only exception is for the few who have known Jesus Christ in the flesh and those saints in the first generation of Christians which are mentioned in the Apostolic writings. Thus the Epistle at the Liturgy of St. Stephen the Protomartyr (December 27) could hardly have been anything else but the account of Stephen's arraignment before the Sanhedrites, his fiery diatribe when, from accused, he turned their accuser, and his death by stoning (Acts 6:8 to 7:5, 47-60). It called, by symbolic correspondance, for reading the parable of the wicked husbandmen who murder the heir of their master and stone his messenger to death (Mt. 21:33-42). But the laconism of the Scriptures and our scanty information on a majority of the earliest saints of the Church have given little guidance to the compilers of the liturgies.

Whereas Vespers lessons, whenever prescribed, are normally taken from the Old Testament, it is significant that those assigned for the feasts of the Apostles are invariably from the

New. The reason for this seems to be that the Apostles and Evangelists performed in the Church a unique, unprecedented office, not to be duplicated in any way: that of eyewitnesses and authentic recorders of the earthly life and work of Christ. No analogy from the Old Testament can possibly apply here. Nor should the charism of bishops, priests and deacons consecrated and ordained to be leaders and ministers of the Church be assimilated to the charism of the Apostles, even though it happened that James "the Just," one of the witness to the Resurrection (1 Cor. 15:7), was counted traditionally as the first bishop of the Holy Zion, "Mother of all the Churches";[71] we may also remember, as a countertest, the difficulties which St. Paul had to face in order to persuade the early Christians— and the other Apostles—of his being an Apostle in his own right. It is true that a number of Saints, like Constantine and Helen, Methodius and Cyril, Vladimir, are labeled "Equal to the Apostles," 'Ισαπόστολοι but this title refers to their labors for the conversion of pagans and the propagation of the faith, in the imitation of the Apostles, *ad instar apostolorum*; the proper charism of the Twelve as witnesses to Christ in the days of his flesh is one that cannot possibly be shared. It is only because he had been associated with the disciples "all the time that the Lord Jesus went in and out with them," that Mathias was numbered with the Eleven after the tragic end of Judas (Acts 1:15-26). In the same way Mary Magdalen, in that she was the first to meet the Risen Lord and that she announced the Resurrection to the Apostles (John 20:11-18), deserved eminently to be called "Equal to the Apostles." Working on those principles, the Church has chosen to read from the first Epistle of Peter at the Vespers of St. Peter and Paul on June 29 (1 Peter 1:3-9; 1:13-19; 2:11-24); from the first Epistle of John at the Vespers of St. John the Evangelist on May 7 (1 John 3:21 to 4:6; 4:11-16; 4:20 to 5:5); from the first Epistle of John (1:1-7), the Epistle of James (1:1-12), and the Epistle of Jude (verses 1-7, 17-25) at the Vespers of James son of Alphaios on October 9, Thomas the Apostle on October 6, and St. Luke the Evangelist on October 18.[72] Vespers lessons for the other Apostles were chosen in a similar manner.

Scripture readings for the Divine Liturgy may be proper:

thus the relation of Peter's confession of Christ at Caesarea
Philippi (Mt. 16:13-19) and St. Paul's account of his raptures
(2 Cor. 11:21 to 12:9) for the feast of the two Apostles on
June 29; St. John's supreme recommendations to his disciples
(1 John 1:1-7) and his standing with Mary at the foot of the
Cross (John 19:25-27 and 21:24-25) for the feast of the Evangelist on May 8; the apparition of the Risen Christ to the
Apostles and to Thomas (John 20:19-31) for the feast of
Thomas the Apostle on October 6. In the majority of cases,
however, the liturgists had to proceed by way of symbolic assi-
milation in their choice of lessons for the other Apostles, of
whom we know very little except their names.[73]

Readings for the feasts of later saints are assigned in ac-
cordance with the traditional categories of the lists of the
Church: martyrs like St. George on April 23 or Demetrius on
October 26: "If the world has persecuted me, it will also perse-
cute you" (John 15:17 to 16:2); confessors, wonderworkers,
unmercenary healers, such as the Three Hierarchs on January
30: "You are the salt of the earth" (Mt. 5:14-19), St. Nicholas
on December 6: "A great multitude came to hear him and to
be healed of their diseases" (Lk. 6:17-23), St. Constantine and
Helen on May 21 or St. Vladimir on July 15, true shepherds
and leaders of their subjects: "The shepherd calls his sheep by
name . . . and the sheep follow him, for they know his voice"
(John 10:1-9). Similar analogies have guided the compilers
of our liturgists for the choice of Old Testament lessons at
Vespers, drawn from the historical, prophetic or wisdom books
when the degree of the feast warrants them.

Epilogue

This book was undertaken as a labor of love. From the very first page, my intention was to be practical. I have refrained from purely technical considerations, except those which appeared to be of immediate interest. On the one hand, the history of our lectionary belongs to the comparative study of ancient liturgies, a discipline which is not of my competence; on the other hand, the task before me was not to write one general commentary of those Scriptures from which we read in our liturgical worship, but rather to examine the lessons of our Orthodox worship in relation to the alternation of seasons and festal occasions through the year. I have aimed at nothing more than providing a help; but nothing can take the place of a direct contact with the Word of God, the word inspired by the Holy Spirit, the word of life, the word we read and hear, the word we sing in our churches, for the chanted word has a virtue of its own. So "let it dwell in you richly, as you teach and admonish one another in all wisdom, and as you sing psalms and hymns and spiritual songs, with thankfulness in your heart to God" (Col. 3:16).

Notes and References

CHAPTER I

[1]A. Kniazeff, "La lecture de l'Ancien et du Nouveau Testament dans le rite byzantin," in *La Prière des Heures,* edited by Mgr. Cassien et Dom Botte (Paris, 1963) p. 201.

[2]They form the three *staseis* of the eighteenth *kathisma.* They seem to have been originally songs of pilgrims on their way to the Temple. According to the Mishnah, they were sung during the festival of *Sukkoth* (Tabernacles) on the steps leading to the court of Israel, when the priests brought water from the fountain of Siloam for the festal libations.

[3]References in J. A. Lamb, *The Psalms in Christian Worship* (London, 1962), p. 61 ff.

[4]J. A. Lamb, *op.cit.,* pp. 14-16.

[5]On the relation of Ps. 104 to the account of the Creation in the first chapter of Genesis, see G. Barrois, *The Face of Christ in the Old Testament* (St. Vladimir's Seminary Press, 1974) pp. 48-49.

[6]To compare with the Latin usage of selected verses for the *antiphonae super Psalmos.*

[7]Typologically applied to the death and resurrection of Christ.

[8]A. Kniazeff, *op.cit.,* pp. 201-202.

[9]*Saint Vladimir's Theological Quarterly* 19 (1975) pp. 75 ff.

[10]This period corresponds to the series of Sundays and weeks "after Pentecost" and "after the Epiphany" in the Roman missals and breviaries.

CHAPTER II

[1]Forty-eight days, *viz.* from the Monday after the Sunday of Forgiveness (Cheesefare) to Great and Holy Saturday inclusively. The length of the Lenten

fast has varied considerably among the churches, according to when the count started and whether the Saturdays and Sundays were included. The Roman Church counts forty-six days, from "Ash Wednesday," *in capite ieiunii*, to Holy Saturday, *sabbato sancto*.

[2]A. Kniazeff, *op.cit.*, pp. 227-228.

[3]Possibly in reaction to the complete abstinence observed for some time by oriental churches, which the Byzantine Church deemed out of order. Cf. Kniazeff, *op.cit.*, p. 229.

[4]For a comprehensive study of the Lenten Triodion, see A. Schmemann, *Great Lent* (St. Vladimir's Seminary Press, 1969).

[5]*Talmud of Babylon*, treatise *Ta'anith*, 12 b.

[6]St. Paul and the early Christians expected the return of Christ in the immediate future.

[7]The parable has frequently been interpreted as an allegory, as if each detail or each character of the story had to be scrutinized and identified. Thus Tertullian, *De pudicitia* 9, saw in the robe which the father orders his servants to put on the prodigal son the status which Adam had forfeited through his transgression. A few moderns find in the two sons a figure of the Jews and the Christians, or in the older son a personification of the Pharisees. Some parables of Jesus contain allegorizing features, but it would be misleading to surcharge the simple story recorded by St. Luke with an overload of allegorical interpretation.

[8]*Expositio in Lucam, lib.* 7. P.L. 15, col. 1847. Reference to Eph. 2:13, 19.

[9]Possibly a saying of St. Paul himself, upholding Christian liberty against the Judaizers, but diverted from its true meaning by the libertines.

[10]Kontakion at the Ninth Hour (transl. Hapgood).

[11]The symbolism is necessarily late, at any rate posterior to the establishment of Christianity in Russia. It is not substantiated by the iconography of the cross in Greek lands.

[12]P.L. 76, col. 1300.

[13]The second part of the verse, "they leave the rest of their substance for their babes," is generally interpreted as describing the unique preoccupation of these men. The text is hopelessly corrupted. It has been suggested that the Psalmist includes the heirs to the evil men in the reprobation of their fathers; if so, then the verse should be regarded as an imprecation against the entire breed.

[14]Hence a certain fluctuation in the thought of the Apostle, manifest in the first and the second Epistle to the Thessalonians.

[15]The early Christians regarded the end of the present age and the return of Christ as imminent.

[16]In most of our Bibles, the chapter ends with verse 23. The liturgical selection adds the doxology of the Epistle, which is placed by a few authorities at the end of chapter 14.

[17]The memorial service of the second Saturday of Lent is in remembrance of "Our Holy Fathers massacred by the Saracens in the Lavra of St. Sabbas"—obviously a Jerusalem feature.

[18]The Book of Joel can hardly be dated earlier than 400 B.C. Joel 3:5-6 quotes explicitly Obadiah (Abdias), verse 17, and mentions the "sons of Yawan," *viz.* the Ionians, that is to say: the Greeks.

[19]The names given to the locusts in Joel 1:4 and 2:25 do not designate several species of insects, but locusts in the various phases of their evolution from hatching to their full development. They have obviously puzzled the King James translators and have been rendered according to etymology accurately, but clumsily, in the Revised Standard Version.

[20]"Between the porch and the altar," the altar of burnt offerings, in the courtyard of the priests, not the altar of incense within the "house."

[21]"The Valley of Jehoshaphath," interpreted etymologically in verse 14 as "Valley of Decision." Fourth-century Christian topographers identified it with the Valley of the Cedron, where a Jewish tomb of the Hellenistic period is now shown as "Tomb of Jehoshaphath," King of Judah.

[22]Counting Nisân (March-April) as the first month.

[23]Our expectation as Christians is founded upon the Resurrection of Christ, when the "Temple" of his body, after death has done its worst to destroy it, arose victorious from the grave (John 2:19-22).

CHAPTER III

[1]We refer once and for all at the beginning of this chapter, to Fr. Schmemann's *Great Lent* (St. Vladimir's Seminary Press, 1969).

[2]A Liturgy of the Presanctified was prescribed in the Roman Missal for Good Friday, when a Host previously consecrated on Holy Thursday was consumed by the celebrant alone after the Elevation.

[3]Forty days, that is, from the Monday after Cheese-Fare Week to Lazarus Saturday. Palm Sunday and Great Week are counted separately.

[4]The only exception is when the Annunciation falls during Great Lent. See chapter VII.

[5]Dates of events during the period of the Hebrew monarchies are given according to the system of chronology of E. Thiele. Other systems vary noticeably. Exact figures are relatively unimportant for the purpose of this book.

[6]This designation is taken from the opening words of chapter 40: "Comfort ye my people."

[7]Namely Is 42:1-9; 49:1-6; 50:4-9 and possibly verses 10 and 11; 52:13 to 53:12.

[8]Verse 6 has sometimes been applied, out of context, to Christ in his Passion. This arbitrary adaptation can be justified indirectly if we consider that Christ did actually take upon himself "the sins of many," that "he was bruised for our iniquities" (Is. 53:5) and that, "while he was without sin, God made him sin for us" (2 Cor. 5:21).

[9]A theme frequent in the Psalms and the Prophets, cf. Is. 22:8-11; 31:1; Ps. 20:7; 146:3.

[10]The rhythm of this piece is that of a Palestinian village song ending on a spiteful note. The Latin liturgy uses verses from the song of the vineyard in the

rite of the "Adoration of the Cross" preceding the Liturgy of the Presanctified on Good Friday.

[11]In 740 B.C., according to the chronology of Thiele.

[12]The very words of the priest to the deacon who has partaken of the Precious Blood.

[13]Cf. G. Barrois, *The Face of Christ in the Old Testament* (St. Vladimir's Seminary Press, 1974) pp. 107-108.

[14]The "Day of Madian." The reference is to the defeat of the Midianites by the Hebrew tribes united under Gideon (Judges, ch. 7 and 8).

[15]Zion, originally the acropolis of the Jebusites conquered by David, who established there his fortified capital. The name was applied later to the rocky area on which Solomon built the Temple and soon was regarded as a specifically religious designation. This sacralization of Zion finally made of the primitive *Rocca* an eschatological symbol.

[16]An implicit quotation from Psalm 103:5. Is it too far-fetched to recall here the symbolic rebirth of the Phoenix?

[17]Cf. Is. 44:6; Apoc. 1:8, "The Alpha and the Omega, who is and was and is to come."

[18]"Yahweh's anointed," in Hebrew *meshiah,* one who has received the unction of the Spirit. Cf. the mission of Elijah, sent to anoint Hazael king of Syria, Jehu king of Israel, and Elisha to the prophetic office (1 Ki. 19:6).

[19]The lectionary, in parcelling out the liturgical sections, did not preserve the integrity of the Servant's songs.

[20]We incline to regard "Israel" in verse 3 as an interpolation of Jewish origin, already extant in the standard Hebrew text.

[21]For a detailed account of the literary composition of the Pentateuch, see Artur Weiser, *The Old Testament in its Formation and Development* (New York, 1958; fifth printing). A more summary presentation, by B. W. Anderson, *Understanding the Old Testament* (New York, 1957) may be sufficient for reading the text of Genesis in the proper perspective.

[22]The Hexaemeron and the seventh day of the Creation are seen as the prototypes of the periodic week, made independent from the phases of the moon: six working days, followed by the sabbath rest, a Jewish institution.

[23]Cf. the Jewish usage of counting the day from sunset to sunset; our liturgical day also begins with Vespers.

[24]Jewish tradition has interpreted this plural in reference to the Hebrew common name for God, Elohim, a plural of majesty, or as implying a counsel of God with the angels, cf. Is. 9:6, in the Greek.

[25]This verse is interpreted by the Church as a first announcement of our salvation, and it has been called appropriately the Protevangel.

[26]On that covenant ritual, see Barrois, *op.cit.,* p. 68.

[27]Literary criticism has interpreted this drama as a legend destined to explain a Mosaic ordinance whereby the first-born of humans must be redeemed by means of a substitutionary sacrifice (Ex. 13:12-13; 34:19 ff.; Num. 18:15 ff., and Lk. 2:23 ff.).

[28]A. Kniazeff, *op.cit.,* pp. 220-222.

[29]We need not be alarmed by the antithesis love *vs.* hatred, a Semitic rhetorical

device eliminating whatever would tune down the opposition of the terms. God, the φιλάνθρωπος, hates no man, yet men have made themselves hateful and are fully responsible for their reprobation.

[30]Changes in personal names, such as Abram becoming Abraham, Saraï becoming Sarah, symbolically explained in the text on the basis of often fanciful etymologies, are indicative of the shift from Aramaic dialects to the "language of Canaan," of which the biblical Hebrew is a variety. A tell-tale clue to this transformation is found in Gen. 31:47 ff: the cairn erected by Jacob and Laban following a convention relative to pasture rights is named Gal'êd (Gilead) in Hebrew, Yegarshahadûthâ in Aramaic; the meaning in both cases is: "the cairn of (God's) witness."

[31]The monumental enclosure built by Herod was turned into a Christian church, the Praesidium ad sanctum Abraham of the Crusaders; under the name Haram el-Khalil, it is today a Moslem sanctuary.

[32]The text and numbering of verses in the Greek is often at variance with the Hebrew, which the English versions follow substantially.

[33]The diversity of sources used by the compiler of the canonical book is in no way detrimental to the homogeneity of the doctrine. Attempts at distinguishing or dating several schools or trends by internal criticism have thus far yielded no significant results with regard to the moral conceptions of the Hebrews in the post-exilic period.

[34]The issue of retribution and sanctions in the world to come is necessarily related to the doctrine of the resurrection of the dead, still controverted in the time of Jesus Christ, and definitely established on the fact of his own Resurrection.

[35]The shéol, one of the names for the abode of the dead, and which the King James renders by "hell."

[36]There is here more than a simple precaution dictated by prudence: a sworn promise or vow would engage God, whose Holy Name "thou shalt not take in vain."

[37]The identification of the Wisdom in the Old Testament with the Logos of St. John became generally accepted by the time of Origen.

[38]J. Meyendorff, Byzantine Theology (New York, 1974) p. 21.

[39]A. Kniazeff, op.cit., pp. 239 ff., and his reference to I. Karabinov, Postnaïa Triod (Saint Petersburg, 1910).

[40]Psalm 95 (Vulg. 94), Venite exsultemus, is recited or chanted at the beginning of Matins (the midnight Office) in the Latin monasteries, and ironically called the "psalm of the lazy ones," because late brethren, if they arrived in the church before the psalm was ended, incurred no penalty.

[41]"Messianic secret," the name given by some moderns to the discretion which Jesus required of his followers in order to avoid malignant interpretations of his claim to be the Messiah. Cf. V. Kesich, The Gospel Image of Christ (St. Vladimir's Seminary Press, 1972) pp. 100-102.

[42]The scribes, γραμματεῖς, doctors and interpreters of the law, belonged either to the party of the Pharisees or of the politically-minded Sadducees.

[43]There is no cogent reason for translating Rom. 1:17 by "he who through faith is righteous," as in the Revised Standard Version, which—inconsequently—

renders Habakkuk and Hebrews, which St. Paul quotes, by "the righteous" or "my righteous one shall live by faith."

[44]The partitioning of the Temple of Solomon and of the Second Temple corresponds to the divisions of the Tabernacle of Moses. The description of Kings makes no mention of a curtain. St. Matthew (27:51) relates how the veil of the Temple was rent asunder when Jesus expired on the Cross.

[45]We may recall a number of occasions on which Christ refused or reluctantly granted a miraculous sign to those requesting it indiscretely. See for instance Mk. 8:12-13; Mt. 16:1-4; Lk. 11-29; John 4:48.

[46]A. Kniazeff, *op.cit.,* p. 242.

CHAPTER IV

[1]The same lesson is read for the Marian celebration (see chapter VII). It is significant that the Akathist is served on the evening of the fifth Friday in Lent.

[2]In some Latin liturgies, these verses are sung as a *responsorium* during the procession which follows the Vespers of Easter and of the following three days.

[3]"His feet," a euphemism for the organs of generation; his descendence shall reign for ever.

[4]Cf. 1 Ki. 11:28, where the Hebrew *Misraïm* does not mean Egypt but rather the district of *Musru* in Cilicia, then under Hittite domination. The cuneiform ideogram for *horse* is tell-tale, composed as it is of the sign for *ass,* and the determinative for *mountain, viz.* the border with a foreign land. Horses were an Asian import.

[5]There is no certainty as to the exact location of Bethphage, hypothetically toward the little chapel and villa of the Franciscans on the eastern face of the Mount of Olives. Bethany is located three quarters of a mile south-east, at a short distance from the modern road to Jericho and the Jordan.

[6]"The Lord," ὁ Κύριος, in this context is a common title, not necessarily understood by the owner of the animals with the exclusive meaning of "the divine Lord," which Jesus could claim for himself and which the Church professes as an article of faith.

[7]It matters little to our purpose to decide during which period of captivity the letter to the Philippians was written.

[8]"Maranatha," a transcription from the Aramaic: "Our Lord comes," or, cutting the letters differently, "Come, O our Lord!"

[9]The mention of palms is proper to John. The Synoptics speak only of green branches and of the garments spread on the road.

[10]Some of the services during Great and Holy Week are usually "anticipated." Moreover the practice of local churches with regard to the hour of the various services varies greatly. We make abstraction of these peculiarities and we abide by the traditional designations.

[11]Services of Great and Holy Week in the St. Vladimir's Seminary translation.

[12]This grouping of the parables is proper to St. Matthew, who organizes his material in large, systematic units. The same pieces figure in Luke in different contexts and order.

[13]The first three verses of the Book of Ezekiel fuse two different introductions, the first one (verse 1) being the prologue of the prophet's vision, the second one (verses 2 and 3) serving as preface to the entire book. The chronological indications given in these verses are not easily reconciled, which anyway is not relevant for our purpose.

[14]See below, chapter VII, and Barrois, *op.cit.,* pp. 79 ff.

[15]A. Kniazeff, *op.cit.,* p. 248.

[16]The lessons are read in the following order: (1) James 5:10-16 and Lk. 10:25-37. (2) Rom. 15:1-7 and Lk. 19:1-10. (3) 1 Cor. 12:27 to 13:8 and Mt. 10:1, 5-8. (4) 2 Cor. 6:17-18 to 7:1 and Mt. 8:14-23. (5) 2 Cor. 1:8-11 and Mt. 25:1-13. (6) Gal. 5:22 to 6:2 and Mt. 15:21-28. (7) 1 Thess. 5:14-23 and Mt. 9:9-13. The Latin Church reckons the anointing of the sick as one of the seven sacraments. It is normally administered in case of severe illness, hence the prevailing denomination "extreme unction."

[17]The sanctuary of Nob—presumed location north-east of the Mount of Olives—had been served by priests descending from Eli of Shiloh. The religious reform of Josias recognized only those priests serving in the Temple of Jerusalem.

[18]In the Latin Church, Holy Thursday has long been regarded as the feast of the Christian priesthood. The custom in France was that the priests would abstain from the celebration of private masses, and received communion from the hand of the bishop or the rector of the church.

[19]The reference should be to Zechariah 11:12-13. The "field of the blood," in Aramaic *hâkel-damâ* (Mt. 27:8), continued for centuries to be a burial ground for paupers and foreigners. The ruins of the charnel house built during the Frankish period are still visible at a short distance from the monastery of St. Onophrios.

[20]The text refers to a legal prescription regarding the paschal lamb. The passage from Zechariah belongs in an eschatological context. The messianic triumph is at the price of suffering and death.

[21]The First, Third, Sixth, and Ninth Hours were read in the Great Church with solemnity on special days or feasts which the Emperor attended; hence the appelation Royal or Imperial Hours.

[22]Psalm 91 (Vulg. 90) is regularly sung at monastic Compline in the Latin Church as the evening prayer of the community before retiring.

[23]*Et erit sepulchrum eius gloriosum,* St. Jerome's interpretation of Isaiah 11:10, in the Hebrew *menûhathô,* his "resting place," Greek ἀνάπαυσις, "his rest."

[24]An ancient rock-cut tomb in the village of Selwân is shown to pilgrims as the tomb of Isaiah, and another one, higher in the valley, as the tomb of the "daughter of Pharaoh." Immediately below Gethsemane, a conspicuous group of monuments from the early Hellenistic period are commonly known as the tomb of Jehoshaphat, the tomb of Absalom (which has nothing to do with the *yad Ashalom* of 2 Sam. 18:18), and the tomb of St. James, which is in reality the mausoleum of the priestly family of the Benê Hézir.

[25]A great latitude is left in practice for the observation of that rubric.

[26]There is no obvious reason for the actual order of the fifteen Vespers lessons on Great and Holy Saturday. An extreme case is that of the ninth lesson, which begins with Isaiah 61:10, while verses 1-9 form the eleventh lesson.

[27]A. Kniazeff, *op.cit.,* pp. 218 ff., gives lists of lessons for Great and Holy Saturday in early lectionaries of the Armenian Church and of the western churches, Mozarabic and Gallican.

[28]We may recall that the Byzantine rite uses the Canticle of Jonah (2:1-10), a mosaic of verses quoted from various thanksgiving psalms, as the sixth of the odes on which the Matins canons are based.

[29]The crossing of a body of water, be it the Red Sea, the Jordan, the Rubicon, or the "Deep River" of the Negro spirituals, involves always a decisive break in what would appear as a continuous chain of happenings.

[30]The personage of Elias reappears frequently in the course of the Byzantine liturgical services. Cf. chapter VII.

[31]The same lesson is also read on September 1, beginning of the Indiction and of the Church year.

[32]Cf. Galatians 3:27: "As many of you as were baptized into Christ have put on Christ," the verse which replaces the singing of the Trisagion on Great and Holy Saturday and several feasts.

[33]Similar usage in the Latin Church. At the Holy Saturday Mass, when the Alleluia interrupted during Lent is resumed, the Dominicans and Regular Canons remove their black *cappa* and appear in their white habit.

[34]Mark 15:40, "Mary, the mother of James" (the younger). St. Luke does not identify the myrrhophorae. John has a different, more detailed version of the apparition to Mary Magdalen (John 20:1-18).

CHAPTER V

[1]As an example of these discrepancies: the women who visit the tomb see "an angel of the Lord ... his raiment white as snow" (Mt. 28:2-3); "a young man dressed in a white robe" (Mk. 16:5); "two men in shining garments" (Lk. 24:4); "two angels in white robes" (John 20:12).

[2]The rubrics specify that the Divine Liturgy must follow the Resurrection Matins immediately.

[3]The prologue to Acts mentions "the former treatise," *viz.* the Gospel of Luke, as having same (unnamed) author and same addressee, the "Most Excellent Theophilus," otherwise not known to us. The Book of Acts begins as an impersonal, elaborate composition, until 16:10, where the style shifts abruptly from verbs in the narrative third person to verbs in the first person plural, "*We* sought to go on ... *We* made a direct voyage ... Seeing that God had called *us* ..." This *we* and *us* hints the correctness of the traditional identification of the author of Acts with St. Luke, the "beloved physician" (Col. 4:14) and faithful companion of St. Paul.

[4]The date of this episode is uncertain. John seems to place it in the early

years of Jesus' public activity, but the Synoptics connect it with the events of Holy Week.

[5]*Peregrinatio Etheriae,* c. 10, sections 287-292. Translation in *Ancient Christian Writers,* vol. 38, p. 92.

[6]A. Kniazeff, *op.cit.,* p. 209.

[7]The transformation of pagan places of worship into Christian sanctuaries is not uncommon, for example the Roman basilica of St. Clement over a *Mithraeum,* or the sanctuary of St. Michael on Monte Gargano on what seems to have been a high place sacred to Baal.

[8]The well of Jacob, close to the ruins of Shechem, is seen in the crypt of the Greek Church; the successive layers of masonry down to the original cavity in the rock where the water is gathered are easily observable.

[9]We cannot but outline our argument, reduced here to the essentials. The entire problem will be discussed elsewhere, on the basis of the available evidence.

[10]The "ascent" to Jerusalem three times a year was bound to remain somewhat theoretical, like the obligation for Moslems to accomplish the pilgrimage to Mecca.

[11]Variously translated as Feast of the Tents, or of the Tabernacles (cf. the Latin *Tabernacula*), or Feast of the Booths or Huts, Σκηνοπηγία.

[12]This supposes a certain adaptation in the case of city-dwellers. Today, observant Jewish families decorate their homes with greenery. In some sections of Jerusalem, they used to remove some roof tiles and replace them with foliage for the duration of the feast.

[13]*Rosh-hashanah,* New Year "for the Kings" on the first day of Tishri (September-October). The first day in Nisân (March-April) marked the New Year "for the Feasts."

[14]The *ordo* of the *Hanukkah* was modelled after the ritual of *Sukkoth.* The feast was sometimes called Σκηνοπηγία τοῦ Χισλεῦ (*Kislew,* the ninth month of the Hebrew calendar, counting from spring: November-December.)

[15]The closing section of the Gospel of Mark is regarded by the critics as a late addition. The lesson of Luke is a marginal gloss incorporated into the text.

[16]Vulg. *angelus faciei eius salvavit eos.* Cf. Is. 9:6, in the versions: μεγάλης βουλῆς ἄγγελος, *magni consilii angelus.*

[17]The ruins of a Byzantine circular church, now a Moslem shrine, marks the traditional site of the Ascension, at a short distance from the Russian monastery.

[18]The context is that of the other Joel oracles which are read on the Wednesday of Cheese-Fare Week.

[19]It would be futile to enlist these texts for a discussion of sacramental *vs.* disciplinary powers in the Church. But they certainly mean that the Church, through its priestly hierarchy, is God's appointed organ of salvation to mankind.

[20]The *de'ath-Yahweh* of the Hebrew prophets, no mere speculative knowledge, but knowledge unto life, both practical and mystical.

CHAPTER VI

[1]The entire passage, Apoc. 7:2-10, is read as the Epistle of the Roman Mass on the feast of All Saints, on November 1.

[2]For its scriptural and hymnological contents, the liturgy of the Zacchaeus Sunday can be regarded as the prelude to the Lenten Triod. Cf. A. Schmemann, *Great Lent* (St. Vladimir's Seminary Press, 1969) pp. 17-18.

[3]A. Kniazeff, *op. cit.,* p. 210-211.

[4]A summary introduction to the technical problems raised by modern Gospel criticism is found in the book of Professor V. Kesich, *The Gospel Image of Christ* (St. Vladimir's Seminary Press, 1972). See also the introductory sections to single books or groups of books of the New Testament in the so-called *Bible of Jerusalem,* originally published in French by a group of Dominicans, now available in an English edition (Doubleday, New York).

[5]The Epistle to Philemon is not read in the course of the lessons *de tempore,* but on the feast of the saint, November 22.

[6]The first Sunday after Pentecost, "All Saints," has its proper Gospel lessons, also taken from Matthew.

[7]The pericope follows immediately the episode of the Transfiguration. See chapter VII.

[8]The sermon "on a level-place" is shorter than the sermon "on the mount." St. Luke seems to have streamlined the discourse held by Jesus, omitting items which would have a lesser appeal for his Greek readers. Matthew, on the contrary, has included some material originally from another context, because it appeared germane to the general theme of the sermon on the mount.

[9]Multiple variants: τῶν Γερασηνῶν, cf. Gerasa, presumably opposite Capernaum, not Gerasa-Djerash in the Adjlûn; τῶν Γαδαρηνῶν, cf. Gadara, a city of the Decapolis, south-east of the lake, rather improbable in our context; and even τῶν Γεργεσηνῶν.

[10]Mentioned in Joshua 15:7 as a key point on the border between Judah and Benjamin.

[11]In classical Greek, διά with the accusative, in the local sense, is used chiefly in poetry. In composition, the values "between, in the interval of," are well attested: διαμερίζω, to divide, to separate; διαμερισμός, partition; the adjective διάμεσος, that which is intermediate, in the interval between two parts.

[12]A note in the Jerusalem Bible observes that the Law demanded a fourfold restitution only in the case of a theft of small cattle (five-fold for a bull), Exodus 22:1 (21:37 in the Hebrew).

CHAPTER VII

[1]"Major Feasts" calling normally for an "all-night vigil," according to the Slavic tradition.

[2]It is important to remember the thirteen-day discrepancy which affects the dates of fixed feasts and fasts of the annual cycle, whether they be computed as in the old Julian calendar or according to the Gregorian calendar.

[3]In the case of some major feasts of the Marian-Incarnation cycle, the singing of a special *megalynarion* is substituted for the *Magnificat* at the ninth ode of the canon.

[4]According to local traditions, in the valley of the Wady Qelt, at or near the monastery of St. George the Khozibite, a few miles from Jericho.

[5]Hebrew: *Beth-Elohim,* "house of God," as an explanation of the name Bethel. It was turned derogatively into Beth-awen, "house of nothingness," by allusion to the schismatic sanctuary of the kings of Israel. In the same way, the name of Babylon, *Bâb-Ilâni,* a Semitic transcription of the Sumerian ideogram KA-DINGIR, "the Gate of the Gods," was interpreted by derision as the unintelligible babble resulting from the confusion of tongues (Gen. 11:9).

[6]The prayer *Supplices te rogamus* of the Latin anaphora, perhaps originally a eucharistic epiclesis.

[7]Stikheron at Great Vespers on "Lord, I have cried," and Akathist, stasis 1.

[8]Cf. Barrois, *op.cit.,* pp. 98 ff.

[9]Second canon of the feast, third ode, translated in the *Festal Menaion.*

[10]The ceremony of the Ὕψωσις, as it is performed in cathedrals and monasteries, manifests the cosmic nature of the feast: the bishop raises the Cross five times, facing east, south, west, north, and again east.

[11]The Constantinian sanctuary, as far as its disposition can be inferred from early relations and archeological research, consisted in a circular esplanade around the Sepulcher; a basilica, the μαρτύριον, oriented east-west; south of the μαρτύριον, the rock of Calvary on which a canopy sheltered the votive Cross erected by order of the Empress. The primitive ordinance was radically changed when the rotunda of the Sepulcher, the basilica, and the Calvary were restored by the Crusaders and enclosed in a single complex, now in course of restoration.

[12]*Ipse lignum tunc notavit damna ligni ut solveret*; in that day, "God himself designated the tree, to repair the harm a tree had wrought."

[13]Vincent and Abel, *Jérusalem Nouvelle,* fasc. 4 (Paris, 1922) p. 942.

[14]Cf. the verse *ad Laudes* of the Dominican breviary: *Dicite in nationibus quia Dominus regnavit a ligno.*

[15]*The Festal Menaion* (London, 1969) p. 50.

[16]*Dictionnaire d'Archéologie Chrétienne et de Liturgie,* vol. 14.2, cols. 1729-31, "Présentation de Marie."

[17]See M. R. James, *The Apocryphal New Testament* (Oxford, 1924) pp. 39-49.

[18]A distribution of space which is sometimes perceptible from the outside of the building, as in the case of some Russian churches.

[19]The High Priesthood is represented pictorially in the icons of Christ the Hierarch, vested and mitred, sitting on a throne.

[20]"Winter festivals." A regionalism: no white Christmas in the southern hemisphere!

[21]The Royal Hours on the eve of the Nativity and of the Theophany, with

their series of Scripture readings, have been composed on the model of the Royal Hours of Great and Holy Friday. Cf. A. Kniazeff, *op.cit.,* p. 205 ff.

[22]This schedule has to be modified when the Nativity or the Theophany falls on a Sunday or a Monday, without changing the essential structure of the services. Our exposititon follows the basic *ordo.* The variations are clearly indicated in the *Festal Menaion,* p. 252.

[23]At Vespers, the prophecy of Micah begins with 4:6-7, heralding the return of the "remnant" of the exiled nation.

[24]The Book of Baruch is extant only in Greek, as an appendix to the Book of Jeremiah, immediately following the Lamentations.

[25]"He was seen on earth" (verse 38), *viz.* God himself, οὗτος (verse 36), cf. the Latin *visus est,* also in the masculine. Modern translators, reluctant to admit a messianic prophecy in the literal sense, prefer to make ἐπιστήμη (verse 37), knowledge personified, the subject of the verbs.

[26]For a more detailed presentation of the Immanuel prophecies, see my article in *St. Vladimir's Theological Quarterly* 16 (1972) p. 109 ff., or *The Face of Christ in the Old Testament,* p. 107 ff.

[27]"For God is with us," the refrain of the verses at Great Compline.

[28]The wailing of Rachel in Ramah, a locality in Benjamin, whose inhabitants, Rachel's children, had been deported into exile. An ancient Judaean tradition locating the tomb of Rachel in the vicinity of Bethlehem prompted St. Matthew to quote Jeremiah 31:15 in relation to the massacre of the infants of Bethlehem.

[29]The pedagogue, παιδαγωγός, was the slave who accompanied the children to school.

[30]Cf. the cult of the Magi in the archdiocese of Cologne, the Romanesque sculptures of the cathedral of Autun (France), and the popular appellation, in French villages, "le jour des Rois." The name of the feast in the Latin West is "the Epiphany," *viz.* the "manifestation."

[31]The site is called by the Arabs of the region Qasr el-Yehûd, the "Castle of the Jews," recalling the crossing of the river by Joshua and the Israelites.

[32]This oracle is akin to the prophecies of the second part of the Book of Isaiah, the so-called "Book of the Consolation of Israel."

[33]Here again, an echo of the psalms: "The sun shall not smite thee by day, nor the moon by night" (Ps. 121:6).

[34]Hence, instead of the typical antiphon at the Divine Liturgy, verses from Psalm 114 are chanted: "What ails you, O Sea, that you flee? O Jordan, that you turn back?" On the possibility of a landslide which would have barred the flow of the river for a few hours, see N. Glueck, *The River Jordan* (Philadelphia, 1946) pp. 143-145, and D. Baly, *The Geography of Palestine* (New York, 1957) p. 98.

[35]The question whether the text should read, "Voice of him who shouts in the desert," or, "Voice of him who shouts: In the desert, prepare ye . . . etc." is immaterial with regard to typology.

[36]Allusion to Ex. 17:5-6; cf. Num. 20:7.

[37]We see no valid reason for opposing the Synoptics and the Johannine tradition, as did Loisy.

[38]It was optional to redeem the first-born of an ass; otherwise it would have been sacrificed like every male firstling of cattle.

[39]Historical reference to the invasion of Egypt by the Assyrians in the seventh century B.C., and to the communities of the Jewish diaspora, typologically projected.

[40]In the western church, the character of the feast as a feast of light is manifested by the offering of the wax-candles for the service of the altar, hence the popular name of the feast as Candlemas or, in French, *la Chandeleur.*

[41]Cf. the western feast of the "Compassion of the Blessed Virgin Mary" on the Friday preceding Palm Sunday; the verse at Lauds: "A sword shall pierce through thy soul, that the thoughts of many hearts may be revealed."

[42]These variations are succinctly but clearly indicated in the *Festal Menaion,* p. 435 ff.

[43]On the significance of the episode of the Burning Bush for the Christian revelation, see Barrois, *op.cit.,* pp. 79-82.

[44]This passage is read also on Christmas eve at the Royal Hours.

[45]A favorite theme of the Fathers and of the hymn writers: John, not yet born, sensed Jesus' presence in the womb of Mary.

[46]Exegesis is bound here to remain in the realm of the phenomenal and can at best explain the terms used by the Evangelist. The question *Cur Deus homo* cannot be answered; the Incarnation is a mystery of God's inscrutable wisdom and love.

[47]The initial words of the second sticheron at the Praises.

[48]Stichera on "Lord, I have cried" and the first ainos.

[49]It may well be that we are in presence of the redaction in duplicate of a single episode, which the compiler of Exodus drew from two different sources; but this is scarcely relevant for the liturgical interpretation of the narratives.

[50]In Exodus 33:18, Moses asks: "Show me thy glory," *eth-kebôdka,* but in LXX (cod. Vat.) ἐμφάνισον μοι σεαυτόν, "Manifest thyself to me." God does not grant the request which he judges indiscrete, and answers elusively (verse 19): "I will make all my goodness, *kol-tûbî,* pass before thee," for which the Greek has substituted a redundant paraphrase: "I shall pass before thee in my glory," ἐγὼ παρελεύσομαι προτέρος σου τῇ δόξῃ μου.

[51]Hebrew: *qol-demamah,* "a murmur of the breeze."

[52]The Evangelists speak of "a mountain," "a high mountain." It was identified since the third century with Mount Tabor, seven miles east south-east of Nazareth. The dome-shaped hilltop rises some 1,500 feet above a northern arm of the plain of Jezréel, *hâ-èmeq.* A Greek monastery and a Latin basilica occupy the summit.

[53]The authenticity of the second Epistle of Peter is a matter of discussion among the critics. It does not seem to have been read in the churches much before the third century. It may have been composed by an unknown disciple of St. Peter; if so, the testimony concerning the Transfiguration loses its directness.

[54]Cf. J. Meyendorff, *Saint Gregory Palamas and Orthodox Spirituality* (St. Vladimir's Seminary Press, 1974).

[55]The feast, prior to the liturgical reform, ranked in the Roman *ordo* as a *duplex secundae classis,* without octave.

[56]The *Liber transitus* was circulated in a number of recensions and translations. A Latin version (presumably fifth century) attributed the original to

Meliton of Sardis (end of the second century). Cf. B. Altaner, *Patrologie* (Freiburg i. Br., 1951) p. 101.

[57]Juvenal, whose episcopal see, thus far under the jurisdiction of the Metropolitan of Caesarea, was declared a Patriarchate at the Council of Chalcedon, had a personal interest in circulating the story, and his testimony is not entirely above suspicion.

[58]Cf. Eugene N. Trubetzkoï, *Icons: Theology in Color* (St. Vladimir's Seminary Press, 1973) p. 50 and color reproductions.

[59]However the modern church of the German Benedictines on Mount Zion was consecrated under the archaic title of the Dormition.

[60]It may not be superfluous to remind our readers that "Immaculate Conception" refers to the conception of Mary by her mother Ann and to the theory according to which she was spared the defilement of original sin from the first moment of her being.

[61]There is no special feast of the Visitation of Mary to her cousin Elizabeth, as in the Roman Church, where it is celebrated on July 2. On that day, the eastern Church commemorates the translation of the veil of the Theotokos to the Blachernae in Constantinople.

[62]The archaeological exploration of Ugarit (Ras Shamra) on the Syrian coast has brought to light rich documentation on the religion of the Canaanites. Clay tablets inscribed with cuneiform alphabetic signs, in a West-Semitic language akin to Biblical Hebrew, contain extensive fragments of religious epics thus far known indirectly through the Greek mythographers. For commented translations of those texts, see Cyrus H. Gordon, *Ugaritic Literature* (Roma, 1949) and G. R. Driver, *Canaanite Myths and Legends* (Edinburgh, 1956).

[63]Elijah is frequently assimilated in popular circles to St. George or to a mythical figure called in Arabic *el-Khidr*. On his cult and its derivatives, see Cl. Kopp, *Elias und Christentum auf dem Karmel* (Paderborn, 1929) and the two volumes of essays published in the *Etudes Carmélitaines* under the title *Elie le Prophète* (Paris, 1956).

[64]Zarephath (Σαρεπτά), between Tyre and Sidon, today Sarafand, with a small "wély" of el-Khidr, in memory of Elijah's miracle.

[65]A Carmelitan tradition sees in that little cloud a figure of the Theotokos. The "White Friars" of Mount Carmel, a medieval order of hermits, claim to be the spiritual descendants of the ascetics who had gathered around Elias and his disciple Elisha.

[66]The bloody episode of the massacre of the priests of Baal at the torrent Kishon offends our sensibility, and some exegetes have interpreted Elijah's cry of despair in the desert (1 Ki. 19:4) as expressing remorse. But the orders which he would receive from God are hardly less harsh. Elijah, the jealous prophet of a jealous God, is by no means a sweet character, and the cycle of Elijah and Elisha narratives is of the epic, not of the idyllic, variety.

[67]The feast is extremely popular in rural France: *La Saint Jean d'été*.

[68]The Nazorite (Hebr. *nasîr*), is a person consecrated to Yahweh by vow on a temporary basis, or for life, Numbers, chapter 6. The author of the Samson story supposes that the dietary interdicts prescribed for the pregnant woman will be binding on her son.

[69]The Latin Vulgate translate the impersonal "justice," *tsédeq* in Hebrew,

δικαιοσύνη in the LXX, by the concrete *justum, viz.* the Messiah, the Just. Cf. the Advent verse at Vespers in the Latin liturgies: *Rorate coeli desuper et nubes pluant Justum; aperiatur terra, et germinet Salvatorem.*

[70]Votive feasts of St. John the Baptist, as the anniversary of the discovery of his head, which several churches (and the Mosque of the Ommayads in Damascus) claim to keep among their relics, use the Epistles and Gospels designated for the two principal feasts.

[71]According to St. Clement of Alexandria, as quoted by Eusebius, *Hist.* II, 1:33.

[72]The critical problem of the authenticity of the so-called Catholic Epistles has little or no bearing on our understanding of the lessons of the Office.

[73]Some accounts of apocryphal acts of the Apostles have been the source of the lessons of the Second Nocturn of the Roman breviaries, prior to the recent liturgical reforms.